The Word of God

THE WORD OF GOD

A Guide to English Versions of the Bible

LLOYD R. BAILEY, editor

John Knox Press
ATLANTA

Library of Congress Cataloging in Publication Data
Main entry under title:

The Word of God.
Expanded from the Duke Divinity School review's spring 1979 issue, entitled: Recent English versions of the Bible.
Bibliography: p.
Includes index.
1. Bible. English—Versions—Addresses, essays, lectures. I. Bailey, Lloyd R., 1936-
BS196.W67 220.5′2 81-85335
ISBN 0-8042-0079-3 AACR2

10 9 8 7 6 5 4 3 2 1
Printed in the United States of America
John Knox Press
Atlanta, Georgia 30365

Preface

Anyone who teaches a course in biblical literature, whether at the seminary, college, or local church level, may anticipate an inevitable question at the first session: "Which Bible should we use?" It is an inquiry made necessary by the proliferation of translations during the last two decades. For Protestants, the dilemma began with the appearance of the RSV (1946, 1952), which was heavily promoted as an "authorized" revision of the traditional KJV. No sooner had it begun to gain acceptance in many circles when another "authorized" version appeared (the NEB in 1961, 1970) and soon thereafter other widely publicized translations became available. A "conservative" backlash, generated by the RSV, ultimately led to the appearance of yet other versions: NASB (1963, 1971) and NIV (1973, 1978). For Roman Catholics, the range of choice was slower in arriving, more limited, and greeted with wider acceptance. Those who were accustomed to the Douay Version (as revised by Challoner) now had alternatives in JB (1966), NAB (1970), and even a Catholic Edition of the RSV (1965, 1966).

Those who seek an informed answer to the question, "Which Bible?" quickly discover that there are few reliable and detailed sources to which they can turn. There are occasional superficial reviews of a given version, usually done in isolation from others; there are large volumes on the history of the English Bible, but they may give no more than a single paragraph to an important modern version; and there are shrill polemics for or against a given translation in denominational publications. The resultant need for detailed discussions of the most popular recent versions, under one cover and written by respected biblical scholars and translators with no theological "axe to grind," has given rise to the present volume. It had its beginnings with the Spring, 1979 issue of The Duke Divinity School Review, entitled *Recent English Versions of the Bible* (Lloyd R. Bailey, Guest Editor). Potential authors were asked to evaluate a given version by whatever criteria they felt to be appropriate, but to give some attention to the following: (1) textual decisions concerning the original manuscripts (e.g., is one reading from a Hebrew or a Greek text at a given point, and do marginal notes indicate what is happening?); (2) interpretation by the translators (e.g., is word-meaning derived from etymology, context, or cognate languages; theological presuppositions of the translators); and (3) English usage (e.g., clarity, level, consistency).

The demand for the resultant collection of essays, from laypersons, clergy, and faculty alike, suggested that it should be made more widely available, and in an expanded form. Consequent additions include: an initial essay which explains that an answer to the question, "Which Bible?" may depend upon the audience for which it is intended; discussion of NASB; an examination of the most popular "study Bibles"; and a glimpse at the personalities and organization of the KJV translators (Appendix 1). Finally, the versions which have previously been discussed are compared at crucial points (Appendix 2).

Attention should be called to the appendix which follows the discussion of each version (with the exception of NASB). Here one will find a list of the translators, which is otherwise not always readily available. The Lockman Foundation, which holds the copyright to NASB, declined to supply the names of the panel members, in keeping with the policy that "no work will ever be personalized."

James Smart's discussion of the Living Bible was originally published under the title, "The Invented Bible," in *The Presbyterian Record* (July-August, 1976), pp. 6-7, 32, and is reprinted here (with small changes) with the permission of the editor and author.

Lloyd R. Bailey, Sr.
Duke Divinity School

The Contributors

Lloyd R. Bailey is Associate Professor of Old Testament at the Divinity School, Duke University.

Robert G. Bratcher is a Translation Consultant for the United Bible Societies. He was the translator of the Good News New Testament and Chair of the Old Testament translation panel for Today's English Version.

Roger A. Bullard is Professor of Religion and Philosophy at Atlantic Christian College. He served on the Old Testament and Apocrypha translation panels for Today's English Version.

Keith R. Crim is Professor of Philosophy and Religious Studies, Virginia Commonwealth University. He served on the Old Testament translation panel for Today's English Version.

Walter J. Harrelson is Professor of Old Testament at the Divinity School, Vanderbilt University. He is a member of the Revised Standard Version Bible Committee.

Bruce M. Metzger is George L. Collord Professor of New Testament Language and Literature at Princeton Theological Seminary. He is Chair of the Revised Standard Version Bible Committee.

Barclay M. Newman, Jr. is a Translation Consultant for the United Bible Societies. He served on the Old Testament and Apocrypha translation panels for Today's English Version.

Eugene A. Nida is a Translation Consultant for the American Bible Society, and for the United Bible Societies.

James D. Smart is Emeritus Professor of Bible Interpretation at Union Theological Seminary, New York. He is a Presbyterian minister and now resides in Toronto.*

William F. Stinespring is Emeritus Professor of Old Testament and Semitics, the Divinity School, Duke University.

Bruce Vawter is Chair of the Department of Religious Studies, DePaul University. He was a member of the New American Bible translation panel.

*Professor Smart died on January 23, 1982.

Abbreviations

ABS: the American Bible Society

ASV: the American Standard Version (the U.S. edition of RV) (1901)

AT: *The Complete Bible: An American Translation* (commonly called "The Chicago Bible") (1939)

AV: Authorized Version, a common designation for KJV, based upon the statement in its preface. (Other versions may legitimately claim that status, however. See H. G. May, "Authorized Versions," in *The Interpreter's Dictionary of the Bible,* Supplementary Volume.)

ERV: the English Revised Version (the British edition of RV) (1881, 1885, 1895)

JB: the Jerusalem Bible (1966)

JPS: see NJV

KJV: the King James Version (1611)

LB: the Living Bible (1967, 1971)

NAB: the New American Bible (1970)

NASB: the New American Standard Bible (1963, 1971)

NEB: the New English Bible (1961, 1970)

NIV: the New International Version (1973, 1978)

NJV: the New Jewish Version (1962, 1978, 1981), issued by the Jewish Publication Society (and thus sometimes called the New JPS Version)

RSV: the Revised Standard Version (1946, 1952, 1957, 1965, 1966, 1977)

RV: the Revised Version (of KJV); see ERV and ASV

TEV: Today's English Version (1976). The New Testament was published first, as Good News for Modern Man (1966). TEV is commonly called "The Good News Bible."

* * * *

LXX: the Septuagint Version, an ancient Greek translation from Hebrew (and Aramaic) produced by Jewish scribes for Greek-speaking Jews (and later used by Greek-speaking Christians)

MT: the Masoretic Text, a medieval Hebrew (and Aramaic) text produced by Jewish scribes as a "standard" text, which included insertion of vowels (pointing) lacking in earlier Hebrew (and Aramaic) manuscripts

Contents

1
Why So Many Bible Translations?

EUGENE A. NIDA

In recent years an amazing number of new translations of the Bible have been published in English. Some of these are rather traditional in wording, for example, the Revised Standard Version, the New American Bible, and the New American Standard Bible. Others, however, depart rather radically from traditional terminology and syntax, as in the case of the New English Bible and the Jerusalem Bible, while Phillips' translation aims at strictly contemporary speech, and Today's English Version (the Good News Bible) represents a type of English usage which may be best called the "common language," since it consists of the overlap area between literary and colloquial levels. In contrast with these linguistic translations there is Clarence Jordan's Cotton Patch Version, which is essentially a "cultural translation," in that it provides an entirely new setting for the gospel message. In the Cotton Patch Version Jesus comes from Valdosta, Georgia, and he is "lynched" rather than crucified. Peter, son of John, is "Rock Johnson," and the scribes and the Sadducees are "seminary professors and denominational executives."

How does it happen that one can now buy at least twenty-five such versions in English, in addition to secondhand copies of such earlier modern-language translations as those by Smith-Goodspeed, Weymouth, and Moffatt? For one thing, new Bible translations seem to be commercially quite profitable, particularly if they are well promoted and especially if they are endorsed by leading television and radio preachers. But the fact that publishing a new Bible translation is commercially profitable may only be a symptom rather than the real cause of so many new translations. In reality, there is a rapidly growing worldwide interest in the Scriptures and this is particularly so in the English-speaking world. In North America alone there are evidently at least 100,000 different groups of laypeople meeting regularly in homes to read and study the Bible together. This interest in the Scriptures is usually not based upon a desire to prove any particular set of theological propositions, but upon an urgent need to gain more insight into personal problems and to understand better how to relate both to God and to family and colleagues. In this respect interest in the Bible seems to be very different than it was in the 1920s and 30s, when there were a number of Bible lecturers going about telling people how the Bible confirms great spiritual truths. Now, interest in the Scriptures is far more personal and reflects more realistically the rapid social change taking place in contemporary society and bringing with it emotional stress, intellectual uncertainty, and personal concern about the future. As a result people are more concerned with the content of the message than with preserving hallowed, traditional wording and grammar.

But rapidly increasing interest in the Scriptures is by no means restricted to the English-speaking world. Some six years ago the total distribution of the Scriptures through the United Bible Societies was 50 million copies of Bibles, New Testaments, portions, and selections. Last year the total was more than 500 million, an increase of 1,000 percent, and yet this distribution by no means met the actual or potential demand. Such an interest in the Scriptures would seem to be an anomaly, especially since persons have been saying for years that present-day people cannot understand the Bible, since documents produced by members of a pre-industrial society some 2,000 to 3,000 years ago cannot be relevant today. How can such books have anything important to say to a society grappling with the problems of urbanization, industrialization, technology, and our incredible capacity for inventiveness? And yet we have not invented a new sin in 2,000 years. Perhaps it is the very timeliness (or timelessness) of the message of the Scriptures which makes it so significant today. People recognize in this "mirror" that the real problems of our world are not material or organizational but essentially personal, for it is from the heart that proceed both good and evil.

In the English-speaking world some people have returned to the King James Version, perhaps as a result of a spiritual nostalgia for more settled times. Some of these persons particularly appreciate the cadence of this version and they like to recite its familiar, though often poorly understood, verses as a kind of Protestant rosary. This may explain various attempts to modernize the King James Version at points, so that it can continue to serve the interests of those who have made it into a present-day Vulgate, in other words, a touchstone of doctrinal purity and exegetical accuracy.

In reality, of course, the multiplicity of Bible translations in English is only a reflection of the heterogeneous nature of our present-day society, in which there are important differences in sociolinguistic dialects, in attitudes toward tradition, and in the multiple roles in which so many people are involved.

Any complex society with highly diverse occupations and varying levels of education will inevitably develop a number of sociolinguistic dialects representing various levels of technical and literary usage. While in earlier times translators were faced with the problems of diverse geographical dialects, recent widespread communication by radio and television is reducing their significance, but it is by no means eliminating the sociolinguistic dialects which reflect varying degrees of educational attainment and occupational specialization. And even within any one of these sociolinguistic dialects there are a number of distinct levels, including ritualized, formal, informal, casual, and intimate forms of language. These differences in language usage quite naturally give rise to marked differences of opinion as to the type of language which should be employed in translations of the Bible. Should the Scriptures, for example, be rendered in a ritualized form of language, or should they be on a formal or informal level? Some people even want the Scriptures translated on a strictly casual level of speech, as in the case of a translation of the Gospel of John in the substandard speech of Harlem in New York City.

In addition to the significant differences in sociolinguistic dialects which influence people's attitudes toward language, there are several fundamentally different attitudes toward tradition. Some constituencies want to break radically with history and in fact have a strong suspicion of anything which is traditional, but others hang on to tradition with great tenacity. Those who reject the implication of tradition are interested in a translation which will speak to present-day people without the overlayer of traditional, ecclesiastical vocabulary, but those for whom tradition is a very important intellectual anchor cling to old-fashioned expressions as being more authoritative.

The fact that people engage in different roles also explains the reason for multiple needs. An active member of a church may be called upon to read the Scriptures during a church service, teach a Sunday school class, and engage in an informal Bible study with friends or colleagues. For public reading such individuals may want a more traditional translation, while in preparing for teaching they will want to know what a passage really means. One Sunday school teacher who had for many years read only the King James Version found that by using Today's English Version he could grasp the meaning so much more readily. He once exclaimed to his class, "It is so much easier to teach if I really know what the text means." Many who attend Bible classes use at least two versions of the Bible: one, a traditional version because it is familiar and respectable, and another, a modern-language version, so that the meaning of the text can be accurately understood. In fact, most people who have any real interest in studying the Bible usually have several different translations.

Multiplicity of translations is actually the policy of the United Bible Societies for all major languages. In the first place, there is a need for a traditional translation which preserves the vocabulary and forms of expression which have become so endeared to a constitutency and which may have been important in various phases of the literary development of a language. But a traditional translation is not adequate to meet the needs of most people, especially those who do not understand or appreciate a historical, literary level of language. These individuals will want the Bible translated into what may be called "common language," the area of language in which the literary and colloquial forms overlap. It is this common language which is closest to the Koine Greek of the New Testament and to much of the Hebrew of the Old Testament. But translations which are based only on traditional or common areas of language will not ultimately satisfy the needs of all people. There should also be in every major language a translation in a present-day form of literary language particularly appropriate for worship.

Present-day developments in Bible translating reflect important advances in biblical studies and in communication theory. Advances in biblical studies have been particularly notable in the area of textual analysis and exegesis. Communication theory has made possible a more realistic and effective focus upon the processes of communication, with particular emphasis upon the roles of the receptors for whom a translation is adequate only if it is really understood.

One of the important areas in which biblical studies has contributed significantly to translation involves Greek and Hebrew texts. Because of the dominance of the King James Version, many people have become emotionally attached to its renderings, which reflect the Textus Receptus, or more accurately, the "traditional" Greek text that has come down to us through the so-called Byzantine tradition. From time to time people ask us in the Bible Society whether we have the King James Version in Japanese, Chinese, or the languages of India, thinking that the King James Version is itself "the Bible." More recently some persons have attempted in pseudo-scientific ways to defend the Textus Receptus. They believe that such a "majority text" must be more reliable than other less numerous types, by assuming that reliability can be determined by the democratic means of "counting noses." For many persons the Textus Receptus also has a theological appeal, in the sense that they are convinced that God would not have permitted the vast majority of manuscripts to have reflected anything less than the original autographs.

Though New Testament text and scholarship made significant advances under the direction of Eberhard Nestle and his son Erwin Nestle, it became clear that something more satisfactory was needed.

A text based simply on two out of three printed Greek texts would not reflect properly the kind of judgment needed about internal as well as external evidence. As a result, the United Bible Societies formed an international, interconfessional committee to be responsible for the preparation of the Greek New Testament text designed especially for translators. The same text, with a somewhat different apparatus, is now published in the 26th edition of the Nestle-Aland series.

One of the major advantages of this text for translators is that it not only reflects the combined judgment of outstanding specialists in the field of New Testament textual criticism but it also evaluates the variants in terms of four grades of certainty as to the probability of the text being correct. A rating of *A* indicates that there is little or no doubt about the rendering in the text. A rating of *B* indicates some doubt; *C* measures a considerable degree of doubt; and *D* implies that "God only knows what was in the original autograph." This text has met with general acceptance by translators and scholars all over the world and has accordingly become the basis for most committees producing translations of the New Testament.

A similar program has been sponsored by the United Bible Societies for the text of the Old Testament. The international and interconfessional committee for the Hebrew Old Testament Text Project has worked for a period of ten years, analyzing some 5,000 passages in the Old Testament in which there are textual difficulties. Already the Bible Societies have published a five-volume preliminary report in French and English, giving translators advice as to what text seems to be the most satisfactory and providing at the same time a rating as to the probability of the text and also some suggestions as to how it can be translated. The final reports of this committee will consist of five volumes of approximately 1,000 pages each, both in French and in English. They will contain not only the reasoning for the committee's decisions, but will also provide all of the relevant background information from early manuscripts and versions, the opinions of leading medieval Jewish scholars, and a summary of modern scholarly opinion.

In dealing with the textual issues of the Old Testament, the committee made no attempt to reconstruct a so-called Ur-Text (initial copy; autograph) on the basis of literary criticism. Rather, they undertook to establish what might be called the second stage in textual development: the earliest form of the text which can be reconstructed on the basis of textual evidence. It has been interesting to see the extent to which the committee's judgments have shown how remarkably reliable the existing Masoretic Text generally is.

The second principal area in which biblical studies have made an important contribution is in a new concept of the exegetical base for translation. Since the rise of historical criticism, there frequently have been discussions among scholars as to what the base should be. Should one, for example, attempt to go behind the existing biblical texts in order to determine what may have been the original form? Or should one accept as the exegetical basis for translation the meaning which the texts had when they were accepted as the authoritative "Word of God"? In other words, in Genesis 1:2 is one to speak of a "mighty wind" as moving over the water, or is it "the power of God" or "the spirit of God"? In the case of the Psalms, is one to base a translation upon the meaning that certain of the phrases have in Ugaritic literature, or is one to assume that the correct meaning is the way in which it must have been understood when it was used by Israelites in temple worship in Jerusalem?

Some persons have contended that in translating the Scriptures it is important to correct what seem to be evident errors. For example, Acts 7:16 states that Jacob and his sons died and their bodies were taken to Shechem where they were buried in the grave which Abraham had bought from Hamor. According to the Old Testament account, Jacob was buried in Hebron (Gen. 50:12-13) and Joseph was buried in Shechem in a field which Jacob had bought (Josh. 24:32). Rather than correct the New Testament on the basis of Old Testament records, some translators want to revise the Old on the basis of the New, presumably thinking that the latter must be more inspired. This tendency becomes particularly evident when translators wish to change passages in the Old Testament which are quoted in the New on the basis of the Septuagint rather than from the Hebrew text.

Many persons have not recognized the fact that in parts of the Bible there is a distinctive literary genre which literary analysts call "dramatic history." In other words, the accounts are not diaries; neither are they based upon stenographic reporting. Rather, the material was selected and arranged in order to highlight themes which had important historical or theological significance. Thus, translators must accept each text in its own right and translate it as a literary entity rather than attempting to alter it for theological reasons on the basis of some related text.

For many years the Koine Greek of the New Testament was regarded as a unique and distinctive form of language. It was regarded by some as a kind of "Holy Spirit language," since in classical literature there were few clear parallels. Later discoveries of numerous papyri in Egypt changed this viewpoint and people began to realize that Koine Greek was simply the "common Greek" of the day. Great emphasis was placed on this new insight into the language of the New Testament. More recently, biblical study has indicated some of the important Semitic characteristics of the language as well. In fact, many scholars have felt that the Greek New Testament has primarily Hebrew concepts in Greek clothing. Accordingly, New Testament expressions such as "covenant," "righteousness," "loving kindness," "blessing," and "faith" should really be interpreted in the light of the corresponding Hebrew terms, as they are translated in the Septuagint (Greek) text coming from the 3rd century B.C.

Study of Hebrew terms has led to significant new insights. As an illustration, the Hebrew term traditionally translated "righteousness" throughout the Old Testament *(tsedaqah)* has sometimes been found to have a different sense, especially in the latter part of the book of Isaiah. In Isaiah 61:11 for example, rather than the "righteousness" of the Lord, what it really meant is "salvation," and in Isaiah 51:8 the term is better rendered as "deliverance." This theme of God's salvation and deliverance is, however, not new to the book of Isaiah, for it already occurs in the Song of Deborah in Judges 5.

A somewhat corresponding development has taken place with the Greek New Testament term *dikaiosunē.* In the Synoptic Gospels this term normally refers to conduct or behavior which conforms to requirements established by God. But in various passages of the Pauline Epistles this term refers to what God has done in putting people right with God. This latter meaning is particularly crucial in Romans 1:17. At least ninety-five percent of readers do not correctly understand the traditional rendering which is "the righteousness of God is revealed from faith to faith." They naturally assume that "righteousness" in this context must refer to God's own personal quality of justice or rightness. In reality, it means what God does in order to put people in right relationships with deity; and the following Semitic expression, literally "from faith to faith," is an idiom meaning "through faith from beginning to end" or "by means of faith and only by faith."

New exegetical insights have not been restricted to the meanings of words; grammatical constructions also carry meaning. However, one cannot assume that a formal structure automatically provides the basis for understanding the meaning of a combination of words. For example, in Romans 1:5 there is a coordinate construction translated traditionally as "grace and apostleship." Even though the structure is syntactically coordinate, the semantic relationships are subordinate, for "apostleship" is essentially the content of the "grace." In other words, this "grace" consists of "being an apostle." Accordingly, one may best translate the first part of Romans 1:5 as "We received the privilege of being an apostle." In this same verse there is an expression translated traditionally as "obedience of faith." Some have understood this in the sense of "obeying the faith," in which case the Greek term translated "faith" is regarded as really a summary of truth. But this subordinate construction ("obedience of faith") is only a nominal transform for a verbal expression which has a coordinate structure, namely, "believe and obey." Hence, what first appears as a coordinate construction, namely, "grace and apostleship" ends up semantically as subordinate, while a syntactically subordinate construction really has a semantic value of coordination, namely, "believe and obey." This latter type of structure appears in Mark 1:4 in the phrase "baptism of repentance." Grammars may speak of the genitive expression (rendered "repentance") as being a "qualitative genitive," but this does not really help much in understanding the meaning or in determining the underlying structure. In reality, "baptism of repentance" is only a nominal restructuring of what is basically a verb phrase, "repent and be baptized."

These types of insights with regard to the meaning of grammar (reflecting, as they do, certain present-day developments in transformational generative grammar) provide important help to translators who, as in the case of Mark 1:4, may very well discover that in many languages there are no nouns for "baptism," "repentance," or even for "forgiveness" or "sins" which follow in the same verse. All of this may mean that in some languages one must translate Mark 1:4 as, "John . . . preached that people should repent and be baptized, and God would forgive their sins."

The other principal contribution to translation in modern times has been the application of communication theory to the problems of the translator. Essentially, this has meant greater consideration for the role of receptors. In the past translators have seemed to be concerned only with what may have been the intent of the author, and they have given little or no consideration to the problems faced by receptors who must understand a text. When persons ask, "Is this a correct translation?" the most satisfactory response is usually another question: "For whom?" Does the intended audience consist of new adult literates, of children, of students of theology, of the well-educated layperson? Who are the presumed receptors who must decode the message and determine its meaning?

In the past many translators have been unaware of the diversity of possible receptors for a particular text. Scholars often have thought only about how other scholars would criticize their work rather than about how the average reader would likely interpret the vocabulary and syntax of their translations. This may explain some of the vocabulary in the rendering of Hebrews in the New English Bible. It uses such terms as *effulgence, ministrant, purgation, marjoram* and *myriads*. Different educational backgrounds and experiences will determine the extent to which such texts can be accurately and readily understood by receptors.

More important than differing educational levels are the differing emotional orientations which people have concerning translation. These attitudes arise from several sources. One source is the experience of studying a foreign language in school, where for the most part one may have thought of translation as being a word-for-word rendering of a foreign-language text. On the other hand, a person's emotional attitude toward translation may be influenced by the aesthetic appeal which a particular translation may convey, and this is true of the King James Version in particular. Reinforcement of emotional attitudes may result from a spiritual experience associated with a particular version. If a translation has led one to experience conversion to Christian faith, undoubtedly the very form of that translation becomes an important factor in one's attitudes.

Another factor which must be taken into consideration is the different circumstances in which the translation will be used. Is it for private reading or for public worship? In the Revised Standard Version there is no problem in reading the phrase "prophesied with the lyre" (1 Chronicles 25:3), but in hearing the passage read in public worship most people will understand "liar" rather than "lyre."

One must also reckon with the different needs which people have. For example, some persons may be keenly interested in studying the form of an original text, since from an analysis of a literal form, they may feel that they can better appreciate the content. Accordingly, some persons attempt to study the New Testament on the basis of an interlinear translation of the Greek. This, however, can be very misleading, as has occurred several times with persons who have misjudged the meaning of John 1:1. They have assumed that the Greek must mean "and the Word was a God," because there is no article with the predicate noun. Not knowing certain syntactic rules of the Greek language, they have been unaware of the fact that a predicate attributive normally does not have an article when placed in a pre-verb position.

In order to understand what has been happening in an increasing number of modern translations, it may be well to emphasize the significance of translation as being a process of reproducing in a receptor language the "closest natural equivalent" of the message in the source language. Since no two words in any two languages have exactly the same denotative and connotative meanings, one cannot expect absolute correspondence, or a strictly concordant translation, but one can always find a functional equivalent. To translate the Greek term *sarx* always as "flesh" is to misunderstand the essential fact of areas of meaning, for words are not "points of meaning" but cover areas of meaning, and there are no two words in two different languages which cover precisely the same semantic area. This means that one must often use different terms in rendering a source-language word if the correct meaning is to be satisfactorily conveyed. In Luke 24:39 one can justifiably translate "a spirit does not have flesh and bones," but to translate the Greek term *sarx* as "flesh" in Romans 11:14 is to distort the meaning of the original, for one does not "provoke to jealousy those of one's flesh," but one can "make the people of my own race jealous." In Acts 2:17 a literal rendering "pour out my Spirit upon all flesh" is relatively meaningless, for the Greek term *sarx* refers here to people, and therefore one must translate "pour out my Spirit upon all people."

An equivalent, however, should be a *natural* equivalent, that is to say, the best translation is one which does not sound like a translation. While the content of the Bible will indicate clearly that the events did not happen in the next town two or three years ago, this does not mean that the grammatical structures and the vocabulary employed by the translator should seem to be strange, foreign, or outlandish.

In being a natural equivalent of an original expression a rendering should also be the *closest* equivalent. It should make explicit only what is structurally implicit. That is to say, it must not add to the text anything which is not to be found structurally implicit in the text itself. For example, in the above translation of Mark 1:4, namely, "John . . . preached that the people should repent and be baptized and God would forgive their sins." Both "the people" and "God" are structurally implicit in this passage, and therefore making them explicit is completely legitimate. But it is not legitimate to add to a text what is not to be found in the lexical or syntactic structure. In the rendering of John 1:17 in the Living Bible, Kenneth Taylor has added as a characterization of the law the following phrase: "with its rigid demands and merciless justice." Such a statement does not occur anywhere in the New Testament. Furthermore, it is completely out of keeping with the theology of the New Testament, for the law is regarded as a positive means of leading people to a recognition of sin and of introducing the believer to the grace of God in Christ (Gal. 3:24).

Equivalence in translating must also be understood in a dynamic rather than in a mechanical sense, for the relationship is not one of mere formal correspondence between terms but between the ways in which the particular message of the Scriptures is understood. Because of the importance which the Scriptures attach to history in the sense of the uniqueness of God's entrance into history in salvation and deliverance, it is not enough for modern receptors to comprehend the message merely in terms of their own personal experience. They must understand something of the particular historical context in which God has been revealed. This implies a corresponding set of relationships and so we define translation as a process in which the meaning of the original text is made sufficiently clear to receptors of a translation that they can understand how the original receptors must have comprehended the message. This does not mean that one is justified in introducing into a translation all of the background information which the original source and receptors must have shared. When necessary, that kind of information can be placed in marginal notes, but because of the two corresponding sets of comprehension, namely, the understanding of present-day receptors in such a way as to be able to appreciate the way in which the original receptors understood the original message, one must speak of dynamic equivalence rather than formal correspondence of item for item.

As a result of focusing attention upon the comprehension of receptors, present-day translations give attention to the problems posed by changes which are constantly occurring in modern languages. Often those terms which have been traditionally used in renderings of the Scriptures are no longer satisfactory, since they have lost their earlier significance. This is particularly true of the English word "grace" as a rendering of the Greek *charis*. The Greek word actually had a considerable chain of related meanings, beginning with "beauty of form" and then developing a series of related meanings involving "beauty of personality," "generosity," "kindness," "gift," and "thankfulness." Though the English term "grace" does share some of these meanings, particularly in the sense of "beauty of form and movement," a high percentage of the meanings are quite different from those which occur in the Greek New Testament for the corresponding word *charis*. In the Random House Dictionary of English, "grace" in the theological sense is listed only as the seventh meaning, and even that requires special identification and explanation.

In the Middle Ages there was a tendency to think of "grace" as being a kind of substance which could be dispensed, but in the New Testament phrases such as "the grace of God" do not refer to a substance or to a personality trait of God. They refer, rather, to what God does in bestowing unmerited favor or blessing. It is no wonder, therefore, that the Greek term *charis* is variously translated. Though in some passages it can be rendered in English as "grace," it is often better rendered as "blessing," as in John 1:16 and Luke 2:40. In Ephesians 4:29 instead of "to minister grace" (KJV), it is far better to speak of "to do good." In Philippians 1:7 the traditional phrase "ye are all partakers of my grace" (KJV) is doubly misleading, and in this context *charis* is really closer in meaning to the English term "love." In Today's English Version this phrase is rendered as "you are always in my heart." In Colossians 4:6 *charis* qualifies the content of what people should say, and therefore it may be far more satisfactory to say "your speech should be pleasant." And in 1 Peter 3:7 instead of "the grace of life" (RSV) a more satisfactory equivalent is "the gift of life."

Because of special emphasis upon the significance of receptors in the communication process, increasing attention in translation is paid to the factor of aesthetic appreciation. Many translators, however, seem to concentrate their attention upon the written form of a text, not realizing that far more people are likely to hear a text read than will ever read it for themselves. In reading a page receptors do pay attention to punctuation marks, but punctuation marks rarely play a significant role in the oral reproduction of a text. Hence, an expression such as "lead us back to the land, Lord" is likely to be understood as "lead us back to the landlord." Or, "see, the enemy is coming" is likely to be understood as simply "see the enemies coming."

The problem of decoding an oral text is in many regards more difficult than interpreting the written form, despite the fact that the former provides many semantic clues by means of intonation. In the oral form, however, there is a problem of temporary memory, for the text is in a lineal order, while in reading one can often decode by chunks as the eye races back and forth on a line or over an area of text. This cannot be as easily done in the oral form of a text, and therefore translators must pay far greater attention to the way in which people are likely to understand a text, based upon the problems posed by the limited span of temporary memory.

One of the serious problems in the style of a translation involves maintaining the same linguistic register. For example, a letter, whether personal or general, should not sound like some kind of legal document, nor in English should poetry start out primarily with basic Anglo-Saxon vocabulary and then shift promptly to heavy Latinized expressions. One aspect of the New English Bible which has been rather extensively criticized is the lack of consistency in register, for the text often shifts abruptly from a rather elevated literary style to almost slang expressions.

An even more dangerous aspect of Bible translating involves the tendency to embellish a text. There is in all cultures a tendency to embellish whatever is particularly appreciated or valued. Accordingly, many translators wish to employ for the entire New Testament a relatively high literary form of language as a means of signaling the importance of the text, but this inevitably wipes out differences between various books.

As a result, the Gospel of Mark ends up sounding like the Epistle to the Hebrews; and 2 Peter, which employs a level of Koine Greek bordering on substandard usage, sounds like 1 Peter, which contains some of the most elaborately structured Greek in the entire New Testament.

Though in the translation of the Bible content obviously has priority over form, nevertheless, there is a message which is communicated by form. For example, the disjunctive anacolutha of the Pauline Epistles (e.g., Rom. 5:12; 9:22-24) and the heavy parenthetical expressions (e.g., 2 Cor. 6:1-3) suggest the intense personal involvement of Paul in the message which he was dictating. This same intensity cannot always be expressed in translation by using sentences which are grammatically incomplete. One may, however, be able to suggest something of the same meaning by a quite different form, namely, short parallel structures. It is a mistake to obliterate stylistic differences between books, and it is equally wrong to embellish a text to the point of making it seem "other worldly."

Communication theory has been important in making significant contributions to the translation of the Scriptures in European languages, but it has been even more crucial for the translation of the Bible into the languages of the Third World, with their vast linguistic and cultural diversities. Perhaps the most obvious problems have involved the necessity for syntactic restructuring. In a number of languages, for example, there are few, if any, so-called "passive constructions," so that one simply cannot translate "Judge not that ye be not judged." In such languages it is essential to indicate clearly who is the agent of the passive construction "be not judged." Most scholars regard this passive expression as an instance of so-called "divine avoidance," that is to say, the avoidance of specifically naming God as the agent, so that a proper interpretation of this passage is "Judge not in order that God will not judge you." This passage certainly does not mean that one should not criticize others simply as a means of avoiding criticism.

Syntactic problems become far more acute in languages in which indirect quotations must be changed into direct ones. But what is more complex are the so-called implied quotations. For example, in some languages one cannot translate literally "praise God," for the term "praise" implies some direct quotation, and therefore it may be necessary to say, "God is great" or "God is wonderful."

A far more complex problem of syntactic restructuring involves the fact that in so many languages there are few if any nouns for events or states of being, so that terms such as "kindness," "goodness," "faith," and "joy" must all be rendered by verbs rather than by nouns. Accordingly, "kindness" must become "to be kind to someone" and "faith" must become "trust" or "believe in."

Most people assume that so-called "primitive languages" (though there is really no such thing, since such languages may be exceedingly complex) lack sufficient words to express biblical truths. The real difficulty which translators have, however, is not in finding sufficient words or phrases, but in sorting out the subtle differences between a number of ways of speaking about essentially the same experience. No two languages have any two corresponding words which have absolutely the same meaning, but there are always sufficient expressions to render such concepts as "love," "trust," "obedience," and "goodness," though it may be necessary to use various idiomatic expressions. For example, in some languages one must speak of "loving God" as "my heart goes away with God," and "obeying God" may be expressed as "listening to God with the heart."

To translate idioms literally is almost always a mistake, for it is very likely that such translations will either be meaningless or carry the wrong meaning. For example, in rendering Psalm 60:8 a translation such as "I cast my shoe on Edom" would certainly be interpreted in most languages as indicating disrespect or contempt for Edom. However, in this passage God is declaring that Edom belongs to him, for in Old Testament times the idiom "to cast one's shoe on" indicated taking possession of something.

If a translator is to communicate God's word in a relevant manner, there must be a constant awareness of local indigenous expressions, even if they may be incredibly strange to those who are not familiar with the culture. For example, in the language of one tribe in the Baiyer River area of New Guinea, the only way to talk about God's forgiveness is to say "God does not hang up jawbones against us," an idiom which reflects a common practice among these former headhunters. People who had lost a member of the family in an enemy raid would rescue the body, remove the jaw, cut away the meat, and then hang the jawbone on the doorpost, as a reminder that some time within the next week, month, year, or even generation, some one in the family must kill a member of the enemy tribe or clan. But when such persons become Christians the most significant ceremony is one in which they take down the jawbones and burn them to indicate that since they have experienced the forgiveness of God, who "does not hang up jawbones," they likewise have forgiven others.

At the present time Translations Consultants and Advisors of the United Bible Societies are engaged in providing help to teams of translators working in some 750 languages, representing over eighty percent of the world's population. In fact, Bible translating is being carried on in practically all major languages of the world, including more than fifty languages in Europe, twelve of which are behind the Iron Curtain. In addition to this enormous program, Bible translating is also going on in some 500 additional languages which are being newly reduced to writing. Much of this work is under the auspices of the Wycliffe Bible Translators, but additional programs are being carried out by the Lutheran Bible Translators, the Pioneer Bible Translators, and the Evangel Bible Translators. These groups have patterned their work to some extent upon the program of the Wycliffe Bible Translators, but normally in much closer cooperation with existing churches and Christian constituencies.

At present there is far more Bible translating being done than at any time in the history of Christendom. A translation of at least some portion of the Scriptures is completed at the average rate of one every two weeks.

2
The Revised Standard Version

Bruce M. Metzger

The New Testament of the Revised Standard Version (RSV) was published in 1946; the Old Testament in 1952; the books of the Apocrypha in 1957; the second edition of the New Testament in 1971; and the expanded edition with the Apocrypha in 1977. The Revised Standard Version is, in fact, still in the making, for the RSV Bible Committee is an ongoing committee, and its annual meetings are devoted to taking into account the discovery and publication of still more ancient manuscripts of the Old and New Testaments as well as the refining of the English expressions chosen to render the original text. At the moment the Committee is also giving attention to the presence of masculine-oriented phraseology imposed on the Bible by earlier translators (see below). The most noteworthy new development was the publication in 1977 of the first truly ecumenical edition of the Bible in English, suited for use by members of all three principal branches of the Christian Church—Protestant, Roman Catholic, and Eastern Orthodox (see below).

In what follows attention is given to the historical background of the RSV Bible, including earlier revisions of the King James Version culminating in the American Standard Version (1901) and the subsequent formation of the RSV Bible Committee. This is followed by consideration of certain problems, old and new, in Bible translating, and the ongoing work of the RSV Committee in preparation of the forthcoming revision of the RSV text.

Earlier Revisions of the King James Version

When King James I of England assembled about fifty scholars in the early seventeenth century, it was not to make an entirely new translation of the Bible, but to revise the English version of 1568 called the Bishops' Bible. Let it be said with all due emphasis that these learned men produced, from a purely literary point of view, a classic rendering of the Scriptures, and the 1611 Bible has deserved the acclaim that it eventually won for itself.

Despite the wide acceptance which the 1611 Bible eventually attained, in subsequent generations occasional proposals were voiced as to the desirability of introducing here and there various corrections and other alterations of phraseology. During the eighteenth and nineteenth centuries several dozen private ventures in Bible translating were undertaken in England and in America. Some of these were merely revisions of the King James Version; others were more independent paraphrases. An example of the former type was John Wesley's revised edition of the Authorized Version of the New Testament, published in 1768 with some 12,000 alterations in all, but none of them, the reader is assured, for altering's sake. The same year saw the publication of a quite paraphrastic rendering in the stilted, verbose style of eighteenth-century English popular in the time of Samuel Johnson. Made by the bibliographer Edward Harwood, an ordained Presbyterian minister, its style can be seen from the grandiose manner in which Harwood renders Jesus' Parable of the Prodigal Son:

> A Gentleman of a splendid family and opulent fortune had two sons. One day the younger approached his father, and begged him in the most importunate and soothing terms to make a partition of his effects betwixt himself and his elder brother—The indulgent father, overcome by his blandishments, immediately divided all his fortunes betwixt them, etc. (Luke 15:11ff.)

Harwood's elaboration of the familiar text of John 3:16 is as follows:

> For the supreme God was affected with such immense compassion and love for the human race, that he deputed his son from heaven to instruct them—in order that everyone who embraces and obeys his religion might not finally perish, but secure everlasting happiness.

In America Noah Webster, the lexicographer, prepared a revision of the King James Version which was published in New Haven in 1833. A Congregational layman who had been admitted to the bar, Webster's purpose was, as he says, to remove obsolete phrases, to remove grammatical infelicities,[1] and to correct mistranslations. To this he added one thing more, which he considered of very grave importance. In his own words:

> To these may be added many words and phrases very offensive to delicacy, and even to decency. In the opinion of all persons with whom I have conversed on the subject, such words and phrases ought not to be retained in the version. Language which cannot be uttered in company without a violation of decorum, or the rules of good breeding, exposes the Scriptures to the scoffs of unbelievers, impairs their authority, and multiplies or confirms the enemies of our holy religion. (Preface to Webster's Bible)

Another American production, similar to Harwood's British monstrosity, was *A New and Corrected Version of the New Testament,* prepared by Rodolphus Dickinson, an Episcopalian rector, and published at Boston in 1833. The preface to this volume is an astonishing exhibition of conceit.

The author condemns the "quaint monotony and affected solemnity" of the King James Version, with its "frequently rude and occasionally barbarous attire," and he declares his purpose to adorn the Scriptures with "a splendid and sweetly flowing diction" suited to the use of "accomplished and refined persons." Here are Mr. Dickinson's renderings of three well-known passages:

> And it happened, that when Elizabeth heard the salutation of Mary, the embryo was joyfully agitated. (Luke 1:41)
>
> His master said to him, Well-done, good and provident servant! you was[2] faithful in a limited sphere, I will give you a more extensive superintendence; participate in the happiness of your master. (Matt. 25:21)
>
> Festus declared with a loud voice, Paul, you are insane! Multiplied research drives you to distraction. (Acts 26:24)

One of the curiosities in the history of the English Bible is the translation of the Scriptures made by Julia E. Smith, the Women's Suffragist of the past century. Published in 1876 at Hartford at her own expense, this version is excessively wooden, using throughout the same English word for the same Hebrew or Greek word. She thought that, as she says in the Preface, this would give "much clearer understanding of the text." The end result, however, of such a policy of mechanical translation was much nonsense and, in some passages, almost complete mistranslation. In historical narratives she rendered Hebrew verbs in the future tense, giving the reader the impression that everything in those narratives, including the acts of creation in Genesis, chapter 1, was yet to happen. The extent of the obscurity is suggested by Jeremiah 22:23, presented as a complete sentence and reading: "Thou dwelling in Lebanon, building a nest in the cedars, how being compassionated in pangs coming to thee the pain as of her bringing forth."

Miss Smith illustrates dramatically a fact which some persons do not appreciate, namely, that most words have more than one meaning, and in translation the more specific meaning of a word in a particular context has to be determined from that context. Perhaps her initial mistake was to seek no help or advice in her venture, as she naively discloses to the reader: "It may be thought by the public in general that I have great confidence in myself in not conferring with the learned in so great a work, but as there is but one book in the Hebrew tongue, and I have defined it word for word, I do not see how anybody can know more about it than I do"!

The Revised Version in England and the Standard Version in America

As time went on, an ever greater need was felt for a thorough revision of the 1611 Bible to be made by a committee comprising representatives of diverse ecclesiastical affiliations. In 1870 both Houses of Convocation of the Anglican Church in England adopted a recommendation which led to the preparation of an "official" revision. A committee of British scholars and divines, numbering at various times twenty-four to twenty-eight, labored for ten and a half years to produce the Revised Version of the New Testament and fourteen years to produce the Old Testament. Soon after work on the revision had begun, an invitation was extended to American scholars to co-operate with the British in this work of common interest. Thereupon an American committee, comprising about thirty members (of which only about twenty members were active), was appointed from nine different denominations, with the eminent church historian Philip Schaff acting as chair.

The Revised Version of the Bible was published and copyrighted by the University Presses of Cambridge and Oxford, the New Testament appearing in 1881, the Old Testament in 1885, and the Apocrypha in 1895. Readings which the American Committee preferred but which the British Committee rejected were printed in an Appendix (for example, the Americans preferred "Jehovah" to represent the Hebrew divine name [tetragrammaton] instead of the traditional word "LORD" printed with a capital and small capitals).[3] The agreement was that after fourteen years the Americans would be allowed to publish an edition of the Revised Version that incorporated into the text itself the several preferences previously listed in the Appendix. Accordingly, in 1901 the American Committee issued through Thomas Nelson and Sons the Standard American Edition of the Revised Version of the Bible (the Apocryphal books were not included). In order to protect the integrity of the version, which came to be called the American Standard Version, its text was copyrighted by the publisher.

The fate of the Revised Version in Great Britain was disappointing. Complaints about its English style began to be made as soon as it appeared. Charles Hadden Spurgeon, the great English preacher at the close of the nineteenth century, put it tersely when he remarked that the Revised New Testament was "strong in Greek, weak in English." The Revisers were often woodenly literal, inverting the natural order of words in English to represent the Greek order; and they carried the translation of the article, and of the tenses, beyond their legitimate limits. An example of rather tortuous order in English in the Revision is Luke 9:17, "And they did eat, and were all filled; and there was taken up that which remained over to them of broken pieces, twelve baskets." These criticisms apply as well to the American Standard Version.

In the United States the work of the Revisers was somewhat more widely adopted than in Britain. But in both countries the revision failed to supplant the King James Version in popular favor. Furthermore, proponents of other versions in a more modern idiom deprecated the Revisers' continued use of archaic speech.

The need, then, for a generally acceptable revision continued, and was accentuated during the twentieth century by the discovery of new evidence for the text and its meaning. Many private translations appeared, representing various interests and emphases. Three widely used modern speech renderings were those of R. F. Weymouth, James Moffatt,[4] and E. J. Goodspeed. More idiosyncratic were the "immersionist" Bible, which uses "immerse" in place of "baptize," and the Jehovah's Witnesses' *New World Translation,* which introduces the word "Jehovah" 237 times into the New Testament.

The Revised Standard Version

Steps to produce a suitable revision of the American Standard Version were undertaken in 1928 when the copyright of that version was acquired by the International Council of Religious Education. In the same year the American Standard Bible Committee was appointed, with an original membership of fifteen scholars, to have charge of the text of the American Standard Version and to make further revision of the text should it be deemed necessary. The chair of the Committee was Luther A. Weigle, Dean of Yale Divinity School and Chair of the Federal Council of Churches of Christ.

For two years the Committee wrestled with the question whether or not a revision should be undertaken; and if so, what should be its nature and extent. At one extreme stood James Hardy Ropes of Harvard, who held that the revisions of the King James Version published in 1881 and 1901 ought not to have been made, and opposed any further revision.[5] At the other extreme was Edgar J. Goodspeed of Chicago, who advocated a new version in present-day colloquial English. Finally, after revisions of representative chapters of the Bible had been made and discussed, a majority of the Committee decided that there should be a thorough revision of the American Standard Version of 1901, which would stay as close to the King James tradition as it could in the light of present knowledge of the Greek text and its meaning on the one hand, and present usage of English on the other.

In 1930 the nation and the churches were going through a serious economic depression and it was not until 1936 that funds could be secured and the work of revision could begin in earnest. A contract was negotiated with Thomas Nelson and Sons, publishers of the American Standard Version, to finance the work of revision by advance royalties, in return for which Nelsons were granted the exclusive right to publish the Revised

Standard Version for a period of ten years. Thereafter it was to be open to other publishers under specific conditions.

With the financial undergirding thus provided, it was possible to schedule regular sessions of both the Old Testament and the New Testament Sections. Travel expenses and lodging and meals for the members were provided. No stipends or honoraria, however, have been given to RSV Committee members, who contribute their time and energies for the good of the cause.

After serious work had begun, a hope was expressed that cooperation of British scholars might be obtained, thus making the version an international translation. The war years of 1939-1945, however, made such collaboration impossible. In the summer of 1946, after the war was over, an effort was made to secure at least a token of international collaboration in the work on the Old Testament, the RSV New Testament having been published in February 1946. Such partial collaboration was not to be forthcoming, for in that same year delegates of several Protestant Churches in Britain decided that they should begin work on a wholly new translation, one which made no attempt to stand within the tradition of the 1611 Bible. The outcome of this effort was the New English Bible published in 1970.

Meanwhile, work continued on the RSV Old Testament. After 81 separate meetings, totalling 450 days of work, the complete Bible was published September 30, 1952, the festival day, appropriately enough, of St. Jerome.[6] The new version was launched with an unprecedented publicity campaign. On the evening of the day of publication, in the United States, in Canada, and in many other places, 3418 community observances were held with over one and a half million persons attending.

The fanfare, however, did not protect the version from adverse criticism. Pamphlets appeared bearing such titles as *The Bible of Antichrist, The New Blasphemous Bible,* and *Whose Unclean Fingers Have Been Tampering with the Holy Bible, God's Pure, Infallible, Verbally Inspired Word?* The last named pamphlet opens with the sentence: "Every informed and intelligent person knows that our government is crawling with communists, or those who sanction and encourage communism"—which indicates the line along which the version was attacked. In fact, those who were looking for an opportunity to calumniate the Federal Council of Churches, under whose auspices the RSV had been produced, managed to influence Senator Joseph McCarthy's investigative committee to bring insidious and absurd charges against several members of the RSV Committee, to the effect that they were either communists or were hospitable to communist ideas—allegations that were eventually printed, of all places, in the United States Air Force Training Manual! As the result of a thorough investigation conducted by non-partisan authorities, this entirely unsupported charge was rebutted on the floor of the House of Representatives in Washington.[7]

Despite these and other criticisms during succeeding years, the RSV made its way in the United States and in other countries where the English language is used. It is a testimony to its qualities that in Great Britain, where it has not enjoyed the intensive "promotion" which it was given in North America, it has made steady headway on the ground of its intrinsic merit.

The Revised Standard Version, Catholic Edition

A new and unexpected development came in the autumn of 1953 when the Chair of the Standard Bible Committee received a letter from the Catholic Biblical Association of Great Britain, asking whether there would be any disposition to confer with them about certain emendations in the RSV which they had in mind, with an eye to the possibility of issuing an adaptation for Roman Catholic readers. After consultation with members of the RSV Committee, Weigle and Gerald E. Knoff, who was then the General Secretary of the Division of Christian Education of the National Council of Churches, began conversations with representatives of the Catholic Biblical Association. By 1956 most of the desired New Testament changes were reviewed, a draft of a Foreword was discussed, and the exact wording on the title page was approved. All seemed to be going well—but the uncertainties of human life interposed a delay. Cardinal Griffin of London, who had written a Foreword for the RSV New Testament, Catholic Edition, died suddenly.

The promoters of the edition in England were faced with a quandary. Did the Cardinal's authorization for the edition still hold? And if technically legal, was it wise and prudent to proceed? As it turned out, Cardinal Griffin's successor, Archbishop William Godfrey, declared in 1958 that he could not sanction the venture, that it would cause a scandal to the faithful to receive a translation of the New Testament that had been made originally by a committee of Protestant scholars.

In the course of time, however, in view of the new climate that began to pervade the Roman Catholic Church after Vatican Council II, negotations were resumed, and finally in the spring of 1965 the Catholic Edition of the RSV New Testament was published by the two branches of Thomas Nelson and Sons, in Edinburgh and in New York. An appendix in the volume lists the 93 verses involving 67 slight changes in the wording required by the Catholic Biblical scholars. (The list includes also the original RSV wording.)

The next stage began when consideration was given to a Catholic

Edition of the RSV Old Testament. As is generally known, the Old Testament in Catholic Bibles includes more than the thirty-nine books of the Hebrew Scriptures. These additional books and parts of books, accepted as Deuterocanonical by Catholics, are regarded by Protestants (with several other books) as Apocryphal. The Apocrypha, originally included in the King James Bible of 1611, were translated by a panel of the RSV Committee (working from 1953 to 1956) and published by Nelson in 1957.

Surprisingly enough, the scholars of the Catholic Biblical Association decided to ask for no changes whatever in the RSV Old Testament (including even the rendering of Isaiah 7:14, "Behold, a young woman shall conceive and bear a son . . ."), or in the RSV Deuterocanonical books, which were placed throughout the Old Testament in accord with their position in the Latin Vulgate Bible. In 1966 the RSV Catholic Edition of the entire Bible was published, with a brief Foreword by Cardinal Heenan in the British edition and one by Cardinal Cushing in the American printing. Catholic notes, as at that time required, were included, but Protestant nomenclature in the titles of the biblical books was adopted.

The Catholic Edition of the RSV was just that—a special edition of the RSV text adapted for Roman Catholic readers. The notes as well as the expanded form of the Old Testament made it unsuited as a common or ecumenical Bible. The steps which led to making such an edition, however, were taken during the following decade.

The First Truly Ecumenical Bible

The first step in the production of a truly ecumenical Bible was taken in 1966 when Richard Cardinal Cushing, Archbishop of Boston, gave his imprimatur to the *Oxford Annotated Bible, with the Apocrypha.* This edition, prepared by Herbert G. May and Bruce M. Metzger, contained the original RSV text, not the text as modified for the Catholic Edition. The books of the Apocrypha were segregated and stood after the New Testament.

The next step was taken in 1971 when the second edition of the RSV New Testament was issued. This incorporated a number of changes that reflect the Greek text as adopted for the third edition of the United Bible Societies' *Greek New Testament,* which serves throughout the world as a standard text for translations and revisions made by Protestants and Catholics alike. Among such changes was the transfer of the ending of the Gospel of Mark and of the *pericope de adultera* (John 7:53—8:12) from the RSV footnotes into the text, though the passages continue to be separated from the context by a blank space to show that they were not part of the original text.

Soon afterward a significant step was taken by scholars of the Catholic Biblical Association of Great Britain. Under the leadership of Dom Bernard Orchard and Reginald C. Fuller, a plan was evolved to divide the books of the Apocrypha into two sections, those which the Catholic Church regards as Deuterocanonical and those which are not so regarded. In an edition issued by Collins Press in 1973 these two sections were bound separately between the Old and New Testaments. The volume, therefore, had four sections: the thirty-nine books of the Old Testament, the twelve Deuterocanonical books, the First and Second Books of Esdras and the Prayer of Manasseh (three books which are part of the traditional Apocrypha but are not included among the Deuterocanonical books), and the twenty-seven books of the New Testament. No Catholic notes were included, since this Bible was to be "common," for use by Roman Catholics and Protestants alike.

It should be noted that in such an arrangement Catholics made a significant departure from the accepted practice of their long history. The separation of the Deuterocanonical books from their places throughout the Old Testament is essentially an accommodation to the Protestant arrangement of the books of the Bible.

In May of 1973 a specially bound copy of the Collins RSV "Common Bible" was presented to Pope Paul. In a private audience granted to a small group comprising the Greek Orthodox Archbishop Athenagoras of London, Lady Priscilla and Sir William Collins, Herbert G. May, and the present writer, Pope Paul accepted the copy as a significant step in furthering ecumenical relations among the churches.

Worthy as the "Common Bible" is, however, it fails to live up to its name, for it lacks the full canon of books recognized as authoritative by Eastern Orthodox Churches. The Greek, the Russian, the Ukrainian, the Bulgarian, the Serbian, the Armenian, and other Eastern Churches accept not only the traditional Deuterocanonical books received by the Roman Catholic Church, but also the Third Book of Maccabees. Furthermore, in Greek Bibles Psalm 151 stands at the close of the Psalter, and the Fourth Book of Maccabees is printed as an Appendix to the Old Testament. Inasmuch as these texts were lacking in the "Common Bible" presented to Pope Paul, on that occasion Archbishop Athenagoras expressed to the present writer the hope that steps might be taken to produce a truly ecumenical edition of the Holy Scriptures.

Actually, in 1972 a subcommittee of the RSV Bible Committee had already been commissioned to prepare a translation of 3 and 4 Maccabees and Psalm 151. The members of the subcommittee were Demetrios J. Constantelos, Sherman E. Johnson, Robert A. Kraft, Allen Wikgren, and the writer. In 1976 the completed translation of the three additional texts was made available to the five publishers licensed to issue the RSV Bible. Oxford University Press took steps immediately to produce an expanded form of *The New Oxford Annotated Bible, with the Apocrypha,* the edition of the RSV which had earlier received the imprimatur of Cardinal Cushing.

This expanded edition[9] was published by the Oxford University Press on May 19, 1977. A special pre-publication copy was presented by the present writer to His All Holiness Demetrios I, the Ecumenical Patriarch of Constantinople and titular head of the several Orthodox Churches. In accepting the gift, the Ecumenical Patriarch expressed satisfaction at the availability of an edition of the sacred Scriptures which English readers in all branches of the Christian Church can use.

Thus, the story of the making of the Revised Standard Version of the Bible with the expanded Apocrypha is an account of the slow but steady triumph of ecumenical concern over more limited sectarian interests. For the first time since the Reformation one edition of the Bible has the blessings of leaders of the Protestant, Roman Catholic, and Eastern Orthodox Churches alike.

The Next Stages

As was mentioned earlier, the RSV Bible Committee is an ongoing committee that meets annually. Like Luther, who in repeated revisions continually sought to refine and polish his German translation of the Scriptures, the RSV Committee has not hesitated "to bring backe to the anuill [anvil] that which we had already hammered"—to quote an expression used in the preface of the King James Bible.

By the late-1980s it is expected that the second edition of the RSV Old Testament will be finished. A certain number of changes will also be introduced into the current second edition of the New Testament. Among significant changes will be the dropping of the archaic second person singular pronouns from the Psalms and other prayers in the Bible. In the sixteenth and seventeenth centuries it was customary to use "thou," "thee," and "thine" in ordinary speech. Twenty-five years ago the RSV Committee abandoned this usage except for the Psalms and other prayers in the Bible. Today the archaic pronouns are being used less and less frequently in contemporary liturgy and public prayers, and the Committee has decided that future editions of the RSV will employ the same forms in addressing the Deity as are used for individuals. Such a step will, in fact, reproduce more accurately the usage of the Hebrew and Greek texts themselves, which make no linguistic differentiation between address to God and to a person.

In another area of English usage the RSV Bible Committee has become sensitive to what is termed masculine-oriented language. Increasing numbers of persons are becoming dissatisfied with the generic use of the word "man" or "men," which traditionally has referred to both men and women. In fact, for some persons such language has become highly offensive, and during the past several years a wide variety of steps have been taken to introduce what is called "inclusive" language. Instead of saying, for example, "The West was settled by the pioneers who, with their wives and children, overcame many difficulties," it is obviously fairer to phrase the statement, "The West was settled by pioneer families, who overcame many difficulties." Several major publishers (including Ginn; Holt, Rinehart and Winston; Houghton Mifflin; McGraw-Hill; Macmillan; Random House; Scott, Foresman and Co.)[10] have prepared guidelines concerning the use of inclusive language for authors who plan to submit manuscripts for consideration. The State of Connecticut has revised its constitution to make equal reference to men and women. Several Protestant denominations, as well as groups within Roman Catholic orders and within Reformed Judaism, have undertaken to rephrase their psalter, liturgy, hymns, and a variety of church standards and constitutional documents.

Now, in earlier versions of the Bible, one finds that translators more than once inserted the word "man" where it is lacking in the original text. In many other passages where the original text permits the rendering "any one" or "no one," the King James translators chose to say "any man" or "no man." This practice limits many statements unduly, and results in occasional infelicities. For example, the original printing of the King James Version of Mark 10:18 read: "And Jesus said unto him, Why callest thou me good? There is no man good, but one, *that is* God." Since this implies that God is a man, the unfortunate rendering was soon altered to read, ". . . there is none good but one, *that is,* God." Revelation 3:20 in the King James Version reads, "Behold I stand at the door, and knock: if any man hear my voice, and open the door, I will come in to him, and sup with him, and he with me." Here the Greek text has no word for "man" and in 1946 the RSV correctly rendered it, ". . . if any one hears my voice. . . ." In Luke 17:34 the King James translators inserted the word "men," contrary to the Greek text, so as to read, "I tell you, in that night there shall be two *men* in one bed; the one shall be taken, and the other shall be left." In the second edition of the RSV (1971) the Committee, for obvious reasons, removed the intrusive word, thus returning more closely to the Greek and, incidentally, to all English translations of the verse in pre-1611 Bibles.

At its annual meetings in recent years the RSV Committee has been giving attention to instances where the traditional English rendering has inserted "man" or "men" without support from the Hebrew or the Greek. For example, in Psalm 54:3 "insolent men" and "ruthless men" will become "the insolent" and "the ruthless"; Psalm 66:6 "men passed through the river on foot" will become "they passed through . . ."; and similarly in 106:16; 119:136; 141:5; 142:4; 143:2.

In John 2:10, the Committee has proposed to change "Every man serves the good wine first; and when men have drunk freely, then the poor wine" to "Everyone serves the good wine first, and then the inferior wine after the guests have become drunk"; in Romans 1:17, "He who through faith is righteous . . ." to "The one who . . ."; and in Romans 2:6, "He will render to every man according to his works" to "He will repay according to each one's works."

Besides passages such as these where earlier translators have inserted the word "man" or "men," though it is lacking in the original text, the RSV Committee is giving attention to instances where it may be possible, without producing contrived English, to render the Hebrew word *'ish* and the Greek word *anthropos* in an inclusive sense. For example, in the first Psalm, the Committee, taking *'ish* as a collective term, has replaced "Blessed is the man who walks not in the counsel of the wicked," with "Blessed are those who do not walk. . . ." The frequently occurring expression, "children of men" or "sons of men" (Ps. 11:4, 12:1, 8; 14:2; 21:10; 31:14; 33:13; 36:7; etc.) has been replaced by a variety of expressions, including "all people," "everyone," and "humankind."

In the Letter to the Romans the RSV Committee has proposed to make the following changes: "wickedness of men who . . . suppress the truth" to "wickedness of people who . . ." (1:18); "exchanged the glory of the immortal God for images resembling mortal man" to ". . . glory of the imperishable God for images resembling perishable humanity" (1:32); "God judges the secrets of men" to ". . . secrets of human beings" (2:16); "His praise is not from men but from God" to ". . . from human beings . . ." (2:29).

Much more perplexing is the problem of what should be done and what can be done with passages that use the third person singular pronoun "he," "him," and "his." The RSV Committee is not prepared to use contrived English or such expressions as "he/she" or "s/he." In its deliberations consideration has been given to the possibility of replacing the third person imperative with the second person imperative; for example, changing "He who has an ear, let him hear what the Spirit says to the churches" (Rev. 3:22) to "If you have an ear, listen to what. . . ." Similarly, in Revelation 3:20, to which reference was made earlier, it is currently proposed to read, "Listen! I am standing at the door and knocking; if any of you hear my voice and open the door, I will come in to you and sup with you."

Revision after Revision

If, as Qoheleth says, "of making many books there is no end" (Eccles. 12:12), one can also add, nor is there an end of making revisions and new translations of the Scriptures. Some of these seek to attain still greater accuracy and felicity of expression; others are prepared for special groups of readers. Among the latter are a rendering of the Gospels, by Frank Shaw (a customs officer) and the Reverend Dick Williams, in "Scouse," the dialect used by dock-workers in Liverpool, and Clarence Jordan's Cotton-Patch Version in the idiom current among laborers in rural Georgia.

While an individual's free-lance translation of the Bible is entirely legitimate—in spite of a phrase in the New Testament itself about "private interpretation"—there are precedents and reasons for having successive revisions undertaken by a committee. The compromises which the individual makes unconsciously when working alone become more conscious when committee members differ in opinion and votes. There is some safety in numbers, since in a discussion more aspects of a problem are presented than any individual would have considered. The substantial unanimity resulting in most cases is reassuring to the translators, though not easily or accurately transmitted to the public. The latter may not understand that every word has to be weighed, even if it is left just as it was translated before, and that the easy flowing wording of a single verse represents at times long and repeated debate, sometimes ending in unity and sometimes in a well-justified difference of judgment. These less-favored alternatives constitute the bulk of the few marginal notes which modern revisers have allowed themselves.

Whatever the scholarly advantages of translations by groups of workers, the process involved provides many pleasant social compensations to those who are thus engaged. Intimate and prolonged sessions of discussion, held annually over a period of years, are conducive to a spirit of camaraderie among the members of the committee. Indeed, the sense of fellowship extends in each generation back over the years to earlier revisers and to the many scholars in many lands.

Other men and women have labored, and we have entered into their labors. This process cannot stop in 1611 or in 1952 or in 1982. Slowly, not spectacularly, knowledge of Hebrew and Greek text and language may be expected to grow, and the English language to change. At some future date a new set of revisers will again echo the words in Preface to the King James Bible of 1611:

> . . . as nothing is begun and perfited at the same time, and the later thoughts are thought to be the wiser: so, if we building upon their foundation that went before us, and being holpen by their labours, doe endeuour to make that better which they left so good; no man, we are sure, hath cause to mislike us; they, we perswade our selues, if they were aliue, would thanke us.

List of Members of RSV Bible Committee (1929-1980)

An asterisk before a name signifies that the person has been chosen for competence in English literature, the conduct of public worship, or Christian education. The abbreviation "Apoc." following a name indicates that the person was a member of the subcommittee (1952-57) that produced the RSV translation of the traditional books of the Apocrypha; the abbreviation "Ap." indicates membership on the subcommittee (1972-76) that produced the RSV translation of 3 and 4 Maccabees and Psalm 151, included in the *New Oxford Annotated Bible, with the Apocrypha,* Expanded Edition (1977). The abbreviations OT and NT are self-explanatory.

Name	*Institution*	*Joined*	*Corresp. Member*	*(Resigned)/ Deceased*
Albright, William F. OT	John Hopkins Univ.	1945	1954	1970
Armstrong, William P. NT	Princeton Theol. Sem.	1930		(1937)
*Beardslee, William NT	Emory Univ.	1972	—	—
Beare, Frank W. NT	Trinity Coll., Toronto	1960	1980	—
Bewer, Julius A. OT	Union Theol. Sem., NYC	1930		1951
Blenkinsopp, Joseph OT	Univ. of Notre Dame	1978	—	—
*Bowie, Walter R. NT	Union Theol. Sem., NYC	1937		1969
Bowman, Raymond A. OT	Univ. of Chicago	1960		(1979)
Burrows, Millar OT; NT; Apoc.	Yale Univ.	1938	1972	1980
Cadbury, Henry J. NT; Apoc.	Harvard Univ.	1930	1972	1975
Constantelos, Demetrios NT; Ap.	Stockton College, NJ	1972	—	—
Craig, Clarence T. NT; Apoc.	Oberlin; Yale Univ.; Drew Th. Sem.	1938		1953
Cross, Frank M. OT	Harvard Univ.	1960	1972	
Dahl, George OT	Yale Univ.	1937		1962
Dentan, Robert C. OT	General Theol. Sem., NYC	1960	—	—
Eiselen, Federal C. OT	Garrett Biblical Institute	1929		1937
Ellis, E. Earle NT	New Brunswick Theol. Sem.	1974		(1978)
Filson, Floyd V. NT; Apoc.	McCormick Theol. Sem.	1953	1972	1980
Fitzmyer, Joseph A. NT	Catholic Univ. of America	1969	1974	
Fuller, Reginald C. NT	165 Copenhagen St., London N1 OSR	1969		(1980)
Goodspeed, Edgar J. NT	Univ. of Chicago	1930		1962
Gordon, Alexander R. OT	United Theol. Coll., Montreal	1930		(1930)
Grant, Frederick C. NT; Apoc.	Seabury-Western; Union Th. Sem., NYC	1937	1968	1972
*Greer, Rowan NT	Yale Univ.	1972		(1974)
Hanson, Paul D. OT	Harvard Divinity School	1978	—	—
Harrelson, Walter OT	Vanderbilt Div. Sch.	1976	—	—

Name	*Institution*	*Joined*	*Corresp. Member*	*(Resigned)/ Deceased*
Holladay, William OT	Andover-Newton	1972	—	—
Hyatt, J. Philip OT	Vanderbilt Univ.	1945		1972
Irwin, William A. OT	Univ. of Chicago	1937		1967
James, Fleming OT	Univ. of South; Berkeley Div. Sch.	1947		1954
Johnson, Sherman E. NT; Apoc.; Ap.	Church Div. Sch. of Pacific	1960	—	—
Knox, John NT	Union Theol. Sem., NYC; Epis. Th. Sem.	1960	1972	
Kraft, Robert NT; Ap.	Univ. of Pennsylvania	1972	—	—
Landes, George M. OT	Union Theol. Sem., NYC	1978	—	—
MacRae, George NT	Harvard Univ.	1972	—	—
Maly, Eugene H. OT	Mt. St. Mary's, Ohio	1969	1975	
May, Herbert G. OT	Oberlin; Vanderbilt	1945		1977
McBride, S. Dean OT	Garrett-Evangelical Theol. Sem.	1978	—	—
McKenzie, John L. OT	Notre Dame; DePaul Univ.	1969		(1977)
Meeks, Wayne NT	Yale Univ.	1972		(1974)
Metzger, Bruce M. NT; Apoc.; Ap.	Princeton Theol. Sem.	1953	—	—
Miller, Patrick OT	Union Theol. Sem., Va.	1974	—	—
Minear, Paul S. NT; Apoc.	Yale Univ.	1966	—	—
Moffatt, James OT; NT	Union Theol. Sem. NYC	1930		1944
Montgomery, James A. OT	Univ. of Pennsylvania	1930		1937
*Mowry, Lucetta NT	Wellesley Coll.	1974	—	—
Muilenburg, James OT	Union Th. Sem., NYC; S. F. Th. Sem.	1945	1972	1974
Murphy, Roland OT	Duke Univ.	1976	—	—
*Orchard, Bernard NT	Ealing Abbey, London, England	1969	1979	
Orlinsky, Harry M. OT	Jewish Inst. Rel.-Heb. Union Coll.	1945	—	—
Pfeiffer, Robert H. OT; Apoc.	Harvard Univ.	1953		1958
Pope, Marvin H. OT	Yale Univ.	1960	—	—
Roberts, J. J. M. OT	Princeton Theol. Sem.	1978	—	—
Robertson, A. T. NT	Southern Bapt. Theol. Sem.	1930		1934
Ropes, James H. NT	Harvard Univ.	1930		(1932)
Sampey, John R. OT	Southern Bapt. Theol. Sem.	1929		1938
Sanders, James A.	Claremont School of Theology	1980	—	—
Sauer, Alfred von Rohr OT	Concordia; Seminex	1960	—	—

Name	*Institution*	*Joined*	*Corresp. Member*	*(Resigned)/ Deceased*
Sledd, Andrew NT	Emory Univ.	1930		1937
Smith, J. M. Powis OT	Univ. of Chicago	1930		1932
*Sperry, Willard L. NT	Harvard Univ.	1937		1959
Stanley, David M. NT	Regis Coll., Ontario	1969	1972	
Swaim, J. Carter NT	Church of Covenant, NYC	1954	1966	
Taylor, William R. OT	Univ. of Toronto	1931		1951
Torrey, Charles C. OT	Yale Univ.	1930		1937
Vawter, Bruce OT	DePaul Univ.	1972	—	—
Waterman, Leroy OT	Univ. of Michigan	1937	1954	1972
*Wedel, Theodore O. NT	Coll. of Preachers, Wash., D.C.	1960		1970
*Weigle, Luther A. OT; NT; Apoc.	Yale Univ.	1929		1976
*Wentz, Abdel Ross NT	Lutheran Theol. Sem., Gettysburg	1938	1966	1976
Wikgren, Allen P. NT; Apoc.; Ap.	Univ. of Chicago	1953	—	—
*Wilder, Amos N. NT	Harvard Univ.	1960	1974	
Yates, Kyle OT	Southern Bapt. Theol. Sem.	1939	1954	1975

3
The New English Bible

Roger A. Bullard

It may seem today that the New English Bible was given a rather unfortunate name; after all, newness is a quality that does not last, whether applied to dishwashing detergents or to Bibles. Still, there is some appropriateness to the title, and it is best appreciated against its background.

The New Testament of the NEB appeared March 14, 1961. At the time, the Revised Standard Version was less than ten years old; its NT was of course some years older, but most people were unaware of it until the appearance of the whole Bible, accompanied as it was by a furor born of the McCarthy era. In 1961 the bookstore shelves were not crowded with new translations, so that the RSV and the NEB had it pretty much to themselves. In that context, the New English Bible was indeed something new. As stunningly different from the familiar King James Version as the RSV had seemed in 1952, increasing exposure had made the literary lineage of the latter version more apparent. The NEB brought into focus the similarities of the RSV to the KJV; it thus stood virtually alone as a genuinely new attempt to put the Scriptures into English.

By the time the Old Testament and the Apocrypha appeared on March 16, 1970, that quality of newness was no longer quite so apparent, at least to readers who kept abreast of developments in translation activity. The Jerusalem Bible had already made its appearance and the NT of Today's English Version had become popular. From Roman Catholic circles, the New American Bible was published the same year as the NEB.

Yet, against the background of the centuries, the claim to newness was still valid. From 1525, when William Tyndale's NT in English first appeared, until 1961, when the NEB NT was published, there really had been no major effort by Protestants at a fresh translation of the Bible into English. Rather, there had been a long series of successive revisions: Tyndale was revised by Coverdale (1535); this was revised by John Rogers (Tyndale's literary executor) as "Matthew's Bible" (1537), which was revised under Coverdale's editorship as the Great Bible (1539), in turn revised as the Bishops' Bible (1568), which was revised by King James' learned men (1611). This was revised as the (English) Revised Version of

1881-85, further developed as the American Standard Version of 1901, revised in turn as the Revised Standard Version of 1946-52. Even such a major translation as the Geneva Bible (1560) draws from this tradition. Seen against this backdrop, the newness of the NEB is apparent; it was the first completely fresh major Protestant translation in almost 450 years.

Similarly, the appearance of the NEB fairly soon after the RSV was not a detraction from its newness, for the beginnings of the NEB date from before the publication of the RSV, which was essentially an American undertaking. The NEB was never conceived as competition for the RSV.

The story of the NEB begins in May 1946, when G. S. Hendry, representing the Presbytery of Stirling and Dunblane, presented to the General Assembly of the Church of Scotland a proposal that a new translation of the Bible be undertaken, "in the language of the present day." This phrase was probably designed to underscore the Assembly's intent that the new effort not be another exercise in neo-archaism, as was the English Revised Version (1885), then the only viable alternative to the KJV. In October of 1946, a conference was held of representatives of the Church of England, the Church of Scotland, and of the Congregationalist, Methodist, and Baptist Churches of Britain. Here the participating churches gave approval to the project, laying down the specific principle that a completely new translation was envisioned, not a revision of any existing version.

A second conference was held in January 1947, this time including, along with representatives of the churches, representatives of the university presses of Oxford and Cambridge. At this time a Joint Committee on the New Translation of the Bible was appointed, to be chaired by J. W. Hunkin, Bishop of Truro. After Hunkin's death in 1950, the post was taken by Alwyn P. T. Williams, Bishop of Durham, later of Winchester. He was succeeded, after his death in 1968, by Donald Coggan, Archbishop of York, later of Canterbury.

This Joint Committee held its first meeting in July of 1947. Membership was expanded by the third meeting in January 1948, when invitations to participate had been accepted by the Presbyterian Church of England, the Society of Friends, the Churches in Wales, the Churches in Ireland, the British and Foreign Bible Society, and the National Bible Society of Scotland. At a later stage of the work, the Roman Catholic Church in England and Scotland sent observers.

The Joint Committee began organizing the work by appointing four panels: three of translators (for the OT, NT, and Apocrypha), and one panel of literary advisors. The translators were selected with no regard for denominational affiliation; competence in biblical scholarship was the criterion. C. H. Dodd was made Convener of the NT Panel as well as

Vice-Chair of the Joint Committee. T. H. Robinson, until his death in 1957, served as Convener of the OT Panel; he was followed by G. R. Driver. W. D. McHardy served as Convener of the Apocrypha Panel.

Dividing the work of translating among specialized committees was nothing new; it was at least as old as the KJV, although the committee method had always been used for revisions, not new translations. Appreciating the importance of literary style as well as of accurate scholarship, the KJV translators had had a subcommittee review the whole by reading it aloud. The KJV succeeded so well in establishing itself as a model of English style that the NEB translators heard, as Brahms said of Beethoven, the footsteps of a giant behind them. With a view then to watching for values literary as well as scholarly, the Literary Panel was appointed. Its members were not scholars of the ancient languages, but recognized masters of current English. While the interpretive decisions of the translators were to be regarded as final, the Literary Panel was to review the text with an eye toward polishing the style into a dignified vehicle. Alwyn Williams, later also Chair of the Joint Committee, was Convener of this panel.

The work was not long underway when, in November 1949, Dodd assumed the additional task of General Director, an office created in an attempt better to coordinate the work of the four panels. Dodd became an *ex officio* member of each. In July 1965 G. R. Driver of the OT Panel became Joint Director with Dodd. McHardy was made Deputy Director in December 1968.

Thus the initials of these three gentlemen, Dodd, Driver, and McHardy, appear at the end of the introductions to the NT, OT, and Apocrypha, respectively. The chairs of the Joint Committee, Alwyn Williams and Donald Coggan, affixed their signatures to the prefaces of the NT (1961) and the whole Bible (1970), respectively. These signatures deserve some explanation, since reputable writers have been mistaking them.[1] Williams' signature appears as "Alwyn Winton," i.e., *Alwyn Wintoniensis,* or Alwyn, (Bishop) of Winchester. Coggan's signature is "Donald Ebor," i.e., *Donald Eboracensis,* or Donald, (Archbishop) of York. This is the customary form for signatures of bishops of the Church of England.

A plan was soon agreed upon for the work to follow. For each book of the Bible, a draft translator was assigned. These were almost always members of the relevant panels, although there were a few exceptions. When the draft translation was ready, it was sent to other members of the panel. When the panel met, the draft was discussed in exhaustive detail. Differences of opinion were resolved either by the panel's reaching a consensus, or in serious cases of disagreement, by the adoption of alternate translations to be published as footnotes to the NEB text. When the translating panel had finished with a book, it was sent on to the literary panel, where it was subjected to a different type of scrutiny. Here the discussion was not about the authenticity of the text translated, or the meaning of some word in the original, or of some ancient grammatical device. The members of this panel concerned themselves only with the level of English employed in the translation. It was their aim to make it consistently dignified, yet appropriate to the genre being translated: poetry, law, narrative, etc. After this analysis, the modified draft went back to the translators, as a guarantee that the intent of the original had not been lost in the process. We are told that especially difficult passages made several trips back and forth between the panels.

These peregrinations completed, the text went to the Joint Committee, with whom lay final responsibility for the project, and who were called on by translators and literary advisors alike for clarifications of policy. Under Dodd's direction, some papers were circulated to the four panels early in the work, indicating some of the general policy regarding the nature of the translation. Dodd himself indicated the purpose of the translation in terms of its intended readership. The new version was not intended primarily to be read in church. Rather, three groups of potential readers were being addressed: those who have little contact with the church, for whom the versions in use were unintelligible; young people, for whom the Bible must be contemporary if it is to mean anything; and intelligent churchgoers for whom the language of the Bible is so familiar that it carries little meaning. It was to be plain enough that any "reasonably intelligent person" could understand it, without its being pedestrian. One should be able to read it aloud with dignity, and it might be hoped that, within these restrictions, the version could produce some "arresting and memorable renderings."[2]

It is convenient, in evaluating the NEB, to consider each of the two testaments and the Apocrypha separately, since observations applying to one part do not necessarily apply to the others.

The textual basis of the NEB New Testament is eclectic. This is a fair representation of the state of NT textual studies today, which, as Dodd's preface to the NT explains, is commanded by no single theory, such as held sway at the time of the RV/ASV revisers. Each reading[3] has been judged on its individual merits, and not in the frame of an overarching theory of textual development and transmission. It may be useful here to record the NEB's decisions on some of the standard problems.

The pericope of the adulteress, John 7:53—8:11, appears as a separate section at the end of the Gospel, where a concise but thorough note explains the problems in placing the narrative.

A change has taken place in the handling of the ending to Mark between the publication of the Bible in 1970 and the appearance of the Oxford Study Edition of 1976. In earlier editions there was a space in the middle of 16:8, separating the text from the so-called "shorter ending." Another space divided this from the so-called "longer ending" (familiar from the KJV), at which point the versification resumed. All but one of the manuscripts which give the shorter ending follow it with the longer, so that the early editions of the NEB reflect the ordering of the relevant manuscripts. In the 1976 edition, the longer ending precedes the shorter, again divided from the text and from each other by spaces. Presumably this is to bring the traditional verse 8 into juxtaposition with the traditional verse 9. The placement of the endings is a matter of small concern, but the student of the text would feel more comfortable had both the endings been separated from the main text by some device more arresting to the eye than a space. For some reason, the "Amen" at the close of the shorter ending in virtually all its witnesses is not translated in either edition. The ending to Mark given in the Freer Gospel manuscript is not translated.

At Mark 1:41 the translators have followed compelling logic and adopted the reading *orgistheis,* though they have drawn back from the full force of the word. Rather than have Jesus "angrily" stretch out his hand, they have him do it "with warm indignation." The more familiar reading, translated "Jesus was sorry for him," is given in a footnote.

Matthew 27:17 gives Bar-Abbas' name as Jesus Bar-Abbas.

Matthew 9:34 is omitted, on Western textual evidence.

Mark 8:26 represents a bold decision; Jesus' saying here, "Do not tell anyone in the village," translates the reading of one Old Latin manuscript. There is no Greek evidence for it at all, but it was thought to explain most satisfactorily the numerous other readings found for this passage.

Luke 22:19b-20 is omitted.

John 19:29 resorts to what is essentially a conjecture (exceptionally rare in NT critical study), although the adopted reading "javelin" is found in one Greek minuscule. All others read "hyssop," which the NEB renders in a footnote as "marjoram." The NEB NT consistently renders this word "marjoram," as does the OT in most cases. Sometimes the OT notes tell us, "*or,* hyssop," and sometimes we are left without this alternative. One suspects the composition of the translating panel differed on the days these passages were discussed. Someone must have held out strongly for "hyssop" and when present was assuaged with a footnote. Psalm 51:7 (Hebrew:9), however, reads "hyssop" in the text, with "*or,* marjoram" as its note. Maybe this was in deference to the familiarity of the passage, to prevent its sounding silly to those who know what marjoram is: "Take marjoram, and sprinkle me." (It is safe to say that many readers will understand hyssop in that verse as a liquid.) Maybe, on the other hand, on the day that Psalm 51 was discussed, the hyssop faction had a better breakfast than the marjoram faction; personal dynamics play a huge role in this kind of committee work.

For those with a knowledge of Greek, an extremely useful guide exists to the textual decisions behind the NEB NT. R.V.G. Tasker published in 1964, under the title *The Greek New Testament* (Oxford and Cambridge), the complete Greek text as translated in the NEB, placing on the page not only the readings adopted, but also the punctuation, capitalization, and versification used by the panel. These 408 pages of legible Greek text are handy, although any second-year Greek student would have little difficulty reconstructing the Greek from the English and a critical apparatus. The real usefulness of the book is in the 35 page appendix, where Tasker gives not only the evidence for certain readings adopted by the translators, but their reasons for doing so. It is a very useful compendium of critical reasoning. Teachers of the Greek NT are overlooking a splendid resource if they do not use it from time to time.

For the most part, the explanations given satisfy, even in cases where one disagrees with the conclusion. An example of an especially good discussion is found on Luke 1:46. (Who sings the Magnificat? Mary or Elizabeth?) Occasionally we do catch some strange reasoning behind the NEB text, however. At Mark 7:3, we are told that the widely attested reading *pugmē* ("fist") and a variant *pukna* ("often") yield no satisfactory sense. Fair enough. In translation, the word is not represented. But we are told in Tasker that the panel decided to relegate both readings to a footnote on the grounds that neither appear in the Sinaitic Syriac or the Sahidic Coptic. It would seem better to attribute the omission to the Committee's uncertainty about intelligible meaning than to blame it on an absence in two obscure versional traditions.

At 1 Corinthians 13:3, the usual reading *kauthēsomai* ("to be burnt") is adopted, but Tasker's explanation seems to give more compelling reasons for the alternate reading *kauchēsomai* ("seek glory by self-sacrifice").

In a note to 1 Corinthians 14:38, Tasker points out an error in the wording of an NEB footnote, where an alternative *translation* is adopted, but introduced by the words "Some witnesses read," misleadingly suggesting an alternative *reading*. Tasker is right: there *is* a textual problem in the verse. But the discussion in the note has to do with the interpretation of a single reading. This was cleaned up in the 1970 edition, where the note does recognize a variant reading, but where the translation of the earlier note has found its way into the text, and *vice versa*.

In Ephesians 1:1 the NEB text includes the highly doubtful phrase "at Ephesus," but only on the very dubious grounds that the book is traditionally known as the Epistle "to the Ephesians." The commentators, we are told, are left to struggle with the problem of destination. The translators seem to have abandoned their responsibility here. The problem of destination is one thing; the authenticity of the reading is another.

Study of Tasker's notes underscores the eclectic methodology explained in Dodd's preface. Though the method is eclectic, it is not erratic. For the most part, ample evidence lies behind the translated text, as well as sound logic. The textual decisions are essentially conservative, though a bit more daring than those of the RSV.

Leaving aside questions of accuracy of text and interpretation, we find that it is in the Englishing that the NEB contributes most to our understanding of the NT. It has succeeded admirably in its goal to avoid traditional renderings, and though there are some serious lapses, it has more than fulfilled Dodd's hope that it might produce "arresting and memorable renderings."

By freeing themselves from the restraints of reproducing Greek structures in English, the translators have provided themselves with increased opportunity to convey the connotative as well as the denotative force of the original. See, for instance, what happens to the present infinitive in Acts 2:1: "While the day of Pentecost was running its course . . ." or to the present participle in Acts 4:1, where it is subordinate to an aorist verb: "They were still addressing the people when the chief priests came upon them. . . ." By transforming the Greek participle into an English main verb, and the Greek main verb into the verb of a subordinate clause, the translators have accented the durative force of the present participle, the punctilear force of the aorist verb, preserved the relation between them, and quickened the progress of the narrative.

Notice how the simple device of moving to an English past perfect in Luke 6:6 preserves the functions of aorist and present tenses: "On another Sabbath he had gone to synagogue and was teaching." Rendering the aorist infinitive by a past perfect, and the present by a present progressive, serves the narrative function of placing the reader immediately in the synagogue rather than putting him through a two-step narrative. Such a device sharpens the movement of the story. Two other points about that sentence can be noted. An *egeneto de* is unrepresented in translation. Since there is no English equivalent, there is no point in trying to invent one. Further, there is no article with "synagogue." Compare our phrase, "went to church." There is great deftness shown in dealing with such fine details.

Consider Luke 5:29. "Afterwards Levi held a big reception in his house for Jesus." Admirable skill lies behind that simple statement. First, note the introductory adverb, which represents *kai*. "Afterwards" is less used than "and"; hence it carries more "information." It makes an immediate impact, binding coherently the paragraph which it opens to the preceding account of the call of Levi. Then, Levi "held" a reception. The verb is *epoiēsen.* It is hard even for seasoned translators to break the habit carried over from "baby Greek" of rendering that word "make," as does the RSV. But in English one does not "make" a feast or reception; we "hold" one. Hence the NEB is translating the sense, not just the word. Further, it is a "reception" that is held, not a "feast" *(douchēn).* Now I suppose one might quibble over whether or not this is an anachronism, suggesting white gloves, punch bowl, and reception line. But on the other hand, Levi is holding this event in Jesus' honor *(autō),* and "reception" is the name we give a social event in which guests are invited in to meet an honored person. It is certainly a word more meaningful to our experience than "feast," which has today inappropriate connotations. Now watch this bold stroke. It is a "big" reception. "Big" is one of those perfectly good words which we avoid in writing, preferring "large" or "great." After all, who ever learned in "baby Greek" that *megas* means "big"? But there are occasions when it is appropriate, and here it contributes to the well-chosen phrase describing the scene. But there is more. Jesus is named, whereas the Greek uses a pronoun. But why not name him? This is a new paragraph, a new topic, and Jesus has not been named since verse 22. This gives immediate clarity to a passage that otherwise would be getting murky with pronouns (cf. RSV). This clarity is also furthered by another deft stroke. Word order is reversed, so that the phrase "in his house" comes before the mention of Jesus. This avoids obscuring the antecedent. A stranger to the story could really not tell from the RSV, for instance, in whose house the feast is being held, Jesus' or Levi's.

As the verse continues, the next *kai* is represented simply by a semi-colon. Initial conjunctions are not a feature of modern English; we do not belabor connections that are quite clear. The Greek text goes on to say "there was a large crowd of tax-collectors and others who were reclining with them." Here the reference is to an unfamiliar social custom which can hardly be brought over literally. The RSV renders by the anachronism "sitting at table." The NEB has simply "among the guests was . . ." which completely avoids the problem, while sacrificing nothing; the context makes it clear that food and drink are involved.

Other examples of small but inspired touches: at Luke 1:1-4, the phrase *kratiste Theophile* has been removed from the end of verse 3, and its semantic components redistributed. Theophilus is named at the beginning ("The author to Theophilus"), and the force of *kratiste* is conveyed by the phrase "Your Excellency," placed in a natural position at the beginning of verse 3.

Acts 1:1 has no "O" before the name Theophilus.

Acts 1:20: " 'The text I have in mind,' Peter continued, 'is in the book of Psalms.' " Using "the text" for the formula "it is written" is brilliant, and the insertion of "Peter continued," representing nothing in Greek, helps resume Peter's speech, which in the preceding verse was badly interrupted by a long parenthetical remark of the author's.

Acts 8:1: "This was the beginning of a time of violent persecution for the church in Jerusalem." This strikingly marks a transition in the narrative. Notice "violent." There is *megas* again, but "violent" is surely a more appropriate modifier for "persecution" than the pale "great."

Use of modern punctuation devices allows the translators increased flexibility, but also commits them to some problems. In John 3, where do Jesus' words to Nicodemus end? The RSV closes the quotation at verse 12 (though I have seen red-letter editions that completely ignore the quotation marks and go rosily on through vs. 21); NEB closes at 21. There is no formal marker in Greek, and one opinion is pretty much as good as another.

But consider the problem in 1 Corinthians. In 6:12, most interpreters agree that Paul is quoting his opponents: "I am free to do anything." NEB makes the quotation clear, not only by the punctuation, but also by inserting after the quote the phrase "you say." The reader *or the hearer* then knows that Paul is playing with a phrase bandied about in Corinth. The same holds at 8:1: "Of course we all 'have knowledge,' as you say." But what of 7:1? Personally, I feel that much mischief has been done by failure to recognize that Paul is quoting his Gnostic opponents when he says, "It is a good thing for a man to have nothing to do with women." But this point is still debated, and the NEB opts for putting this interpretation, with the clarifying "you say," in the footnote.

Strange things and unexpected do lurk in the NEB NT. It is startling to find Paul, in 1 Corinthians 16:8, speaking of staying at Ephesus until Whitsuntide. (Was Paul Anglican?) And it is a little disappointing to find that later editions have not winnowed out two infelicitous remarks long noted, 2 Corinthians 5:9: "You must have nothing to do with loose livers," and Revelation 16:16: "thou hast given them blood to drink. They have their deserts!" By and large, however, the NT is free from this sort of thing.

Turning to the Old Testament, we must take immediate note that the textual terrain here is quite different from that of the New. Virtually none of the OT books are invested with the same degree of textual certainty that is characteristic of the NT as a whole; some of the books (e.g., Samuel, Hosea) are in a fairly bad state of disrepair. It is standard operating procedure for modern translations to resort to versional evidence and to conjectural emendations to produce meaningful readings in places where the Masoretic Text (a highly standardized Hebrew text of early medieval origin, almost universally used as a basis for OT study and translation) is obscure; there are a great many such places.

The NEB OT panel has obviously devoted intense thought to these textual matters, and has been remarkably bold about resorting to emendation, whether supported by evidence or not, when this was felt to be the proper route. Footnotes alert the reader to the presence of problems—*sometimes.* Here is one of the difficulties the user of the NEB OT faces. There are two sets of notes. The "Library Edition" of 1970 has a full panoply of notes, but most editions, including, most surprisingly, the "Oxford Study Edition" of 1976, have an abbreviated set. Since the complete notes would not occupy an untoward amount of space, it is somewhat mystifying that there is not one set only, and that in every edition. The difference is that only the Library Edition indicates where the text is based on the reading of other Hebrew manuscripts or of the versions. The Library Edition also has notes giving a literal rendering of the Hebrew at places where it was felt that the chosen translation was so different as to merit a comment.

Not having these notational references to the versions in the other NEB editions deprives most users of helpful information, especially where one might wonder about insertions into or omissions from the familiar text. Genesis 2:2 tells us, "On the sixth day God completed all the work he had been doing," but most versions will say that this was on the seventh day. Genesis 4:8 has Cain say to Abel, "Let us go into the open country," a phrase not found in the Hebrew. One has to consult the Library Edition to discover that the change to "sixth" and the inclusion of Cain's words are based on the Samaritan Pentateuch.

One can quibble with the wording of these notes. Where an emendation is made, the Masoretic Text is translated in the notes, unless the panel thought the Hebrew hopeless. In these instances, the Hebrew is said to be either "obscure" or "unintelligible." I assume it is simply a subjective value judgment which is used. However, the reading in the NEB text is termed in the note the "probable reading," even in places where the most dubious conjectures have been made. In Proverbs 12:12 we find a Hebrew text that is just about as obscure as one is apt to find (the note translates it, however). The note refers only to the first line of the verse translated, "The stronghold of the wicked crumbles like clay," which is called the "probable reading." Now this reading must be arrived at by repointing at least one word, rearranging the order of three words, and giving one word the meaning of a cognate root in Arabic. The proposal goes back to Hitzig (1858), and it is certainly one way to force sense from a difficult line, but it is by no stretch of the imagination "probable." The second line is also obscure, but the repointing of the verb and its investment with an Arabic meaning apparently made it clear to the panel.

The reference to Arabic brings up one of the most notorious features of the NEB OT, a trait which puts it in sharp contrast to every other mainline translation, and which more than any other single feature has made scholars wary of it.

In the past decades, great strides have been made in our understanding of the classical Hebrew lexicon. Largely this has been due to the exacting labors that have been expended on languages cognate with Hebrew, such as Ugaritic, Akkadian, and Arabic. Meanings can now be suggested, with some confidence, for words that have long been obscure in meaning. Many such have found their way into Koehler-Baumgartner's *Lexicon in Veteris Testamenti Libros.* A large number of others have been, until the NEB, lying dormant in the scholarly literature. The basic assumption of this philology is that a Hebrew word may have had a meaning in biblical times which was later forgotten—thus distorting the sense of the passages where it was used—but which may be recovered by examining the meaning of a cognate root in a related language. For instance, one familiar with only the modern sense of the English "ghost" might well wonder about religious usage of the term "Holy Ghost." Modern English would not illumine the phrase at all, but reference to the cognate German "Geist" would. Now the course that semantic change has taken in the European languages in modern times is well documented, but for the ancient Semitic tongues it is not. If any generalization can be made from the observed phenomena of semantic change, it is that it is completely unpredictable. There is absolutely no guarantee that a root in Ugaritic (*pace* Dahood) would have the same meaning in Hebrew, or that a root in Arabic (*pace* Driver, Reider, et al.) would have the same meaning in Hebrew. They well might. But they might not. (English "worm" and German *Wurst,* "sausage," are derived from a common Indo-European root.) In the nature of the case, hypotheses of common meaning in two ancient languages for the same root must remain speculations. James Barr, in his *Comparative Philology and the Text of the Old Testament* (Oxford, 1968), which was published after the work on the NEB had been done, offers a detailed and well-reasoned criticism of this methodology, which should make us highly skeptical of its results.

The relevance of all this lies in the fact that the NEB OT reflects on virtually every page (it seems) these studies in comparative philology. By now the most famous such instance is Judges 1:14 (parallel in Josh. 15:18), where the main verb *(ṣānaḥ)* in the sentence, "As she sat on the ass, she broke wind," carries a meaning teased out of Arabic. (Not to make it sound any worse than it is, the ass is an animal, although it has not been mentioned in the story previously.) In the Oxford Study Edition of 1976 this has been toned down a bit to "she made a noise," which, though less blatant, renders the English almost as obscure as the Hebrew. (In Job 32:18ff, we come across an unexpected attack of gas in a fairly familiar passage, where the sufferer seeks relief by talking.) The only other time the word is used is Judges 4:21, where the translators have apparently given it a different meaning. (I don't know this; they may well be letting the hypothetical root-meaning of the Arabic root color this rendering as well.) It is a graphic picture they paint "his brains oozed out *[ṣānaḥ]* on the ground." In the first place, it is not clear how they have determined the subject of this verb, since it is not expressed; Sisera's previously-mentioned "skull" is a possibility, I suppose, although this would force them to give the one occurrence of the word *(raqqāh)* two different meanings ("skull" and "brains"). What the panel has done with this word is a mystery to me, and this is only one example of something frequently recurring.

In all honesty, the verb used in those passages is obscure (though to my knowledge no one has ever suggested the meaning "break wind"). More unsettling is the constant use of this methodology to discover new meanings in quite familiar Hebrew words. As an example, in the familiar opening lines of Moses' victory song in Exodus 15:2, there occur three common Hebrew words, translated in the RSV "The LORD is my strength and my song." NEB renders this "The LORD[4] is my refuge and my defence." How do we get from "song" to "defence"? Not by any conventional emendation or objective versional evidence, but by assuming that the root has the same meaning as a cognate Arabic root.

I keep talking about Arabic here, but other Semitic languages are drawn on as well. I believe it fair to say that the general stream of OT scholarship today has been far more receptive to illumination on Hebrew from Ugaritic than from any other related language—certainly more so than from Arabic. (There are of course historical and geographical reasons for this.) Now I cannot claim to have fully researched the matter, but in the work I have done it surely seems to me that in the NEB Arabic is resorted to much more often for new meanings for Hebrew words than any other ancient language. One finds it very difficult to believe that it is only a coincidence that Godfrey Driver, Convener of the OT panel, is a renowned Arabist, many of whose published researches are reflected in the renderings of the NEB. If it is not a coincidence, one is driven to speculate, perhaps unfairly, that the chair was overly insistent on its own way.[5]

Now the legitimacy of this type of philological research is not in question. Further, when the NEB panel adopts a suggestion from this realm, its relevance to the context in question is usually apparent. It is the canonizing of large numbers of such newfound meanings in the text of a major translation of the Bible that is unnerving. Some of these are bound to be right, just as some of the noncanonical sayings of Jesus that survive from antiquity are bound to be genuine. The problem in each instance is that we have no way of telling which ones these are. The consistent application of this philological method, based itself on dubious assumptions, and the acceptance of so many of its results do not represent the mainstream of current OT scholarship. This has unfortunately given the NEB OT an element of eccentricity not characteristic of the NT or of the Apocrypha.

Of particular concern is that there is no system of footnoting in any edition to inform either the curious reader or the professional scholar about the sources of these often remarkable translations. Consequently, scholarship eagerly awaited the publication of the textual decisions of the panel. This was provided in *The Hebrew Text of the Old Testament,* prepared by L. H. Brockington (Oxford and Cambridge, 1973). Now in all fairness, Brockington was surely providing exactly the kind of material he was commissioned to prepare, but the book proved to be a stupendous disappointment. It is simply a listing of reconstructed Hebrew readings adopted, on whatever evidence, by the OT panel for those passages where they chose not to read the Masoretic Text. There is no explanation whatever for any of these readings; most of them are the kind of thing that can be dug out of the apparatus in Kittel's Hebrew Bible. Most distressing of all is the fact that the book is not concerned at all with the philological work of the panel. A persistent scholar can find explanations for the peculiar renderings of the NEB OT if he plows through enough journals and *Festschriften,* but some of these problems are enveloped in considerable obscurity.[6]

There are certainly things that evade my understanding. Maybe I have missed something very obvious, but I am at an utter loss to know whence came the line in Hosea 9:6, "the sands of Syrtes shall wreck them." Neither the Library Edition nor Brockington offer any help. A number of years ago a student asked me to explain to him why the NEB in 2 Samuel 15:30 has David bare-headed, when every other version has his head covered. I couldn't explain it then and I can't explain it now.

Regarding the English style of the OT, it is on the whole impressively vigorous, vibrant, and muscular, with touches of translational excellence, though I must confess sensing a bit of stodginess in the prose and a bit of preciousness in the poetry on occasions—qualities I do not find in the NT or Apocrypha. But I hasten to add these are occasional lapses and not characteristic of the OT as a whole.[7]

Consider a few examples out of many that could be mentioned: Amos' condemnatory refrain in the first chapter reads, "For crime after crime of Damascus (Gaza, Tyre, etc.). . . ." This accomplishes its purpose of expressing a crescendo of guilt without leaving the reader wondering about what the literal "three or four" things are. The introduction to the Babel story in Genesis 11:1, "Once upon a time," is bold and brilliant. A panel that produced Jeremiah 46:17, "Give Pharaoh of Egypt the title King Bombast, the man who missed his moment," cannot be accused of lack of imagination and inspiration. Referring to a pigeon rather than a dove in Hosea 7:11, "Ephraim is a silly senseless pigeon," shows a real appreciation of connotative values.

Although the poetry of the NEB is usually compelling and resonant, graceful but sturdy, its appearance on the printed page is awkward and mystifying. As is the usual practice with modern translations, Hebrew poetry is translated as poetry, but a strange criterion indeed has been adopted to determine indentation of lines—a device instrinsic to the English, that properly has nothing to do with the Hebrew at all. The indentation reflects the number of beats in the Hebrew meter; the more beats to the line, the farther to the left the English line extends. Clever, but it gives the poetry a weird appearance, and gives the reader no useful information or insight at all. In the Oxford Study Edition it is mangled even further by a two-column arrangement of the text on the page. For some reason, Job and Proverbs are set up with an even margin.

The quest for accuracy becomes a bit amusing at times. The rose in Sharon (Song of Songs 2:1) has become—are you ready?—an asphodel. It doesn't bother me particulary to learn that the flower in question is not a rose, but at least "rose" carries the freight of centuries of connotative imagery. Before reading the NEB, had someone asked me what an asphodel was, I might have answered with anything from a chemical to a surgical instrument. From reading the list of unclean birds in Leviticus 11:13ff, you would think we had a pretty good idea of what these birds were: griffon-vultures, fisher-owls and hoopoes are pretty specific. But we don't know all that. The notes to the passage do reveal some lack of certainty; there is a series of them reading, "*or* eagle, *or* ossifrage, *or* raven, *or* heron. . . ." The next one is "*or* whatever," which may seem suggestively appropriate, even if unrelated to the previous list. (Would you believe the next note is "*or* weasel"?)

Certainly, no great effort was expended in keeping the vocabulary level within a reasonable range. At least, I found I needed a dictionary at hand to discover meanings of unfamiliar English words: felloe, stook, reck, distrain, keen (verb), etc.

As expected, archaisms are not in evidence, but I wonder if "Hark" is much of an improvement over "Behold." There are anachronisms; the "castles" that occasionally appear have a medieval ring, and the "shirt collar" of Job 30:18 sounds rather modern. In Proverbs 18:10 we discover the Bible quoting Shakespeare (*Richard III,* 5, iii, 12). For all I know, there is good reason for it, but I must say it sounds odd to have buffaloes (1 Kings 1:19, 25) sacrificed on the altar. It has a kind of Wild West ring to it; but then, we read that Abram "journeyed by stages" (Gen. 12:9). Later on, we get more modern: Isaiah cries out for us to "clear the track" (Isa. 57:14), one might suppose for the "baggage-trains" of Isaiah 29:7, or the "trolleys" of 2 Kings 7:27-37.

All of this I say in affectionate fun, but there are, unfortunately, a great many passages that sound funny to the point of being ludicrous. Proverbs 5:4, "For though the lips of an adulteress drip honey . . . in the end she is more bitter than wormwood." Jeremiah 20:7, "O LORD, thou has duped me, and I have been thy dupe." Job 7:20, "Why hast thou made me thy butt?" Jeremiah 51:20, "You are my battle-ax." Deuteronomy 25:17-18, "Remember what the Amalekites did to you . . . how they met you on the road when you were faint and weary and cut off your rear." Genesis 43:18, "He means to trump up some charge against us and victimize us, seize our asses and make us his slaves." Proverbs 19:29, "There is a rod in pickle for the arrogant." Jeremiah 38:6, "So they took Jeremiah and threw him into the pit . . . letting him down with ropes." One who reads the NEB in public would be well advised to look it over beforehand, lest a passage like Job 18:11 provide an embarrassing surprise.

The titles of the psalms are omitted, on the grounds that they are not original. No great loss, but in the light of that reasoning, one wonders why we find rubrics inserted for the Song of Songs. In most cases, of course, the speakers are clear enough in Hebrew, where gender of speaker and addressee can be indicated by grammatical inflection; since it is clear in Hebrew, it is quite legitimate to indicate the speakers in English as NEB has done. But there is no particular virtue in referring to LXX manuscripts as some kind of authority for these rubrics of dialogue (1:1, note).

A feature that will particularly bother many people is the panel's readiness to transpose rather sizable chunks of material, interrupting the traditional verse numbering. If the translators really feel that they are reconstructing the original order of the book, they are to be commended for their boldness. Kindness to the reader, however, would have dictated some kind of typographical device more eyecatching than an inconspicuous footnote to call attention to what is happening. In Job, a book suspected to have undergone considerable textual displacement, there are twenty-three transpositions of material from the "canonical" place to some other.

For better or worse, the book of Job has come down to us as Scripture in a certain form. However it was originally written, it was canonized in the order of verses with which we are familiar. Just how far can we feel justified in allowing our scholarly instincts to reconstruct hypothetical originals? Surely we are not going to try to dissect the Pentateuchal strands in translation, or isolate the genuine memoirs of Nehemiah, or push Psalm 29 all the way back to a hypothetical Canaanite original. Nonetheless, questions of canonical criticism and architectural analysis have much to say to translators. This is one of the frontiers on which future translational activity will take place. Meanwhile we will have to be content with the subjective eclecticism evident in the NEB and virtually every other translation around today.[8]

The question of the original meaning, as well as arrangement, often plagues the conscientious translator. In Genesis 1:2, it is a "mighty wind" rather than the "Spirit of God" that is over the waters of chaos. This has been debated for some time, and it may well be true that at some early stage of the development of the material, the phrase was indeed understood as "mighty wind." One wonders if it really meant this by Exilic times, however. I do not quarrel with the translation—indeed, I rather like it—but I use it to point out a problem. Here the translators have used linguistic archeology to bring to light a new sense for the familiar phrase. But they have failed to do so when the body of water, *yam suph,* is called the "Red Sea" even when it clearly refers to the Gulf of Elath (2 Kings 9:26)—bowing to what is obviously a later interpretation of the Hebrew phrase.

Reviews of the NEB, including this one, have given pretty short shrift to the Apocrypha; this is too bad, for there is some good stuff here. Those interested in the difficult textual problems should consult McHardy's introduction. For our purposes here, it may suffice to say that Ecclesiasticus (the name unfortunately used for "Sirach" in the NEB) has been translated from the Greek text of Vaticanus (found in Swete's LXX) "with constant reference . . . to the various forms of the Hebrew text." In fact, the Hebrew readings have not been used a great deal, far less than in the New American Bible or Today's English Version. (In this book, the use of Hebrew at all raises serious canonical questions for those who accept Ecclesiasticus as canonical.) Most conveniently, the entirety of the Greek Esther is provided.

The translators have succeeded brilliantly in their endeavor "to convey the meaning of the original in language which will be the closest natural equivalent." A touch such as found in Ecclesiasticus 46:11, "Then there are the judges, name after famous name . . ." leaves one with some translating experience breathless with admiration. Or consider 31:12, "If you are sitting at a grand table, do not lick your lips and exclaim, 'What a spread.' " One may well cower at the slow measured threat of 18:24, laden with doom: "Think of the wrath you must face in the hour of death, when the time of reckoning comes and he [the Lord] turns away his face." And we may marvel at the psychological insight of the Wisdom of Solomon, as mediated to us by the NEB panel at 17:12-13: "Fear is nothing but an abandonment of the aid that comes from reason; and hope, defeated by this inward weakness, capitulates before ignorance of the cause by which the torment comes."

Future translators of this material will hear the footsteps of a giant behind them, as the TEV panel already has. For sheer translational deftness, dexterity, and brilliance, the NEB Apocrypha is one of the finest achievements in the history of the English Bible.

One comment about policy, as it applies to the entire NEB. The archaic second person pronoun and verb forms have been retained in address to God. This is unfortunate, and out of keeping with the thrust of the translation. It is perhaps understandable, though, bearing in mind that its genesis was in 1946, before the RSV was available, let alone the more adventuresome translations following it. It is interesting, however, that Adam addresses God as "you" before the fall, and that Satan in Job 1 addresses God as "you."

The appearance of commentaries and other study helps based on the NEB is a good indication of its acceptance, as well as incentive for increased use. The Oxford Study Edition (counterpart to the Oxford Annotated of the RSV) is an American production offering brief but expert notes and introductory statements. Its essay on "Literary Forms of the Bible" is masterfully done. Cambridge, for its part, is publishing, as the New Cambridge Bible, a series of commentaries based on the NEB text. A. E. Harvey's *Companion to the New Testament of the New Engish Bible* (Oxford and Cambridge, 1970) is a useful one-volume commentary.

In spite of the misgivings I have expressed about some aspects of the OT, I am basically an admirer of both the scholarship and the English expression of the New English Bible. Pedantry is not much in evidence, and the whole of it is free of the musty smell of a translation. It does not read like a translation; that in itself is a splendid accomplishment, but its marshalling of the vigorous resources of contemporary English idiom into such forceful array makes it a triumph.

Officers, Committee Members, and Panel Members for the New English Bible Translation Project

OFFICERS OF THE JOINT COMMITTEE—Chair: J. W. Hunkin (1947-50), A. T. P. Williams (1950-68), Donald Coggan (from 1968); *Vice-Chair:* C. H. Dodd; *General Director* (1947-65): C. H. Dodd; *Joint Directors* (from 1965): C. H. Dodd, G. R. Driver; *Deputy Director* (from 1968): W. D. McHardy; *Secretary:* G. S. Hendry (1947-49), J. K. S. Reid (from 1949)

OTHER MEMBERS OF THE JOINT COMMITTEE: George Boobyer (Society of Friends), John Brown (Oxford Univ. Press), R. L. Child (Baptist Union), R. W. David (Cambridge Univ. Press), C. F. Eccleshare (Cambridge Univ. Press), J. L. M. Haire (Churches in Ireland), Thomas Hanlon (Roman Catholic Observer), C. L. Mitton (Methodist Church), H. K. Moulton (British and Foreign Bible Society), D. E. Nineham (Church of England), J. C. O'Neill (Presbyterian Church of England), E. A. Payne (Baptist Union), N. W. Porteous (Church of Scotland), C. H. Roberts (Oxford Univ. Press), C. J. Stranks (Church of England)

THE OLD TESTAMENT PANEL: T. H. Robinson (*Convener* until his death in 1957), G. R. Driver (second *Convener*), L. H. Brockington, J. A. Emerton, A. R. Johnson, W. D. McHardy, N. W. Porteous, B. J. Roberts, H. H. Rowley, C. A. Simpson, N. H. Snaith

THE APOCRYPHA PANEL: W. D. McHardy *(Convener),* W. Barclay, W. H. Cadman, G. B. Caird, C. F. D. Moule, J. R. Porter, G. M. Styler

THE NEW TESTAMENT PANEL: C. H. Dodd *(Convener),* G. S. Duncan, W. F. Howard, G. D. Kilpatrick, T. W. Manson, C. F. D. Moule, J. A. T. Robinson, G. M. Styler, R. V. G. Tasker

OTHER CONTRIBUTING TRANSLATORS: G. W. Anderson, Matthew Black, J. Y. Campbell, J. A. F. Gregg, H. St. J. Hart, F. S. Marsh, John Mauchline, H. G. Meecham, C. R. North, O. S. Rankin, Nigel Turner

THE LITERARY PANEL: A. T. P. Williams *(Convener),* John Carey, Adam Fox, Herbert Grierson, F. H. Kendon, E. Milner-White, Roger Mynors, Arthur Norrington, W. F. Oakeshott, Anne Ridler, Basil Willey

(Information above found in Geoffrey Hunt, *About the New English Bible* [Oxford Univ. Press, 1970], pp. 79-82)

4
The New Jewish Version

KEITH R. CRIM

When the Jewish Publication Society (JPS) decided to prepare a new English translation of the Hebrew Scriptures they were breaking with an old tradition and joining the main stream of a new tradition. The old was reliance on existing Christian translations as the standard for style and diction. This is evident in the 1917 translation which JPS produced and distributed. The new tradition is that of using fully contemporary language and avoiding wooden, literal phrases and sentences, as other recent English translations have also done. But this is not simply another version; it is a fresh translation produced by some of the leading contemporary Jewish scholars, who have made outstanding contributions to biblical scholarship. In addition they have brought to their work a familiarity with the Bible in life and worship and a knowledge of centuries of scholarship in the Jewish community.

Publication to Date

The NJV has been appearing piecemeal since 1962, when *The Torah* was published. Jewish attitudes toward the Scripture and the liturgical need of the Jewish community are reflected in the choice of the first five books of the Bible to launch the new version. Basic to the Jewish view of life, Torah was the obvious choice. The prescribed readings for the year carry the community through the Torah from autumn to autumn.

Then in 1969 we were given *The Five Megilloth and Jonah,* the six smaller books of the Bible that are used on the various holy days. (*Megilloth* ["Scrolls"] is a designation for the books of Esther, Lamentations, Ruth, Ecclesiastes, and the Song of Solomon.) This is the only NJV portion to appear in a diglot, with Hebrew and English in parallel columns. In Hebrew book tradition, this volume starts from what would be the back of an English book, and unlike *The Torah* is illustrated with striking line drawings.

Publication of "The Writings," third division of the Hebrew canon, which was begun with *The Five Megilloth,* took a step forward with *The Book of Psalms* in 1973 and *The Book of Job* in 1980. The entire translation was brought to completion with the publication in 1981 of *The Writings—*

Kethubim. The portion of "The Writings" not previously published appeared too late for discussion in this review.

Isaiah appeared in 1973 in a coffee table edition, with drawings on green pages that contrast with the white pages of the text. Simultaneously it appeared in a less expensive and smaller version. Later the same year *Jeremiah* was issued in a coffee table edition with woodcuts, in my estimate, the most pleasing illustrations of any of the separate editions. Both Isaiah and Jeremiah were included in the completed *The Prophets—Nevi'im* in 1978. This volume is identical in format to *The Torah* and completes the second division of the Hebrew canon. ("Former Prophets": Joshua, Judges, 1 and 2 Samuel, 1 and 2 Kings; and "Latter Prophets": Isaiah, Jeremiah, Ezekiel, and "The Twelve" [Minor Prophets])

Orlinsky's Notes on the New Translation of the Torah

Each separate volume has an introduction that tells something of the nature of the translation project. But the most detailed account is given by Harry M. Orlinsky, Editor-in-Chief of the NJV, in the introduction to his *Notes* (1969). In the remainder of this invaluable volume he gives specific explanations of the reasoning behind the translation of key passages. The notes are fullest for Genesis, but he carries them through all five books of the Pentateuch.

He tells also about the organization of the work. It was begun with a committee of seven: three biblical scholars, the editor of the Jewish Publication Society, and one representative of each of the three sections of organized religious Jewish life in America—Conservative, Reform, and Orthodox. In order to expedite the work an additional committee was created in 1966 to translate the third division of the Hebrew canon, the *Kethubim,* or "Writings."

The procedures followed represent standard practices for such a translation. One person (for *The Torah,* the Editor-in-Chief) prepared a draft translation which was circulated to the other members, along with comments and explanations of the reasons for particular readings. The other members sent in their comments, and on the average of once every two weeks the entire committee met for a full day. Most decisions were made by consensus, but whenever a vote was necessary, a majority of those voting decided the issue.

How to Study the NJV

NJV has a great deal to offer the non-Jewish reader. It can be read systematically or selectively as an alternative to other English versions. It can be read for pleasure or spiritual benefit. It is also a good Bible for scholarly study, and its differences from other versions will stimulate you to explore the differences and try to understand the reasons for them.

The place to begin for scholarly study is with the footnotes in NJV. These are essentially translator's notes, explaining to the reader what the translators have done. The detailed comments later on in this article give guidance in how to use the notes. But in addition to the notes, the text itself is waiting to yield up new insights. Almost any familiar translation can serve as a starting point, and comparing the familiar with the unfamiliar will throw new light on both.

Not that I am suggesting a search for wording that confirms what you already believe. A preacher once told me that he had had to consult eight different translations of his text before he found one that supported what he had already decided to say in his sermon. I am suggesting a search for ways to let the text speak for itself. It can be done by taking a specific passage as a whole, examining its parts in each translation you are using, and seeing the role each phrase, sentence, and paragraph plays in the total meaning of the passage.

Another basis for comparison is the rendering of special terminology. Take a word like "righteousness" and with the help of a concordance locate a number of representative passages in the RSV which use the word. (Note, however, that while the RSV is often quite literal, it does at times vary the translation of a word to fit a particular context.) Then look at the way NJV renders that term in each passage. Does NJV's term fit the context better? Is it more natural English usage? Does it suggest some aspect of the concept that a more literal, woodenly consistent rendering might miss? Is the word that is appropriate in one context slightly misleading in another? Some concrete examples are given below.

One word of caution. NJV follows the verse and chapter divisions of the Hebrew text, and these are often different from the English Bible. RSV usually points out such differences in a footnote, e.g., Malachi 4:1-6. In the Hebrew Bible the Psalm titles have verse numbers, so that sometimes there may be as much as two verses difference between Hebrew and English. For example, in Psalms 19, 20, 21, and 22 verse 1 is the title so that the English verse 1 is Hebrew verse 2. In Psalm 51 English verse 1 is Hebrew verse 3.

The Steps in Translation

Any translator of an ancient document must raise three questions, representing three stages of the translation process. First is the question of the text itself. Where the Hebrew text is unclear, scholars may turn to various ancient translations or they may make more or less informed guesses based on modern knowledge of biblical backgrounds or linguistic processes. And sometimes recently discovered manuscripts give what appears to be a clearer, more accurate text. So decisions must be made. Second, the translator must ask what the text means. This includes not just individual words but the larger units in which the words occur. A translator may get words right, but have wrong reference of pronouns, incorrect transitions, and word order that misplaces the emphasis. Third, the translator must find a natural, easily understood way of expressing the meaning in English. Involved here is the level of usage, which may range from colloquial speech to highly formal language. Since the NJV is intended for liturgical usage, it tends to move on a fairly formal level. We shall now examine these three stages of the translation process as evidenced in NJV.

Determining the Text

The answer to the *first,* textual, question is clear. Both *The Torah* and *The Prophets* say on the title page, "A new translation of the Holy Scriptures according to the Masoretic text." This claim is borne out by examination of the translation. The translators have endeavored to bring over into English the meaning of the traditional Masoretic text (produced by the labors of medieval Jewish scholars to agree upon a "standard" text). In so doing, they have chosen not to employ more recently discovered pre-Masoretic Hebrew manuscripts or to engage in a hypothetical reconstruction of the received text based on ancient translations or in subjective "corrections" based on a feeling that the traditional text was "somehow" wrong. Nevertheless, there are many places where there are genuine difficulties in this procedure. Let us look at the ways NJV dealt with some problem passages.

The simplest way is to recognize that there is a difficulty and translate as best one can, then add a footnote acknowledging what has been done. NJV has notes such as "Heb. obscure," "Meaning of Heb. uncertain," "Exact force of Heb. uncertain," etc. The book of Ezekiel presents many difficulties of this sort. Ezekiel 19:10 reads in NJV "Your mother was like a vine [b]-in your blood,-[b]" with the note "Meaning of Heb. uncertain; emendation yields 'in a vineyard.' " Certainly the Hebrew text is puzzling and the emendation (followed also by RSV) makes more sense. But perhaps such a correction is too easy, and to make it gives the modern reader more certainty about the verse than is justified.

Emendation, then, is a second solution, but one that NJV consistently avoids. The notes "emendation yields" are frequent, but angel-like, the translators feared to tread on this ground. A careful comparison of these rejected emendations in NJV with what was done in the same passages in RSV and other versions will bring into focus the implications of emending the text. Can modern scholars solve these ancient problems? What authority, then, does an emended text have compared to a text that leaves the problem unresolved?

The translator, if not on firm ground, is at least on less mirey clay when following the ancient versions, especially the Septuagint (LXX) in Greek, and the Targums in Aramaic. Jeremiah 12:4b reads in NJV, "Must beasts and birds perish, / because of the evil of its inhabitants / Who say, 'He will not look upon our future'?[b]" The note says "[b]Septuagint reads 'ways.' " RSV takes no notice of this problem, and TEV follows LXX. "He will not look upon our future" seems to imply that God may not survive as long as we do. "Ways" implies that God is indifferent to what we do. Certainly there is a problem here, and NJV may have chosen the best way by leaving the question open.

The discovery of the Dead Sea Scrolls provided the oldest Hebrew manuscript evidence available and NJV takes note of this, especially in Isaiah. At Isaiah 11:6 NJV notes that the Isaiah scroll from Qumran (IQIs[a]) and the LXX agree, but still the traditional Masoretic reading is kept in the text.

Yet another approach is to assign a new meaning to a Hebrew word in light of usage elsewhere in the Bible (see Ps. 39:2 [Hebrew:3]) or in view of the context (Ps. 49:11 [Hebrew: 12]). Being alert to this type of procedure, always marked by a footnote, can provide helpful comparisons to other versions.

Isaiah 13:8e reads, "Their faces livid with fright." The reason for departing from the usual translation is given in a note: "Taking the root *lhb* as a variant of *bhl:* others 'shall be faces of flame.' " This presupposes a reversal of consonants in the Hebrew, a common enough occurrence in language. If the reversal took place in the copying of a text, it is an error. If it took place in the spoken language often enough that a native speaker would regard the two forms as simple variants of each other, then NJV is justified in translating as it did without saying this is an emendation. Whatever the nature of the change, it does make sense.

All translators encounter problems with the text of Samuel. NJV was able to consult an ancient manuscript (4QSam[a]) that is in private hands and has not been published or made available to the scholarly world. It is therefore impossible to evaluate its usefulness, but NJV often refers to it in footnotes, especially when it agrees with the LXX. In this connection the footnote at 1 Samuel 1:23 seems unprecedented in modern Bible translations: "The translators herewith express their thanks to Frank M. Cross, Jr., for graciously making available to them copies of his unpublished Samuel fragments."

Sometimes part of the Hebrew text seems to be out of order, and some translations shift verses to a place where they seem to fit better. Isaiah

38:21-22 seems to fit better between verses 6 and 7, the place where they are found in the parallel passage in 2 Kings 20:9-11. NJV does not make this move, although it does rearrange verses elsewhere. In Isaiah 10, part of verse 18 is moved to the end of verse 16 "for clarity" and in Isaiah 9, part of verse 16 is placed after verse 17.

NJV gives the overall impression of a respectful attitude toward the traditional text, recognizing that there are insoluble problems and alerting the reader to their presence.

Establishing the Meaning

In examining the *second* stage of the translation process, the footnotes help us see what the translators have done, and Orlinsky's *Notes* give explanations of some of the most consistent changes, especially the free rendering of idioms. Orlinsky gives several examples of the idiomatic "take in one's hand," which means simply "take along," "take with." This is beautifully illustrated in Isaiah 6:6. RSV says that one of the seraphim flew down to Isaiah, "having in his hand a burning coal which he had taken with tongs from the altar." If he could hold it in his hands, he didn't need tongs in the first place. NJV gives the correct picture: "one of the seraphs flew over to me with a live coal, which he had taken from the altar with a pair of tongs." By recognizing Hebrew idioms as idioms (often, as in this case, they are dead or atrophied metaphors), NJV has given the meaning accurately. No note was deemed necessary.

Other metaphors are more striking, and NJV has preserved them, while giving an explanation in the margin, e.g., Isaiah 37:3: "The babes have reached the birthstool, but the strength to give birth is lacking." The footnote explains: "i.e. the situation is desperate, and we are at a loss." Could the idiom have been retained in a somewhat less literal form? As NJV now stands, the concrete object "birthstool" represents the event of birth, but the reader's initial impression may be that the babes are already born, although this is contradicted by the second clause. RSV by slight departures from literalism has a better reading. Still better is NEB, which makes the comparison explicit and the whole sentence clear English: "We are like a woman who has no strength to bear the child who is coming to birth." Note, however, that the two subordinate clauses starting with "who" made the sentence more complicated than necessary. TEV goes a step further and uses coordinate clauses: "We are like a woman who is ready to give birth, but is too weak to do it." As a result the structure of the sentence reflects the natural order of thought in the entire figure of speech.

The study of comparatively easy problems like this will give increasing skill in the use of several modern versions to cast light on a given passage, skill that will come in handy in the study of more difficult problems in the Bible.

Where the metaphor is not so striking, NJV puts the natural English equivalent in the text (e.g., "grant me relief," Ps. 31:9 [English: 8]), and the literal translation in the margin ("make my feet stand in a broad place"). It may be asking too much to wonder whether there was a principle at work here, or whether each time there was an *ad hoc* decision as to what went into the margin and what into the text.

In many passages there are legitimate differences of opinion, which NJV identifies in the footnote as being held by "others." In Exodus 1:10 NJV interprets Pharaoh's fear as being that the Israelites will "gain ascendancy over the country." RSV is among the "others" who see it as a fear that the Israelites will "get them up out of the country," i.e., escape. At Exodus 21:6 a slave is to be taken "before God" in a certain situation. The alternate interpretation given in the note is that the Hebrew word *elohim* (God) refers to human judges. This is probably another metaphor familiar in the language of devotion, when a worshiper in a sanctuary feels he or she is in the "presence of God," whoever the officiating human being may be. From the human point of view, one is taken before a judge, but the important participant, though unseen, is God. Each translation must decide which differences of interpretation are important enough to merit mention in a footnote.

Sometimes the meaning depends on knowledge of ancient customs, knowledge shared by the original readers or hearers, but which we lack. Jeremiah 32:7 deals with the right of a near kinsman to repurchase land that might otherwise be lost to the extended family. NJV has a clear statement in the text and the literal rendering in a note. In some passages this procedure may result in loss of poetic quality, as it clearly does in Psalm 78:63. "And their maidens remained unwed" is prose, while NJV's note on that passage "had no nuptial song" retains the pathos of poetry.

Especially high marks are due to NJV for dealing creatively with the idiomatic meaning of "kidneys," called "reins" in King James English. While it sounds dignified for God to "try the reins," it doesn't sound right to say he "tries the kidneys." We assign psychological functions to the heart, but not to the kidneys in our society. NJV has identified the kidneys as the seat of the conscience and abandoned the metaphorical use of the organ. Note how well this fits the context of Psalms 7:10 (English: 9); 16:7. We also no longer have "bowels of compassion," but we have "gut feelings," something rather different. Now the "bowels" of Jeremiah 31:20 have become a yearning heart in NJV, and most other modern translations (although NEB could not resist saying in a note that it literally is "bowels rumble"!).

Rather different problems confront the translator when dealing with abstract terminology. The Hebrew word *ṣᵉdhāqāh* has usually been translated as "righteousness" or "justice." NJV gave a number of different equivalents in the attempt to express the proper shade of meaning in each context. In Psalm 106:31 the activity of Phineas "was reckoned to his merit." In Psalms 22:32 (English: 31); 69:28 (English: 27) God's attitude toward the people is in focus, so a good equivalent is "beneficence." The reader might object to the word as unpoetic and a bit high flown, but it is in the proper area of meaning. In Psalm 24:5 it is "a just reward from God," and in Psalm 98:2, "triumph," that is, God's having overcome the enemies. "Triumph" is also the translation in Isaiah 51:6; in Isaiah 46:12 we find "victory." Yet another meaning is disclosed in Isaiah 45:23, where it is the "truth" of what God proclaims which is in focus.

Here in these few passages is illustrated the important point that there is great gain in distinguishing the significance of some terms in each specific context, and not mechanically translating them the same way every time they occur. When the quality of *ṣᵉdhāqāh* is accorded to a person for some deed performed, it is "merit" or "reward." When it is God's attitude toward humans it is "beneficence," and when it is the quality of God's statements it is "truth." As the culmination of God's successful activity, it is "triumph" or "victory." These examples ought to arouse the curiosity of a serious student of English versions to go on to examine other passages and compare the way translators have tried to bring out the meaning of this term, so rich in nuances in Hebrew, and so flexible in fitting such varied contexts.

Again and again NJV has succeeded in finding the most appropriate English idiom for expressing the meaning of the Hebrew, but the translators were not consistent in calling attention to the so-called literal equivalents. A word may be the literal equivalent of one segment of meaning of a term it is chosen to translate, but by omitting other, equally important elements of meaning it may be a serious distortion. This can be seen in some instances where square brackets are used to mark departures from literalism. In Judges 1:2 it is obvious that it is not the then long-dead individual Judah who is to attack the Canaanites, but the tribe that claimed descent from him. So it is correct to say, "Let the tribe of Judah go up." But NJV encloses "the tribe of" in brackets. In the very next verse we have "Judah then said to their brother-tribe Simeon," and "tribe" is not marked by brackets. It is implicit in the text that two tribes are meant, not two individuals, so it is semantically appropriate to identify the two entities as tribes. No brackets are needed, but if brackets are used in verse 2 they are also called for in verse 3.

Another type of example is provided by Joshua 7:5, "And the heart of the troops sank in utter dismay." A footnote gives the literal equivalent as "melted and turned to water." Clearly the reading in the text is superior to that in the note, which is of help only to someone comparing the English and the Hebrew. But only three verses later the text reads, "Israel has turned tail before its enemies," a good vigorous idiom, but not a literal translation. Yet the translators did not feel obligated to provide a note saying, "lit. 'turned the back of their necks.' "

Finding the Best Way to Say It in English

The question of meaning as discussed above merges almost imperceptibly with the *third* question of how to say it in the target language, in this case, English. Three dimensions of this question call for particular attention: archaic language or contemporary language; simple style or more formal style; and appropriateness of literary genre, e.g., prose or poetry.

Any ancient book will sound as if it came from another era. The customs are different from ours, the world-view is quaint, the means of transportation, communication, and warfare are outmoded. There is no need to resort to archaic language, as the RSV does, to make the Bible sound venerable. NJV wisely opted for contemporary usage, most conspicuously in the abandonment of archaic pronouns and verb forms, as all other truly contemporary translations have done. Being modern, however, is not always easy, and the NJV uses such archaic words as "lest," "lo," "hark, hearken," and "of yore." As a result there are numerous passages that lose something of the immediacy they should have if they are to confront the reader in everyday life at the end of the twentieth century. A living language changes fast enough as it is without encumbering a translation with words that have already passed out of common usage.

As for stylistic level, NJV in general chose the elegant and the formal rather than the simple. This choice accords with the purpose of the translation to be suitable for use in worship and to appeal to a well-educated audience. The vocabulary is rich and varied, and I have not found any passages where I thought a word was avoided simply because it was rare. The effect of this is most apparent when extended passages are read and the majesty of the Bible is underlined by the cumulative effect of the vocabulary and the manner in which sentences and paragraphs are structured.

There is, however, at least one conspicuous instance in which NJV chose a term that is not only unusual but also imprecise and inadequate. The RSV uses the phrase "utterly destroyed" to describe the process (*ḥerem*) whereby Canaanite towns were not looted, but all valuable material items and persons found there were destroyed (Judg. 1:17 *et passim*). NJV chose the rare word "proscribe," which in addition to being rare is usually used in the sense of "banish," "prohibit," or "condemn." This seems to be a case where the search for the *mot juste* went astray. If the reader does not know the practice that lies behind the word, there is no way to understand the English term in this context by looking it up in a dictionary.

Perhaps no category can contain or account for one distinctive decision of the NJV translators, although it is appropriate in the Jewish tradition. The divine name YHWH, which is by long tradition not pronounced, is a perennial problem for the translator. Most English versions follow the custom of using "Lord" as the best equivalent and, to distinguish it from the translation of the Hebrew *adonai* as "Lord," print it in small capitals: "LORD." NJV does this in every instance except Exodus 6:3, where God reveals this sacred name to Moses. Instead of translating it, NJV simply prints the four Hebrew letters יהוה (YHWH)! Alas for the reader who knows no Hebrew.

NJV is sensitive to problems of sentence structure. Biblical Hebrew uses comparatively few subordinate clauses, and coordination is the normal means of bringing thought together. One of the definite aims of the NJV was to avoid translating every "and" in the Hebrew Bible, and by doing so they have produced a much more readable translation. Orlinsky (*Notes,* p. 20) points to Gen. 31:54—32:1 (English 31:54-55) as a good example of the way NJV used subordination. In passages such as this, NJV uses many types of transitional words and phrases to help the story flow smoothly.

It is often hard to bring out the emotional tone of a particular passage. Note, however, the highly successful way in which the NJV expresses biting sarcasm in Isaiah 10:15, "As though the rod swung him who lifts it, / As though the staff lifted the man!" As you read NJV be alert for ways in which irony, grief, joy, anger are highlighted by the choice of vocabulary and by sentence structure.

One of the great treasures of the Hebrew Scriptures is the variety of literary genres. In Jeremiah the contrast of prose sermons (e.g., chap. 7), biographical narrative (e.g., chaps. 26—29), poetic oracles (e.g., chap. 2) and passionate "confessions" in verse (e.g., 15:15-18) can be readily seen in NJV. As has become customary in modern translations, NJV distinguishes passages that are in Hebrew verse by printing them as English verse. In many instances a genuinely poetic quality is achieved, but this is not always maintained consistently. Ecclesiastes 1:6 is beautiful. "Southward blowing, / Turning northward, / Ever turning blows the wind; / On its rounds the wind returns." But the verses before and after it are less successful. The quality of The Song of Songs is generally high, preserving a sensuous quality of the poetry and marking most transitions well. The reader would be able to follow it better, however, if there were indication in the margin to identify the speakers and mark the alternation between the man and the woman. In the Hebrew original grammatical gender gives many clues that cannot readily be brought over into English without notational indications.

Considering all the problems that are involved in finding the best way to phrase a translation in English, it is inevitable that any translation makes many compromises in style, sometimes under the pressure of striving for precision and accuracy, sometimes under the pressure of the needs of the community that will use the translation. After all, not only are the Hebrew Scriptures the sacred book of ongoing communities of faith, but its parts are highly diverse in content and style. The NJV teams of translators have, by their skill and diligence, given the world a work that repays all efforts devoted to its study and, in addition, stimulates further study, thought, and mediation. The words come alive, the meaning challenges us to respond, the purpose of the whole of Scripture, which is to give glory to God, becomes part of our lives.

Editors and Translators for the New Jewish Version

Torah (Law), Nevi'im (Prophets), and the Five Megilloth (Scrolls): Editor-in-Chief, Harry M. Orlinsky (Hebrew Union College-Jewish Institute of Religion), H.L. Ginsberg (Jewish Theological Seminary), Ephraim A. Speiser (University of Pennsylvania), Rabbi Max Arzt (Rabbinical Assembly [Conservative]), Rabbi Bernard J. Bamberger (Central Conference of American Rabbis [Reform]), Rabbi Harry Freedman (Rabbinical Council of America [Orthodox]), Solomon Grayzel (Editor of the Jewish Publication Society)

Kethubim (Writings): Moshe Greenberg (Hebrew University), Jonas C. Greenfield (Hebrew University), Nahum M. Sarna (Brandeis University), Rabbi Saul Leeman (Conservative), Rabbi Martin S. Rozenburg (Reform), Rabbi David Shapiro (Orthodox), Chaim Potok (Editor of the Jewish Publication Society)

5
The New American Standard Bible

BARCLAY M. NEWMAN, JR.

The *New American Standard Bible* (NASB) is a publication of the Lockman Foundation, which describes itself both as "Producers of Amplified Translations" and as "a corporation not for profit in the State of California." The foundation has a "Fourfold Aim":

1. These publications shall be true to the original Hebrew and Greek.
2. They shall be grammatically correct.
3. They shall be understandable to the masses.
4. They shall give the Lord Jesus Christ His proper place, the place which the Word gives Him; no work will ever be personalized.

"Imbued with the conviction that interest in the American Standard Version 1901 should be renewed and increased," the NASB Editorial Board set out "to adhere as closely as possible to the original languages of the Holy Scriptures, and to make the translation in a fluent and readable style according to current English usage." Two paragraphs extracted from their "Principles of Revision" describe in more detail the goals of the revision:

> Modern English Usage: The attempt has been made to render the grammar and terminology of the ASV in contemporary English. When it was felt that the word-for-word literalness of the ASV was unacceptable to the modern reader, a change was made in the direction of a more current English idiom. In the instances where this has been done, the more literal rendering has been indicated in the margin.
>
> Marginal Readings: In addition to the more literal renderings, the marginal notations have been made to include alternate translations, readings of variant manuscripts and explanatory equivalents of the text. Only such notations have been used as have been felt justified in assisting the reader's comprehension of the terms used by the original author.

In summary, the Editorial Board of NASB avers that the publication was "released with strong confidence that those who seek a knowledge of the Scriptures will find herein a source of genuine satisfaction for a clear and accurate rendering of divinely-revealed truth."

Accuracy of translation. Clarity of English. Adequacy of notes. These are the stated goals of the Editorial Board, and so a review of NASB will require examination of the Reference Edition, since it is this edition which contains the plenary set of marginal notations.

Translational Distortions

There are two areas where it becomes particularly obvious that the substitution of theological presuppositions for sound exegetical and linguistic considerations has led to a distortion of the biblical text.

Attempts at Harmonization

An examination of the manner in which the Hebrew verb "lead astray/seduce/stir up" *(sûṯ)* and the noun phrase "anger of the Lord" are rendered in their various occurrences will lead to the conclusion that the translators of NASB attempted both to harmonize two Old Testament passages and to upgrade the image of God in the Old Testament.

Five times this Hebrew verb is rendered with the meaning "mislead" (2 Kings 18:32; Isa. 36:18; Jer. 38:22; 2 Chron. 32:11, 15); three times as "entice" (Deut. 13:6; Job 36:16, 18); three times the meaning is given as "incite" (2 Sam. 24:1; Jer. 43:3; Job 2:3); in 2 Chronicles 18:2 it appears as "induced," and in verse 31 of the same chapter the verb is rendered "diverted." In each of these fourteen instances the usage may be classified as having a negative connotation.

In the four other places where the verb is used in the Old Testament, it moves toward a more neutral connotation. In the parallel passages at Joshua 15:18 and Judges 1:14 it is rendered "persuaded" ("She persuaded him to ask her father for a field"). In 1 Samuel 26:19, where the Hebrew text specifies the Lord as subject, the translators render: "If the Lord has *stirred* you *up* against me. . . ." Finally, even Satan's image is improved somewhat by the translators: "Then Satan stood up against Israel and *moved* David to number Israel" (1 Chron. 21:1).

We will now return to take a closer look at 2 Samuel 24:1, for it is here that the translators have indulged themselves in a game of translational gymnastics. Compare the rendering of the NASB (right column below) with that of its progenitor, the ASV (left column).

ASV	NASB
And again the anger of Jehovah was kindled against Israel, and *he* moved David against them . . .	Now again the anger of the Lord burned against Israel, and *it* incited David against them . . .

In this verse NASB distinguishes itself from ASV by at least four alterations: (1) the shift from "Jehovah" to "Lord"; (2) the replacement of "was kindled against" by "burned against"; (3) a shift from "he" (= the Lord) to "it" (= anger) as subject; (4) the introduction of the verb "incited" where ASV has "moved."

The use of "Lord" in place of "Jehovah" is in keeping with the stated principles of NASB, and it is a definite improvement over ASV. "Burned against" may represent an attempt to move away from what was felt to have been a more archaic rendering, though this is doubtful, since "kindled" is used elsewhere in NASB. The third change, the replacement of "he" by "it," accomplishes two goals: (1) it avoids making the Lord the cause of David's sinful deed, and (2) it eases the contradiction between this verse and 1 Chronicles 21:1. Why the translators used "moved" in 1 Chronicles 21:1 and "incited" in this verse is a puzzle, unless it was felt that it was more in keeping with "anger . . . burned against" than was the more neutral "moved against" of ASV. Purely as a point of interest, KJV has "he moved . . . against" (2 Sam. 24:1) and "Satan . . . provoked" (1 Chron. 21:1), which is somewhat opposite from NASB.

If we now look more closely at this third alteration, and compare it with the other passages in the Old Testament where "the anger of the Lord" is used as subject, then a pattern emerges. In particular we are concerned with those passages where the clause which follows "the anger of the Lord" as subject has a third person singular pronominal subject, which may refer either to "anger" or "Lord." The relevant passages are as follows:

(1) "So the anger of the Lord burned against them and *He* departed." (Num. 12:9)
(2) "So the Lord's anger burned against Israel, and *He* made them wander." (Num. 32:13)
(3) ". . . otherwise the anger of the Lord your God will be kindled against you, and *He* will wipe you off the face of the earth."(Deut. 6:15)
(4) ". . . then the anger of the Lord will be kindled against you, and *He* will quickly destroy you." (Deut. 7:4).
(5) "Or the anger of the Lord will be kindled against you, and *He* will shut up the heavens." (Deut. 11:17)
(6) "And the anger of the Lord burned against Israel, and *He* gave them into the hands of plunderers." (Judg. 2:14)
(7) "So the anger of the Lord burned against Israel, and *He* said." (Judg. 2:20)
(8) "Then the anger of the Lord was kindled against Israel, so that *He* sold them." (Judg. 3:8).
(9) "And the anger of the Lord burned against Israel, and *He* sold them." (Judg. 10:7)
(10) "Now again the anger of the Lord burned agaist Israel, and *it* incited David against them." (2 Sam. 24:1)
(11) "So the anger of the Lord was kindled against Israel, and *He* gave them continually." (2 Kings 13:3)
(12) "On this account the anger of the Lord has burned against His people, And *He* has stretched out His hand." (Isa. 5:25).
(13) "The anger of the Lord will not turn back Until *He* has performed." (Jer. 23:20)
(14) "Therefore the anger of the Lord was kindled against His people, And *He* abhorred His inheritance." (Ps. 106:40).

(15) "And the anger of the Lord burned against Uzza, so *He* struck him down." (1 Chron. 13:10)
(16) "Then the anger of the Lord burned against Amaziah, and *He* sent him a prophet." (2 Chron. 25:15)

Of the 16 passages cited above, only the verbs "departed" (Num. 12:9), "said" (Judg. 2:20), "has stretched out" (Isa. 5:25), "abhor" (Ps. 106:40), and "sent" (2 Chron. 25:15) may be said to *require* that the subject be "the Lord" as opposed to "anger." Striking, however, is 2 Samuel 24:1, where NASB has "anger of the Lord . . . it" as opposed to "anger of the Lord . . . he" of the 15 other passages. Perhaps the closest parallel to 2 Samuel 24:1 occurs in 2 Samuel 6:7, where NASB translates: "And the anger of the Lord burned against Uzzah, and God struck him down. . . ." There is, of course, no way that the NASB translators could alter this verse, since "God" is there explicitly identified by the Hebrew author as the subject of the verb "struck . . . down." Moreover, the NASB translators would not have objected to God's striking Uzzah down, since other passages speak of God/the Lord in similar capacity. Apparently what did disturb these translators is the existence of two parallel passages, one of which speaks of the Lord's doing X to David and the other of Satan's doing X to David. The conclusion is obvious: theological presuppositions, rather than exegetical considerations, have determined the translation of 2 Samuel 24:1.

A comparison of the three accounts of Paul's conversion (Acts 9:7, 22:9; 26:14) also hints of an attempt at harmonization. The problem is that at Acts 9:7 the men who traveled with Paul are said to have heard the voice from heaven, while at Acts 22:9 the text indicates that they did *not* hear the voice. The account at 26:14 is open; there Paul relates that he heard the voice, but he makes no mention of his traveling companions. So the two passages that are of concern are 9:7 and 22:9, which together with their respective notes, read as follows in NASB:

> And the men who traveled with him stood speechless, hearing the *voice, but seeing no one. (9:7)
>
> *Or, *sound*
>
> And those who were with me beheld the light, to be sure, but did not *understand the voice of the One who was speaking to me. (22:9)
>
> *Or, *hear* (with comprehension)

The translators would doubtless appeal to the Greek as the basis for these narrow distinctions; they would call to our attention that at 9:7 the genitive case is used as object of the verb "hear," thus indicating hearing *without* comprehension, while it would be pointed out that at 22:9 the accusative case follows the verb "hear," indicating hearing *with* comprehension. This would explain both the alternative rendering "sound" at 9:7 and the translation "understand" with its note "*hear* (with comprehension)" at 22:9.

But this disctinction between the use of an accusative and a genitive as object of this verb does not exist in the book of Acts, and the documentation for it elsewhere in the New Testament is also lacking. Moreover, why was a similar note not appended to the translation at the other relevant passages in Acts? For example, at 11:7 the word "voice" is used in the genitive case as object of "heard," and no note explains that the meaning may also be "sound": "And I also heard a voice saying to me, 'Arise Peter; kill and eat.' " At 12:14 "she recognized Peter's voice," has "voice" in the accusative case, yet no note is included indicating "hearing with comprehension."

But most revealing in this regard is the absence of a note at Acts 22:7, where the genitive again appears as object (as opposed to the accusative of 22:9):

> and I fell to the ground and heard a voice saying to me, Saul, Saul, why are you persecuting me?

To have appended a note "Or, *sound*" (as at 9:7) would have been ludicrous, though consistency requires it if the note at 9:7 is purely linguistic and not an attempt at harmonization.

Reading the New Testament into the Old Testament

At several places the integrity of the Old Testament is totally violated by a translation which forces upon it explicit references to Jesus Christ. Perhaps this methodology is in keeping with the fourth aim of the Lockman Foundation ("They shall give the Lord Jesus Christ His proper place, the place which the Word gives Him . . ."). This principle must indeed be followed, where it is relevant, but it does not apply to the translation of the Old Testament. And when, under the compulsion of theological presuppositions, the translators make explicit reference to Jesus Christ in the Old Testament, they are no longer giving him "the place which the Word gives him." They have in fact gone beyond "the Word," placing him in contexts where Scripture clearly does not do so.

In the section entitled "Explanation of General Format," the editors state: "PERSONAL PRONOUNS are capitalized when pertaining to Deity." The adoption of this principle does not necessarily do violence to the text, although the writers of Scripture did not follow it in the original manuscripts. But the manner in which the NASB translators apply this principle in certain Old Testament passages immediately uproots them from their historical setting. Note, for example, that the king of Psalm 2 has now become "His Anointed" (2:2), "My King" (2:6), "My Son" (2:7), and "the Son" (2:12). At Psalm 16:10 the parallelism between "soul" and "Holy One" is obliterated by making the second line refer to Jesus Christ:

> For Thou wilt not abandon my soul to Sheol;
> Neither wilt Thou allow Thy Holy One to see the pit.

The tragic rendering of Psalm 45:1b ("I address my verses to the King") is worsened by the note: "Probably refers to Solomon as a type of Christ." Of similarly sad proportions is the note at Psalm 72:2: "Many of the pronouns in this Psalm may be rendered *He* since the typical reference is to the Messiah." As would be expected, Psalm 110:1 is overloaded with capitals:

> The Lord says to my Lord: Sit at My right hand,
> Until I make Thine enemies a footstool for Thy feet.

It comes as no surprise that the pronouns of Isaiah 53 suffer from acute overcapitalization. And the servant of Isaiah 49:3 is burdened with capitals, even though when specifically identified as the nation Israel: "And He said to Me 'You are My Servant, Israel, in Whom I will show My glory.' " Numerous other examples could be cited, but these are symptomatic of what is found throughout the Old Testament.

Isaiah 7:14 is worthy of comment for at least two reasons. First, the word "son" is not capitalized[1] ("Behold, a virgin will be with child and bear a son . . ."), while the possessive pronoun "His" which refers to this son is capitalized (". . . and she will call His name Immanuel"). The second thing of interest is that the rendering "virgin" appears in the text with the alternative "maiden" in the margin. This positioning of "virgin"/"maiden" is especially noteworthy, not because it represents the unexpected, but because it contrasts with what is done with every other occurrence of this same Hebrew noun *('almāh)* in the Old Testament, as the chart below will reveal:

Passage	Text	Margin
Genesis 24:43	"maiden"	———
Exodus 2:8	"girl"	———
1 Chronicles 15:20	"alamoth"	———
Psalm 46 (superscription)	"Alamoth"	"Possibly 'for soprano voices' "
Psalm 68:25	"maidens"	———
Proverbs 30:19	"maid"	———
Song of Songs 1:3	"maidens"	"virgins"
Song of Songs 6:8	"maidens"	"virgins"
Isaiah 7:14	"virgin"	"maiden"

Apart from the two nonsense passages (1 Chron. 15:20; Ps. 46:1), the translation reflects a definite pattern. Although there is nothing in the Hebrew text which even hints in the direction of "virgin" for Isaiah 7:14, the translators have opted for this rendering, obviously on the basis of their principle to "give the Lord Jesus Christ His proper place." The result is an annihilation of the historical character of the Isaiah text and a distortion of its message.

Awkward English

To comment on the English of NASB is to attack a straw person with fiery darts. By no standard may the language be described as either "contemporary English" or "a fluent and readable style according to current English usage."

This failure may not be attributed in its entirety to unconscious "translationese"; the introductory pages themselves are not alien to awkward English constructions or to the lack of cohesion within paragraphs.[2] The concern of this review, however, is with the quality of the English used in the translation itself.

In a recent article on the readability level of another contemporary formal equivalent translation, the present author demonstrated that it revealed "a serious lack of readableness due to long sentences, heavy grammatical arrangements, use of ecclesiastical 'in-group' language, occasional ambiguity of pronominal antecedents, lack of discourse continuity, ambiguities which may emerge in public reading, arbitrary shifts in language level and other factors."[3] All of these judgments (and more!) may be leveled against the NASB. A few random samplings will indicate the insensitivity of the translators in this regard.

Pronominal ambiguities may be found without effort. One of the more glaring occurs in Psalm 3:2, unless the psalmist's soul was masculine:

> Many are saying of my *soul,*
> There is no deliverance for *him* in God.

Joshua 5:7-8 narrates what must have been a wild circumcision party, and it is difficult, if not impossible, to determine who circumcised whom:

> [7]And their children whom He raised up in their place, Joshua circumcised; for they were uncircumcised, because they had not circumcised them along the way.
> [8]Now it came about when they had finished circumcising all the nation, that they remained in their places in the camp until they were healed.

Joseph's dream is somewhat muddled; no wonder he awoke:

> Yet when they had devoured them it could not be detected that they had devoured them; for they were just as ugly as before. Then I awoke. (Gen. 41:21)

See also at Genesis 40:20-22; 44:5 ("the one"); Acts 8:14-17.

Closely related to this matter of pronominal ambiguity is the lack of continuity within a discourse unit. At this the NASB translators are without rival, even within brief passages. Chapter eleven of Genesis opens: "Now *the whole earth* used the same language and the same words. And it came about as *they* journeyed east, that *they* found a plain in the land of Shinar and settled there." The textual and exegetical difficulties of Psalm 110:3 are legendary, but even these comprise no excuse for what results in NASB:

> Thy people will volunteer freely in the day of Thy power;
> In holy array, from the womb of the dawn,
> Thy youth are to Thee as the dew.

See also Psalm 71:3; Ecclesiastes 12:13-14 ("this"); Lamentations 1:9; Ezekiel 27:10-11.

The person who has a copy of NASB in hand has some hope, because the answers can always be looked up in another translation. But for the person who must rely upon the *hearing* of the Scriptures, the situation will be quite different. At Luke 19:13, 16 the translators have introduced a new parable, "the Multiplying Minnows," or at least that is how it may be heard:

> 13And he called ten of his slaves, and gave them ten minas, and said to them, "Do business with this until I come back."
> 16And the first appeared, saying, "Master, your mina has made ten minas more."

Further ambiguities will emerge in public reading at 2 Samuel 24:24: "I will not offer burnt offerings to the Lord my God which cost me nothing." According to 2 Chronicles 11:1 Rehoboam was a great builder for "when Rehoboam had come to Jerusalem, he assembled the house of Judah and Benjamin." Then the hearer will learn that in ancient times sailors took their wives to sea with them: "And each man said to his mate" (Jon. 1:7).

Occasionally the translation either states or implies the opposite of what is intended by the text. Psalm 16:3 apparently praises the glorious departed saints:

> As for the saints who are *in* the earth,
> They are the majestic ones in whom is all my delight.

For the English speaker, the implication of the rhetorical question at Isaiah 29:16b is that the potter should be considered *inferior* to the clay: "Shall the potter be considered as equal with the clay . . . ?" At Hebrews 13:2 "this" should properly be considered as a reference to the neglect to show hospitality: "Do not *neglect* to show hospitality, for by *this* some have entertained angels without knowing it."

Frequently the failure to heed the canons of English grammar results in comical, yet tragic, translations. At 2 Chronicles 33:19 the reader wonders if one is really reading English:

> His prayer also and how God was entreated by him, and all his sin, his unfaithfulness, and the sites on which he built high places and erected the Asherim and the carved images, before he humbled himself, behold, they are written in the records of the Hozai.

Surely the translators should have known better than to perpetuate the notoriously nonsensical rendering of 1 Chronicles 26:18: "At the Parbar on the west there were four at the highway and two at the Parbar." See also 1 Chronicles 15:20-21.

Esther was neither woman nor virgin: "And the king loved Esther more than all the women, and she found favor and kindness with him more than all the virgins . . ." (Esther 2:17). The inclusion of "other" at two places in the text would at least have been a step in the right direction. Logic demands that Ishmael was illegitimate, since according to Hebrews 11:17 Isaac was Abraham's "only begotten son." Hannah must have had the appearance of a unicorn; she prays:

> My heart exults in the Lord;
> My horn is exhalted in the Lord,
> My mouth speaks boldly against my enemies,
> Because I rejoice in Thy salvation. (1 Sam. 2:1)

Here one observes also the unnatural sequence of "the Lord . . . Thy salvation." But the Lord suffers more at the hands of NASB translators than do we mortals. God may be eternal, yet still has "elders," as Isaiah 24:23 notes:

> For the Lord of hosts will reign on Mount Zion and in Jerusalem,
> And His glory will be before His elders.

God is not dead, but seems to be either anemic or else a vampire: "For He who requires blood remembers them" (Ps. 9:12).

Noisome Notes

As with the noisome plagues that fell upon ancient Egypt, so the notes of NASB Reference Edition constantly harass the reader. Some few notes dispersed throughout the text are of value but their usefulness is considerably diminished by the overwhelming majority of anomalous notes. In fact, more than anywhere else the tragedy of this translation is reflected in its marginal notes, and for this reason the major portion of this review will concern itself with these notes. For convenience, they may be cataloged as follows.

Absurd or Ridiculous Notes

The best that may be said about many of the notes is that they are absurd, based upon the erroneous presupposition that the English reader will benefit from literalisms and/or transliterations of the Hebrew and Greek texts. Several random samplings will aptly illustrate this point. Appended to the word "married" in Genesis 20:3 is the note "Lit., *married to a husband.*" One is made to wonder if on occasion Hebrew women married something other than husbands! "Consult her wishes" is found in the text at Genesis 24:57; a note follows "Lit., *ask her mouth.*" The translators relish marginal readings where "mouth" appears as a literal member of the Hebrew text. At Genesis 25:28 it is said of Esau that "he had a taste for game"; accompanying the text is the splendid marginal note "Lit., *game was in his mouth.*" Dispersed throughout the translation is the note "Lit., *mouth,*" occurring with highest frequency in the book of Numbers, where it accompanies either "command" or "commandment" (see, e.g, 4:27, 37, 41, 49; 9:18, 23; 10:13). At Numbers 32:24 "what you have promised" is clarified by the notation "Lit., *that which has come out of your mouth.*" Two interesting notes, related to those of the mouth, are found in Exodus. At 2:7 the text reads "a nurse," and the note "Lit., *a woman giving suck*"; in 6:12 the text is "unskilled in speech" with note "Lit., *uncircumcised of lips*" (so also 6:30).

Moving from the lips to the ears, the reader is enlightened by two related notes: "Lit., *uncover your ear*" for "inform you" (Ruth 4:4) and "Lit., *uncovered the ear of*" for "made a revelation to" (2 Sam. 7:27). At Jeremiah 6:10 the text reads "Behold, their ears are closed" with a note before "closed": "Lit., *uncircumcised.*" At 1 Kings 13:6 a pair of notes gives attention to the entire face: "Lit., *soften the face of*" for "entreat" and "Lit., *softened the face of*" for "entreated." Then at 2 Chronicles 32:21 "in shame" is "Lit., *in shame of face.*"

Nor is the inner man (better, inner child!) neglected in this array of anatomical information; at 1 Kings 17:21, we learn that "to him" is "Lit., *upon his inward part.*" And for those who may have missed the clue at verse 21, the note is repeated in the next verse!

In this era of equal rights, the reader will find some satisfaction in the realization that the translators have also given some attention to the other extreme of the anatomy. At 2 Samuel 7:12 a portion of the promise which the Lord made to David is translated: "I will raise up your descendant after you, who will come forth from you." A note follows "descendant" ("Lit., *seed*"), but the more edifying note is the one attached to the pronoun "you," which reads "Lit., *your bowels.*"[4]

A survey of the manner in which the NASB translators have dealt with the Hebrew word rendered "bowels" *(me'îm)* in the note of 2 Samuel 7:12 will suggest something of their general carelessness in the handling of the biblical text. In a similar passage in the same book, the text reads "my son who came out from me" (2 Sam. 16:11), where "me" represents "bowels" of the 7:12 note. Here a note accompanies the pronoun "me": "Lit., *my body.*" The same Hebrew construction is found three other times in the Old Testament. At Genesis 15:4 the text reads "body" with marginal comment "Lit., *inward parts*"; at 25:23 the text is "separated from your body" with no accompanying note; at Isaiah 48:19 the text is "your offspring" with note "Lit., *the offspring of your inward parts.*" At 2 Chronicles 21:15, 18, 19 the word is rendered "bowels," but of the more than thirty occurrences of the Hebrew word in the Old Testament, this is the only passage where this particular rendering appears, and in all of the places where a "literal" rendering is given in the margin, the word "bowels" is never used again except at Song of Songs 5:4.

In translation the word appears either as "stomach" (Num. 5:22), "body" (Isa. 49:1), "soul" (Jer. 4:19), "heart" (Ps. 40:8), "womb" (Ruth 1:11), "inward parts" (2 Sam. 20:10, "spirit" (Lam. 1:20), "abdomen" (Song of Songs 5:14), "bowels" (2 Chron. 21:15), or "feelings" (Song of Songs 5:4). Where literal renderings are put in the margin, they are given either as "bowels" (2 Sam. 7:12), "body" (2 Sam. 16:11), "inward parts" (Gen. 15:4), or "entrails" (Isa. 16:11).

The translators' carelessness is most vividly illustrated by the Isaiah 16:11 passage. There the Hebrew noun is translated (together with the verb that follows it) as "heart intones" with note "Lit., *entrails murmur,*" while another Hebrew noun is translated "inward feelings" in the text, with note "Lit., *inward parts.*" Any reader who takes all these notes seriously is going to end up frustrated and confused. The same Hebrew word is said to be literally (1) "bowels," (2) "body," (3) "inward parts," or (4) "entrails," while yet a second Hebrew word is also literally "inward parts." One is given pause to wonder what may have been the outcome had the translators been consistent in maintaining "bowels" as the literal rendering in the margin. For example, the note does follow the noun "feelings" in the clause "And my feelings were aroused for him" (Song of Songs 5:4), but ten verses later in the clause "his abdomen is carved ivory" (5:14), no note is given to indicate that "abdomen" is also literally "bowels."

Among others, the following marginal readings also strike the reader as ludicrous: "us odious"/"Lit., *our savor to stink*" (Exod. 5:21); "she cannot afford a lamb"/"Lit., *her hand does not find a sufficiency of a lamb*" (Lev. 12:8); "incest"/"Lit., *confusion;* i.e., a violation of divine order" (Lev. 20:12); "that creeps on the ground"/"Lit., *with which the ground creeps*" (Lev. 20:25); "she happened to come to"/"Lit., *her chance chanced upon*" (Ruth 2:3); "Make your peace with me"/"Lit., *Make with me a blessing*" (2 Kings 18:31); "Mourn"/"Lit., *Make for yourself mourning*" (Jer. 6:26); "their first-born"/"Lit., *that which opens the womb*" (Ezek. 20:26).

The New Testament is not without its ludicrous notes: "attendants of the bridegroom"/"Lit., *sons of the bridalchamber*" (Matt. 9:15); "His coming"/"Lit., *the face of His entering*" (Acts 13:24); and, "tutor" with note "Lit., *a child-conductor*" (Gal. 3:24).

Useless Notes

There are a number of notes which are useless for the ordinary reader and unnecessary for the scholar. Many such notes are found in conjunction with the superscriptions to the Psalms. The phrase "for flute accompaniment" precedes Psalm 5 with the word "flute" given a note: "Heb., *Nehiloth.*" At Psalm 60, however, the order is reversed so that one reads in the text "according to Shushan Eduth" with the English equivalent in the note: "Lit., *The lily of testimony.*" The latter procedure of providing a transliteration in the text and a literal rendering in the margin is also adopted at Psalm 53, but the note there takes a different form: the word "mahalath" receives an explanation rather than a translation: "I.e., sickness, a sad tone." Where the transliterated word "Maskil" occurs in the superscriptions, a note emerges which is reminiscent of many *Amplified Bible* renderings: "Possibly, Contemplative, or Didactic, or Skillful Psalm" (45; 53; 54). And the word "Mikhtam" is handled similarly: "Possibly, Epigrammatic Poem, or Atonement Psalm" (56; 57). But the note on "Jonath elem rehokim" is even more impressive: "Or, *The silent dove of those who are far off,* or, *The dove of the distant terebinths*" (Ps. 56). One also discovers that the translators do not always distinguish between literal renderings and transliterations. For example, at Job 42:11 "piece of money" is followed by the note "Lit., *Qesitah.*"[5] But this is not a literal rendering of the text; it is rather a transliteration of a Hebrew word which, literally rendered, would be "measure of weight."

Isaiah 62:4 comes replete with a series of four notes, each of which is a transliteration of the Hebrew:

> It will no longer be said to you, '[1]Forsaken,'
> Nor to your land will it any longer be said, '[2]Desolate';
> But you will be called, '[3]My delight is in her,'
> And your land, '[4]Married';
> For the Lord delights in you,
> And to Him your land will be married.
>
> 1 I.e., *Azubah*
> 2 I.e., *Shemamah*
> 3 I.e., *Hephzibah*
> 4 I.e., *Beulah*

Similar notes are supplied with some frequency throughout the text: "threshing floor of Atad"/"Heb., *Goren ha-Atad*" (Gen. 50:10); "treatise"/"Heb., *midrash*" (2 Chron. 13:22; 24:27); "offering"/"Heb., *qorban*" (Lev. 1:2); "giant"/"Heb., *Raphah*" (2 Sam. 21:18); "destruction"/"Heb., *Belial*" (2 Sam. 22:5); "accursed"/"Gr. *anathema*" (1 Cor. 12:3).[6] The most fascinating set of transliterations appears at Exodus 16:31 ("manna"/"Heb., *man,* cf. v. 15") and 16:15 ("What is it?"/"Heb., *man hu,* cf. vs. 31"), where there is an attempt to mark the play on words; but the reader would have to know Hebrew to understand what is being done. Job 1:15 suffers from notes as much as Job suffered from sores. There we learn: "the Sabeans" are "Lit., *Sheba*"; "attacked" is "Lit., *fell upon*"; "slew" is "Lit., *smote*" and "I alone" is "Lit., *only I alone.*"

The notes on Urim and Thummim are totally valueless, and the translation of the Hebrew "give Urim" at 1 Samuel 14:41 as "give a perfect lot," appearing in the context in which it does, makes no sense whatsoever. The phrase "Urim and Thummim" occurs four times in the Old Testament. At Ezra 2:63 and Nehemiah 7:65 it is translated without comment, but a note is given at Exodus 28:30 ("i.e., Lights and the Perfections") and at Leviticus 8:8 ("i.e., the Lights and Perfections"). Other than at 1 Samuel 14:41, the noun "Urim" is used by itself at Numbers 27:21 and 1 Samuel 28:6, where it appears without note, as does the phrase "Thy Thummim and Thy Urim" at Deuternomy 33:8. The omission of the note at two places where "Urim and Thummim" occur as a unit, as well as the appearance of the note in two separate forms where it is given, is typical of the sloppy editorial work that characterizes NASB.

At Jeremiah 5:19 "When they say" is accompanied by a note concerning the pronoun "they"; it reads "Or, *you.*" The hapless reader is left to guess why he is given this choice. Little does he suspect that the alternative represents a different Hebrew text. He will be further astonished to discover in the margin at Acts 7:45 that "Joshua" of the text is actually "Gr., *Jesus.*" In this instance the note is not only of no help to the reader, but it is of negative value since it is misleading. "Jesus" also appears in the Greek text at Hebrews 4:8, where a note is lacking.

Inadequate Notes

Some of the notes to be discussed in this section could also be included below under "Inconsistent Notes." But inadequacy, especially where notes could throw light on a poor translation, does need special attention in itself. Compare, for example, Job 29:4 with 29:6.

At Job 29:4 the text and notes read:

As I was in [1]the prime of my days,
When the [2]friendship of God was over my tent;

1 Lit., *the days of my autumn*
2 Lit., *counsel*

The rendering of the first line is a step away from literalism in the direction of a dynamic equivalent, but the note is of questionable merit. The second line strikes the reader as somewhat unusual in its structure, though the abnormal English could be attributed to poetic license. Now observe 29:6:

When my steps were bathed in butter,
And the rock poured out for me streams of oil!

Here, two verses later, the translators have slipped back into a literalism and have missed the opportunity either to translate dynamically or else to provide an explanation in the margin.

In verse 8 the English reader would conclude that Job is complaining about the disrespectful actions of young men who "saw me and hid themselves," though in Job's own culture such an action was a show of respect. Then in verse 9 one might gather that the princes were making fun of Job when he approached:

The princes stopped talking,
And put their hands on their mouths;

According to verse 18, Job thought two things: (a) "I shall die in my nest," and (b) "I shall multiply my days as the sand." Two miscues are even more significant than the comical second line. First, the reader does not know if Job is speaking of favorable or unfavorable circumstances when he talks about dying in his nest. Second, the inclusion of a note "Lit., *with*" in conjunction with the preposition "in" compounds the confusion, since in English this might well imply that Job was bemoaning the fact that he was about to die together with his nest, and that this death was imminent.[7]

The inadequacy of the existing notes is further revealed in such passages as "He claps his hands among us . . ." (Job 34:37) and "Thus says the Lord God, 'Clap your hand, stamp your foot' . . ." (Ezek. 6:11).[8] In each of these passages the literal renderings provide false clues for the English reader, for whom applause generally implies approval. A cultural note could easily clarify the significance of the action in the two contexts.

The inadequacy and the inconsistency of the attempt to meet the stated goal of providing "literal renderings" in the margin is illustrated in the following texts. At John 2:4 the text reads "what do I have to do with you?" which is followed by note "Lit., *what to Me and to you* (a Hebrew idiom)."[9] But they fail to indicate that "What is between you and me . . . ?"

(Judg. 11:12) and "What have I to do with you . . . ?" (2 Sam. 16:10) also translate the same Hebrew idiom, except that "you" of 2 Samuel 16:10 is plural. Observe also at Matthew 16:23 which in part reads ". . . for you are not setting your mind on God's interests, but man's." A note precedes "God's": "Lit., *the things of God.*" But why do they fail to indicate that "man's" is "Lit., *the things of men*"?

A pair of inadequate notes emerges at Acts 10:2 and 10:4, attached to the rendering "alms." At verse 2 the note reads "Or, *gifts of charity*" and at verse 4 it reads "Or, *deeds of charity*" (so also at verse 31). The note explains the same Greek word in the same context, and the reader is offered no hint for alternating between "gifts" and "deeds" in the margin. At Acts 24:17 the comment differs only slightly from that of 10:2: "Or, *gifts to charity.*" Acts 3:2 has the singular (still as a comment on the plural rendering "alms"): "Or, *a gift of charity.*" No comments are given at 3:10; a note is also absent from 9:36, but the translation reads, "deeds of . . . charity."

Inconsistent Notes

A disturbing number of inconsistencies is found throughout the marginal notes. A note on "tax collectors" appears in no less than three forms: (1) "Publicans who collected Roman taxes on commission" (Matt. 5:46; Luke 3:12; 7:29); (2) "Publicans who collected Roman taxes for profit" (Matt. 9:10; Mark 2:15; Luke 5:27; 15:1; 18:10; 19:2); and (3) "A publican who collected Roman taxes" (Matt. 18:17; 21:31).

Some of the most disturbing inconsistencies are found in conjunction with the abbreviation "Lit." (meaning "literally"), which is apparently used as ambiguously and as inconsistently as is the conjunction "Or" in the notes. One wonders what the translators actually meant by the term "literal" and what they hoped to accomplish by the menagerie of queer sounding notes prefaced by it. Genesis 1:11 reads, "fruit trees bearing fruit after their kind" and a note supplements the text: "their" is "Lit., *its.*" But these same translators fail to indicate that the noun "trees" is also singular in Hebrew, as is the noun "trees" in the following verse. At Exodus 8:6 they do supply the information that "frogs" is "Lit., *frog,*" from which the reader may conclude that it must have been a huge frog, since it "came up and covered the land of Egypt." In Revelation 9:19 the translation reads, "For the power of the horses is in their mouths and in their tails." But alas, we are not informed that in Greek "mouths" is singular (literally "mouth") while "tails" is plural. On the other hand, in Revelation 19:18 the word "flesh" occurs five times in the plural, and in each instance it is translated "flesh" without a note.

The Hebrew word traditionally rendered "spirit" *(rûaḥ)* receives inconsistent treatment, as may be seen by a survey of several places where it is used in the book of Job. At Job 4:9 it is translated "blast" in the clause: "And by the blast of His anger they come to an end." A note accompanies "blast" ("Lit., *wind*"). At Exodus 15:8 the word is also rendered "blast" ("at the blast of Thy nostrils"), but without note. And in the same Exodus passage (15:10) the word is rendered "wind," also without note. Moreover, in the phrases "at the blast of the breath of His nostrils" (2 Sam. 22:16) and "At the blast of the breath of Thy nostrils" (Ps. 18:15), the word is translated "breath" without note. Then at Job 4:15 the rendering is "spirit" with note "Or, *breath,*" while at 19:17 the rendering is "breath" without note. At 21:4 "I" appears in the text with note "Lit., *my spirit,*" and at 27:3 "breath" is given in the text with note "Or, *spirit.*" But then at 26:4 "spirit was expressed" is given a note "Lit., *breath has gone forth.*"[10] At 34:14 the translation is "spirit" without note, as it is at 32:18. The variations in the translation of the word are of no concern, for the same word may have many different meanings according to the context in which it appears. However, of genuine concern is the observation that the same Hebrew word should be given three different literal renderings ("breath"; "wind"; "spirit"), and this within the same Old Testament book!

The Hebrew noun generally rendered "word" *(dabar)* fares no better at the hands of NASB translators. In the book of Esther the noun is translated "command" four times, each of them without note (1:12; 2:8; 3:15; 8:14), and at 3:1 the plural is translated "events," also without notation. Then at 2:20 the text reads "what Mordecai told her," followed by the note "Lit., *the word of Mordecai*" (compare 5:5: "as Esther desires"/"Lit., *the word of Esther*"). At 2:22 the rendering is "plot" with comment: "Lit., *matter,* so also vs. 23." At 5:14 the rendering is "advice" and the note "Lit., *thing.*" Attached to the renderings "instructions" (9:31) and "customs" (9:32) is the note: "Lit., *words.*" So here, in the brief book of Esther the same Hebrew word is said literally to be "word," "matter," and "thing." The translator of Ezra 10:5 gave his readers a double choice; the text is "proposal" and the note "Lit., *word, thing.*"

The translation "GOD says" in Jeremiah 3:1 provides an interesting study in the art of inconsistency. In conjunction with the verb "says" is a note "Heb., *saying.*"[11] But the translators fail to inform the reader that the word "God" (appearing in the text in oversized capital letters) is *not* in the Hebrew. The translators could also have indicated that the participle "saying" is not present in some ancient translations.[12]

NASB is not even consistent in doing what it overtly claims to do. In the introduction to the Reference Edition there is a section entitled "Greek tenses," where the first paragraph in part reads:

> A careful distinction has been made in the treatment of the Greek aorist tense . . . and the Greek imperfect tense. . . .

First of all, "Greek aorist tense" would more accurately be "Greek aorist indicative tense," for the subjunctive, imperative, and optative of the Greek aorist tense are future by nature. Second, this "careful distinction" is not so carefully maintained throughout the text. For example, at John 11:5 and 13:23 the imperfect tense of the Greek verb *agapao* is rendered "loved" without accompanying note. But at 11:36 and 20:2 the imperfect tense of the Greek verb *phileo* is rendered "loved" with note "Lit., *was loving*." One might conclude that there is something in the nature of these two verbs that distinguishes them from one another, so that the imperfect tense of one deserves a note while the imperfect tense of the other does not. But this illusion quickly vanishes when the reader turns to John 21, and discovers that *agapao* is used twice in the imperfect tense and translated "loved" in both instances. But whereas there is a note at verse 7 ("Lit., *was loving*"), the same form contains no note at verse 20.

This inconsistency in dealing with verb forms extends even to participles. In Acts 6:11 two participles are used; the first is rendered as an infinitive "to say" with note "Lit., *saying*," while the second is translated as a finite verb "speak" without note. Every student of the Greek language knows that the perfect participle occasionally functions as an imperative. Observe how the translators have dealt with the perfect participle of the verb "be subject to" in its five occurrences in the New Testament. At Ephesians 5:21 it is translated "be subject to" with note "Lit., *being subject*." At 1 Peter 2:18; 3:1 it is translated as an imperative ("be submissive to") without a note, while it is translated as a participle at Titus 2:5 ("being subject to") and 1 Peter 3:5 ("being submissive to").

Inaccurate or Misleading Notes

The translators of NASB evidently assumed that the inclusion of notes which represent literal renderings of the Greek or Hebrew text would be of value for the Engish reader. However, this assumption is based upon the erroneous presupposition that all languages express themselves similarly, and that unusual sounding collocations of words in Greek or Hebrew must therefore have some special significance. But this is not the case, for these expressions which may sound strange to the English speaker were perfectly natural to the biblical writers. Just as their cultures differed from ours today, so the form and idiomatic expressions of their languages were also different. Fallacious also is the presupposition that a literal rendering of the original text represents a faithful translation. This is certainly not true; in fact, the form in which something is expressed in one language may frequently convey either an opposite or wrong meaning in another language. But our main concern for the present is to suggest that if such notes are included, they surely ought to be both accurate and comprehensive, which is not what one finds in NASB.

Mark 4:1 is significant, as much for the lack of a note at one point as for the note that does accompany the translation. In NASB the phrase "by the seashore" occurs twice in this verse, and it deserves a note more than many of the other phrases which do receive notes in NASB. First, the word rendered "seashore" by NASB is literally "sea" or "lake"; there is no place in the New Testament or in Classical Greek where the word means "seashore." Second, in Greek the preposition translated "by" is different in each of these phrases. In its first occurrence "by" translates a preposition meaning "along beside," while in its second occurrence it represents a preposition, the root meaning of which is "facing." Why did the translators fail to call these matters to the attention of the readers?

But these errors of omission are not nearly so serious as the error that is made in the note that they do include in this verse. Accompanying the verb "gathered" is the note "Lit., *is gathered.*" Since the present tense in Greek frequently denotes action in progress, one could just as easily say "Lit., *is being gathered.*" However, that is of minor significance. What is important is that the verb, in the form in which it occurs in this verse, may be reflexive as well as passive. If it is taken to be reflexive, then "gathered" is just as much a literal rendering as is the marginal proposal "is gathered." In fact, at Luke 22:66 and Acts 13:44 the aorist passive form of the verb is translated with a reflexive force as "assembled." But the same aorist passive form (except in the plural) is rendered as a passive at Matthew 26:3: "Then the chief priests and the elders of the people were gathered together. . . ." Here the context is similar to that of Luke 22:66, and a reflexive interpretation of the verb is certainly more satisfactory.

At Luke 2:49 the text reads "Did you not know that I had to be in my Father's house?"; accompanying "house" is the note "Or, *affairs;* lit., *in the things of My Father.*" The problem here is twofold. (1) NASB places "house" in italics, indicating that it is not a part of the Greek text. (2) The so-called literal rendering placed in the margin is misleading, since this particular Greek structure is sufficiently documented from other sources as an idiomatic expression meaning "in the house of. . . ." Although NASB has apparently chosen the correct interpretation of the text, the combination of italics in the translation with the marginal reading will leave the reader to assume that the correct translation is the one given in the margin.

At Matthew 4:12 "been taken into custody" is given a marginal note "Lit., *been delivered up.*" Except for persons who use archaic English, the Greek verb used here can in no way be construed to mean "delivered up," and to present this as a literal meaning is certainly inaccurate. In error also is the note at Acts 2:47. The relevant sentence there reads: "And the Lord was adding to their number day by day those who were being saved." Before the preposition "to" a numeral indicates a marginal note, "Lit., *together*." The first problem that the reader encounters is that of determining precisely how much of the text is covered in the note (this is actually a recurring obstacle in NASB). That is, does the note cover merely the preposition "to" or does it include the entire phrase "to their number"? Evidently the latter is meant, though one can be sure only through checking the Greek text. But having done so, one then discovers that the phrase is literally "upon the same," which may be used as a designation of place (a meaning which it has at 2:1, where NASB translates "in one place" without note). It may also mean "together," but this is not the "literal" meaning, and it is translated that way by NASB in 2:44, also without note.

In the second chapter of Acts another inaccurate note may be pointed out. At 2:43 NASB has ". . . everyone kept feeling a sense of awe" to which is appended a note "Lit., *fear was occurring to every soul.*" If indeed, "a careful distinction has been made in the treatment of the Greek aorist tense . . . and the Greek imperfect tense . . ." then the verb "was occurring to" should not be rendered as a past progressive, for it is *aorist* indicative, not an imperfect.[13]

Occasionally the translators will give a note following "children" to indicate that the Hebrew is literally "sons" (see Jer. 7:18), but on other occasions they will let the translation stand without comment (see Ps. 73:15). The failure to be consistent at this level could possibly be attributed to editorial failure, but there is no excuse for the manner in which text and note are dealt with at Numbers 13:22, 28. In verse 22 the text reads "descendants" with note "Lit., *children*"; in verse 28 the text reads "descendants" with note "Lit., *born ones.*" Why should the translators extend themselves to come up with such a ridiculous sounding phrase as "born ones" when the Hebrew word in both verses is precisely the same?

The Hebrew word translated "mercy seat" occurs twenty-nine times in the Old Testament, twenty-seven of which are accompanied by the note "Lit., *propitiatory.*" The exceptions are at Exodus 37:8 (notes do occur at verses 6, 9) and 1 Chronicles 28:11. Although one of the standard Hebrew lexicons does give "propitiatory" as a meaning for this word, the reader is ill-advised to consider this the literal meaning.

Even the womb and the belly do not find sanctuary from the onslaught of these erroneous notes. For example, a Hebrew expression which occurs four times in the book of Proverbs is translated "innermost parts of the body" (18:8; 26:22), "innermost parts of his being" (20:27), and "innermost parts" (20:30). The variety of translation is justifiable, but not the variation in the notes: "Lit., *chambers of the belly*" (18:8; 26:22) and "Lit., *chambers of the body*" (20:27, 30). Moreover, the Hebrew noun *(beten)* given the literal meanings of "belly" and "body" in the Proverbs passages is translated "birth" at Psalms 58:3 with note "Lit., *the womb.*" Then at Isaiah 48:8 the same translation appears as at Psalms 58:3, but with note "Lit., *the belly.*"

It is true that this Hebrew noun may be used of the womb as of the belly. But there is another noun in Hebrew *(rehem)* which has "womb" as its primary meaning, and it is used in two places in the Old Testament immediately after the preposition "from" and without the definite article (Job 3:11; Ps. 22:10).[14] The note that accompanies the Job passage reads "Lit., *from the womb,*" while the note in Psalms has "Lit., *a womb.*"[15]

What the NASB translators did with Hosea 9:11 is worthy of attention; the translation is dynamic and no note accompanies the text:

> As for Ephraim, their glory will fly away like a bird—No birth, no pregnancy, and no conception!

For this restructuring the translators are doubtless indebted to ASV, which reads in the second line: "there shall be no birth, and none with child, and no conception." But a more literal rendering of the verse is represented in KJV, where the second line is "from the birth, and from the womb, and from the conception." Here one can observe that a literal rendering of the Hebrew does not occur either in the text or in the margin and that the expected italicized words (representing those absent from the original Hebrew) have flown away with the birds! All that remains is a miscarriage of NASB translation principles![16]

Anomalous Textual Notes

Of all the notes contained in NASB, those on the Hebrew, Aramaic, and Greek texts constitute the greatest mystery. The manner in which these notes are introduced is in itself absolute chaos, as the following Old Testament samplings reveal:

(1) "Some mss. read," "Many mss. read," "Most mss. read," "Some ancient mss. read," "So some ancient mss," "Reading of many mss.," "So several ancient mss.," "Or, with many mss.," "So with some mss."

(2) "Some ancient versions read," "Some versions read," "So with many versions, MT omits," "So with some ancient versions; Heb.," "So some ancient versions; Heb.," "So with ancient versions; Heb.," "Some ancient versions render," "So with some ancient versions; MT," "So ancient versions," "Ancient versions read," "So with the versions; MT," "So the versions; MT," "So with many ancient versions; Heb."

(3) "So some mss. and versions"; "Heb.," "So with several mss. and versions; MT," "So some ancient mss. and versions; MT," "So many ancient mss. and versions; MT," "Many mss. and ancient versions read," "So with some mss and the ancient versions," "So with mss. and ancient versions," "With some ancient mss. and versions; MT," "Many mss. and the ancient versions read."

(4) "So with Gk. and other ancient versions," "So with Gk.; MT," "So with Gk.; Heb.," "Gk. version renders," "Gk. and Syr. read," "So with Gk. and some ancient mss; MT," "So Gk. and Heb. mss.," "So with two Heb. mss. and Syriac; MT," "So with Gk. & versions; MT," "So the Gk.; Heb.," "So Gk.; Heb.," "So with Gk.," "Gk. reads," "So the Gk. and the Latin; Heb. omits," "So with Gk. and Syr.; MT omits," "So with DSS; MT," "So DSS; MT," "Targum and DSS read," "So Targum; MT," "Or, *monuments* as in Ugaritic," "Aramaic," "Aram.," "Another reading is."

(5) "A suggested reading is," "Some render as," "Some commentators read," "Some authorities read."

The abbreviations DSS, Gk., Heb., and MT are each given token definitions in the introduction to the translation, though it is really doubtful if the general reader is provided enough information to distinguish, for example, between what is meant by the Hebrew text and the Masoretic text: "Heb.—Hebrew text, usually Masoretic. MT—Masoretic text." A conscientious, but uninformed reader will end up more confounded and confused than ever, after referring to this truncated, and somewhat tricky, explanation. And even if this explanation were sufficient, there still would remain the abbreviations "Syr." (1 Sam. 12:11; Job 21:24; 23:2) and "Aram." (Ezra 6:6), to say nothing of the words "Targum" (Isa. 38:15; Ezek. 19:7) and "Ugaritic" (Ezek. 43:7, 9). What distinction is to be made between "versions" (Gen. 30:11) and "ancient versions" (Gen. 6:3)? What is indicated by the frequently occurring "another reading" (Exod. 21:8; 2 Sam. 22:33, 34)? Who are the "authorities" (Ps. 60:5), the "commentators" (Ps. 25:17; 139:11), and how much weight is one to attribute to their witness?

In a rapid check of the Old Testament, the only verses found to admit of obscurity are (1) Ezra 1:9, which reads "duplicates" with note "Heb. obscure, other possible meanings are *knives, censers*" and (2) Haggai 2:17, where the Hebrew is surely no less obscure than the relation between the translation and the marginal reading:

> . . . yet you did not *come back to me
>
> *Heb. obscure; perhaps, *but what did we have in common?*

If one attempts to work the alternative into the text, the result is ". . . yet you did not but what did we have in common," which certainly is not what the translators intended. Isaiah 14:4b approximates the admission of an obscurity, and the reader will doubtless agree:

How the oppressor has ceased,
And how *fury has ceased!

*Amended from the meaningless *medhebah* to *marshebah*

At Jeremiah 5:26 the translators felt some hesitation, where the text reads, "They watch like fowlers *lying in wait," with annotation "*Perhaps, *crouching down.*"

"Envoys" of Psalm 68:31 cannot be said to render the obscure word of the Hebrew text; rather it represents the reading of three ancient versions. Yet the translation appears without notation. On the other hand, at the equally obscure Proverbs 26:10 they adopt a conjectural emendation (a scholarly guess!) for the reading "archer" in the text, and the reader is merely given an alternative rendering for the entire verse with a note introduced "Or, *A master*. . . ." As noted above, the reader of NASB is deceived on multiple occasions by the notes introduced "Or,. . . ." There is no consistency in the notations introduced either by this brief formula or by its companion "Another reading is. . . ."

The textual notes of the New Testament also assume an equally intriguing bevy of format, and the reader will delight in attempting to distinguish between "mss." (Matt. 5:22), "earliest mss." (Matt. 6:13), "late mss." (Matt. 17:21), "ancient mss." (Matt. 18:11), "early mss." (Matt. 19:9), "the best ancient mss." (Mark 9:43), "oldest mss." (Mark 16:9), and "Greek mss." (John 10:18). The reader's investigative instincts will be aroused to search out who the "others" are, when we encounter, "Or, *Beelzebul;* others read, *Beelzebub.*" Then one can delve into the mysteries of the "authorities," some of whom are said to "insert" (John 5:4) and others to "add" (John 7:8), while at other places "many ancient authorities read" (John 14:4). Will the reader be prejudiced against those manuscripts which are said either to "insert" (Mark 10:24), "add" (Mark 14:68), "omit" (Luke 24:6), or "use" (1 Corinthians 2:10)? Finally, note the textual source cited at Luke 6:18. The text reads "* who had come to hear Him," with the note: "*Most English versions begin verse 18 with, *and those who.*"

This shifting back and forth in the form of the texual notes is more than obvious even within a single book, such as Revelation: "mss." (6:1, 3, 5, 7; 13:1, 18), "ancient mss." (9:13; 11:8; 13:15; 14:3; 15:3; 16:4; 17:8; 18:3; 21:3; 22:21), and "authorities" (16:16). In the last of these passages, the text reads "Har-Magedon" with the note, "Some authorities read, *Armageddon.*" But the note is incorrect, whatever is indicated by the term "authorities." There are orthographic differences in the Greek manuscripts, but the reading "armageddon" (with double "d") is nothing more than the traditional English spelling of the Greek noun used in the verse.[17] The Greek word may more properly be *transliterated* as "Harmagedon" (single "d" with initial "h" representing the "rough" breath marker of the Greek), but both "Armageddon" (of modern English translations) and "Harmagedon" represent the same Greek text. A more precise note would have been "Some mss. read *Mageddon;* others read *Magedon;* and other mss. have still other readings." But no note is really required, for the reading "Armageddon/Harmagedon" has sufficient textual evidence in its support, and for English speakers "Armageddon" has come to be the accepted spelling.

Epilogue

By way of bringing this review to its conclusion, some points of difference between NASB and its forerunner, the ASV, will be briefly noted.

(1) *Paragraphing.* ASV makes effective use of paragraphing, while in the prose sections of the text, NASB reverts to printing each verse as an isolated unit. In the "poetic" sections of NASB all lines are marginally equal, and each line begins with a capital; in ASV this is also true, except that the double column page format of ASV makes it appear otherwise.

(2) *Name for God.* The avoidance of *Jehovah* in NASB is a welcome improvement over ASV.

(3) *Pagination.* The use of single column pages in NASB afforded the translators excellent opportunities, which were unavailable to the ASV translators. This is especially true of the poetic sections, where translators of poetic inclination could have done creative restructuring without multiples of run-on lines on every page. But the NASB threw away this advantage; instead, the use of single columns merely enabled them to squander more pages.

(4) *Marginal notations.* The notes of NASB frequently become doctrinal (especially in the Old Testament), whereas the ASV notes remain, for the most part, either textual, exegetical, or translational.

(5) *Miscellaneous improvements of NASB over ASV.* (a) There are occasional grammatical improvements; (b) sometimes the referents of pronouns are made explicit in the translation; (c) in the Song of Songs the speakers are identified in the margin; (d) notes are included which identify the "Red Sea" as "Lit., *Sea of Reeds.*"

In summary, the translators of NASB have dreamed the impossible dream, only to create a nightmare. Should readers feel the need for a formal equivalent translation, other, more accurate and readable versions are available. And if a choice must be made between ASV and NASB, it cannot be doubted that old wine is better. The initial marginal note of NASB is prophetic: "a waste and an emptiness."

Translators

The list of translators for the NASB was requested from the publisher (The Lockman Foundation), but the request was not honored, in accordance with the version's preface, "no work will ever be personalized."

6
The Jerusalem Bible

Bruce Vawter, C.M.

To understand the considerable success, as well as the virtues and shortcomings of The Jerusalem Bible, one must make the effort to recall, or to learn for the first time, as the case may be, what was the situation facing English-speaking Roman Catholics a quarter-century ago when they wanted to read the Bible. I speak of making an effort, for in these relaxed and ecumenical days it is hard to conjure up that quarter-century ago from the ashes of the past. It is worth the effort, though, and not only for English-speaking Roman Catholics. I intend to make critical remarks about that unecumenical and unrelaxed time in respect to my own church (Roman Catholic), since it is of course the one I know best. If I might venture one fascinating speculation, it would be to wonder about what additional travails might have been experienced by a Revised Standard Version then being burnt in fundamentalist pulpits and raising questions on the floor of a McCarthyite Congress, had Catholics been sitting on its board of editors and translators as they do now.

What was the situation that confronted Roman Catholics in their access to a vernacular Bible? First of all, at least officially they were forbidden any translation (or, for that matter, edition of the biblical text in the original languages) that had been brought out under non-Catholic auspices. That was, and is, the provision of canon 1399, 1° of the Code of Canon Law.[1] It is true, canon 1400 effectively nullified this proscription by permitting the use of such books "only to those who are engaged *quovis modo* (= in any manner whatever) in theological or biblical studies."[2] This is an instance of that built-in dispensational characteristic of Roman law that is often bewildering to people accustomed to a common law that does not take into account privilege. The purpose of these seemingly conflicting laws was to allow relatively free access to the Bible, but only after it had been asserted in uncompromising language that its publication and divulgation were regarded as an exclusive prerogative of the Roman church. Judged in this light the law of the Code was, in fact, quite liberal: at least a reversal of purely negative legislation inherited from pre-Reformation heresy-hunting in the late Middle Ages.[3] On the other hand, as anyone who was teaching Scripture in Catholic schools at that time can readily testify, when the law came to be implemented on the level that affected most people, it was often enforced by those who knew all about canon 1399, 1°, but had never heard of canon 1400 or did not understand it, and this despite the fact that in the Roman as well as in other systems of law, doubtful laws are no laws at all and the presumption of the law is supposed to favor freedom from the law.

Secondly, another canon, no. 1391, managed by its negative phraseology to give the impression that access to the Bible should be made difficult rather than easy. Translations were forbidden, said the canon, "unless they be approved by the Apostolic See, or unless they be published under the bishops' supervision and with notes taken principally from the holy Fathers of the Church and from learned and catholic writers." Quite properly, of course, a Latinate and Italianate Holy See had not to that point, and has not subsequently, "approved" any translation of the Bible into English, French, German, Flemish, or Choctaw. The "bishops' supervision" of which the canon spoke probably envisaged nothing more complex than the imprimatur of a local ordinary (such as took place, for example, in 1965 when Cardinal Cushing of Boston authorized a "Catholic edition" of the RSV New Testament). It was popularly assumed, however, that such translations could be approved only for "private devotion," and that any "official" version would require a more general approbation of the church. Specifically, it would have to be in conformity with the Bible used in the church's liturgy which, by and large and with slight differences, was the Sixto-Clementine Vulgate of 1592. (It must be remembered that at this time the liturgy of the church was in Latin and that the reading of the scriptural word in the vernacular—usually made from the altar and not from a pulpit—was a dispensable concession to the better understanding of the Latin liturgy, simply translating the pericopes in the Roman Missal.) As for the requirement that a translation have notes, the intention of course was to safeguard orthodoxy from the perilous possibility of "private interpretation" which would arise from study of the unadorned word of God. In these days and times, however, there is hardly need to argue the merits of an annotated Bible, when even the Bible Societies have recognized their "without note or comment" formula to be sadly unreal.[4]

Finally, as has already been suggested, there was a persuasion that to be really serviceable in the church and not merely a scholarly curiosity or private source of study, a biblical translation had to be based upon the Vulgate, which the Council of Trent[5] had declared "authentic for public lectures, disputations, preaching, and explanation, so that no one should dare or presume to reject it under any pretext." There is no doubt that this persuasion was very well founded in the letter of the law, which continued to emerge from Rome from time to time almost till the eve of *l'encyclique libératrice* of Pope Pius XII, the *Divino afflante Spiritu* of 1943. It was only then that Catholics of the Anglo-Saxon world discovered that a revisionism had been going on in the law of the church on whose intellectual and ideological periphery they had long been habituated to dwell. Suddenly it was revealed to them that the intention of Trent had been to confer on the Vulgate only a "juridic," not a critical, authority, so that the Vulgate might be textually corrected with impunity, and that even "official" national or regional vernacular translations could and should be made from the original biblical texts without respect to the Vulgate.[6] The Catholic Biblical Association of America, founded in 1937 with one of its principal aims to provide the English-speaking Catholic world with a more serviceable Bible than it then possessed, was at that moment (1943) in process of biblical translation—from the Vulgate, of course. Immediately after *Divino afflante Spiritu* came a shifting of the Association's gears, and a decade later would see the emergence of the beginning of what would eventually become the New American Bible, translated completely from the original biblical languages. Apace, however, in more fruitful and sensitive soil, had already been sown the seeds of The Jerusalem Bible.

Besides the law concerning it, the actuality of Catholic biblical publication must also be known in order to appreciate properly what The Jerusalem Bible brought in its time. The Bible used by English speaking Roman Catholics then was variously called the Douay Version, the Douay-Rheims, or the Challoner-Rheims. None of these titles was especially accurate. What had happened was that English Catholics in exile under Queen Elizabeth I, Oxford scholars all, had produced at Rheims in 1582 an English translation of the New Testament, and again at Douai in 1609 a translation of the Old Testament. Both of these had been made from the Vulgate—out of principle and not because texts in the biblical languages were unavailable, as in the case of the old Wycliffe versions. The translators of the Authorised (King James) Version of 1611 make reference to the Douay-Rheims version disparagingly in their famous preface, neglecting to note how much they had profited from its precedents, especially from its rendering of the Greek definite article that lay behind the anarthrous Latin of the Vulgate by means of the English definite and indefinite articles. (This was a petty conceit on their part, to be sure, since every translation of the Scripture has been in debt to its predecessors, at least from the time of the Targumists and the Septuagint onward.)

The "Douay Bible" that was in the possession of Catholic families in our generation, however, was actually largely the product of Bishop

Richard Challoner (1691-1781). Challoner, who was innocent of the biblical languages, "revised" this version in 1749, again in 1750, drastically in 1752, and later as well. His aim was to make the language more readable which, generally speaking, meant that he adjusted it to that of the Authorised Version. Subsequent to his time the text entered upon a recensional history of its own, picking up variants from the carelessness of printers and the deliberate changes introduced by copyeditors. In England the text tended to be printed as a blend of the first two Challoner revisions, while in America more of the changes from the third revision were included. Probably no two publishers ever produced precisely the same "Douay Bible."[7]

So at length we come to 1966 and the appearance in England and America of The Jerusalem Bible, the realization of an idea whose time most everyone probably agreed had come. There was officially available for the Catholic reader only the Challoner mishmash just described, filled with childishly apologetic footnotes, and hardly the work of "learned and catholic writers." Efforts to replace it had been unsuccessful, and alternatives to it were still aborning. To be sure, at least in the United States, a better edition of the New Testament was available. In 1941 members of the Catholic Biblical Association under the patronage of the episcopal committee of the Confraternity of Christian Doctrine had published a revision of the Challoner-Rheims which was, in effect, a new translation, still officially of the Vulgate (but of critical editions, this time) but with consultation of the Greek so that all major variants between Greek and Latin were noted. Various American publishers of the "Douay Bible" printed this revision for their New Testament. There was also, from England, the version of the entire Bible, made from the (Sixto-Clementine) Vulgate by Monsignor Ronald Knox, the New Testament first published in 1945 and the Old Testament in 1949. The Knox Bible was adopted by the Catholic hierarchy of England and Wales as an official version and also enjoyed considerable success in America. But there was no version done from the original texts. What would eventually become the New American Bible (then known as the CCD or Confraternity Version, begun in 1943) was appearing part by provisional part, but the *editio princeps* of that completed Bible would not be published until 1970. Other "private" translations of the original Greek or Hebrew—such as the New Testament of Aloysius Spencer, posthumously published in 1936, the New Testament of James Kleist and Joseph Lilly, published in 1954, the Westminster Version of the entire Bible begun in 1913 and never completed—enjoyed limited circulation and were mainly regarded as curiosities, though each had its own merits.

What The Jerusalem Bible did, therefore, was, precisely at the right time, to present the English-speaking Catholic world with a version of the Scripture done from the original text, turned into a dignified and highly readable form of our mother tongue, under impeccable Roman Catholic auspices (including, therefore, the Old Testament books and parts of books traditional in the Catholic canon and excluded from the "Protestant" and the Jewish). The introductions and annotations were both critical and scholarly, rarely apologetic. Its success was immediately assured.

The Jerusalem Bible also wisely chose to guarantee its ecumenical acceptance by eschewing the parochial "Catholic" spelling of proper names that had long challenged the good will of non-Catholics seeking to make use of scholarly articles and reference works done by Roman Catholics. The spelling of the biblical names of people and places is, of course, purely conventional. Hardly any normal reader would recognize who is meant by names like Yirmĕyahu or Yesha'yahu, which is the way they read in the Masoretic (Hebrew) text. The Septuagint had rendered them as Ieremias and Isaias (the final *s* to make them declinable) and thus they passed into the Vulgate. Thus they passed also into most modern languages. The early English translators, however, restored to them a bogus Hebrew flavor by substituting an *h* for the final *s*. The spelling of the names was already too well established for more to be done than this. For less well established names, however, more could be done, and generally it was to turn them into a rough-and-ready equivalent of the Masoretic spellings, using some equivalences that were probably lost on even their first readers, such as the *z* which was to stand for the Hebrew *ṣādê* (a Yiddishism). (Though even in the Authorised Version, in the New Testament at least, such forms remain as Elias in Mark 9:5 [RSV, Elijah] and Zacharias in Luke 1:5 [RSV, Zechariah].) Now in many cases the Vulgate, following the Septuagint, had preserved more authentic pronunciations than those devised by the Masoretes. Nabuchodonosor, for example, is certainly closer to the Babylonian Nabukuduruṣūr than is the Nebuchadnezzar or even the Nebuchadrezzar of our English versions. On the other hand, many of the Vulgate spellings simply reflected the inadequacies of Latin or Greek to reproduce Hebrew aspirate sounds. When such forms were then mechanically "Englished," this resulted in sounds not originally intended—Lachis, Ezechias, Osee (Hosea). Other spellings had become transmogrified into bizarre forms with no etymological justification in any language, such as Aggaeus (Haggai) and Eliseus (Elisha). Compounding these confusions in Catholic biblical language were others inherited from the Septuagint which were not really the fault of the Vulgate: Paralipomenon, for example (a Greek genitive plural for works Jerome had called the books of Chronicles), and 1-4

Kings (the Septuagint actually had "Kingdoms") for the books Jerome had distinguished as 1-2 Samuel and 1-2 Kings.

All academic questions aside, the point was that a conventional English rendering of biblical terminology had been arrived at over a period of some centuries, and the alternate "Catholic" usages could only co-exist with it as some kind of ghetto dialect. The Jerusalem Bible led the way in producing a Catholic version of the Bible, English in its spelling as in all else. The Confraternity Version did not adopt this principle until 1969 (at the publication of its final portion of the Old Testament, the historical books from Samuel through Maccabees), one year before the *editio princeps* of the New American Bible which would extend the principle to the Bible throughout. Up to this point only half-hearted gestures in this direction had been made, resulting in such anomalous forms as Isaia, Jeremia, Abdia (from Abdias = Obadiah), Sophonia (from Sophonias = Zephaniah in conventional English), etc. It was with these anomalous forms that the *New Catholic Encyclopedia* was caught when it appeared in 1967, and thus it is locked in with an English biblical vocabulary that is now gone forever.

What primarily made The Jerusalem Bible possible, however, was nothing English at all, but something quintessentially French.

During the late '40s and early '50s there appeared in 43 separate fascicules what was originally conceived and was eventually accomplished as an entirely new, highly critical, translation into French of the complete Bible from the original languages. Each fascicule was the work of at least one internationally recognized biblical scholar. Hardly at that time could any other part of the Catholic world than the francophone have gathered such a cadre as that which produced this Bible. Some of the fascicules were eventually to go through as many as two subsequent revisions, revisions which would be substantive and by no means confined to mere stylistic niceties. Style was, it is true, very important, as one would expect in a French publication, and each fascicule had passed the test of good language as well as good scholarship. What made this Bible of such import in the Catholic world outside of France, however, were the extensive introductions and notes that accompanied each biblical work, amounting in effect to a series of biblical commentaries. (Indeed, for many of the biblical books the best commentary available at that time produced under Catholic auspices was to be found in these fascicules.) In 1956 a one-volume edition was published, understandably with highly compressed introductions and notes, but also with the addition of an admirable system of marginal cross-referencing. This was *La Sainte Bible traduite en français sous la direction de l'École Biblique de Jérusalem.* The title recognized the great part played in this production by members of the

Dominican biblical school in Jerusalem, a part that was proportionately even greater in the publication of the one-volume edition than in the fascicules, which represented the collaboration of some forty translators and editors. It is this Bible, of course, that is the basis of what was published in English in 1966 under the title The Jerusalem Bible. It is not to denigrate the qualities of the twenty-eight "principal collaborators" named in the credits of this latter publication to add that a comparable version in English would have been impossible without dependence on the French. English-speaking Roman Catholicism simply had not yet had the time to gather the resources which had been longer possessed by their numerically superior Continental coreligionists. The necessary dependence is, therefore, clear and undisputed. What is not altogether clear is the degree of dependence, acknowledged or unacknowledged.

An unsigned note following the imprimatur of Cardinal Heenan in the first edition of The Jerusalem Bible states:

> The introduction and notes of this Bible are, with minor variations and revisions a translation of those which appear in *La Bible de Jérusalem* [actually this was not, as yet, an official title] published by Les Editions du Cerf, Paris, (one volume edition, 1961) [actually, as we have seen, 1956] under the general editorship of Père Roland de Vaux, O.P. [The 1956 French Bible lists a far more complex Comité de revision.] The English text of the Bible itself, though translated from the ancient texts, owes a large debt to the work of the many scholars who collaborated to produce *La Bible de Jérusalem,* a debt which the publishers of this English Bible gratefully acknowledge.

In the Foreword by Alexander Jones, General Editor of The Jerusalem Bible, the source of which "this present volume is the English equivalent" is correctly identified as the one-volume 1956 French version "known popularly as *La Bible de Jérusalem.*" The introduction and notes are acknowledged to be "a direct translation from the French, though revised and brought up to date in some places—account being taken of the decisions and general implications of the Second Vatican Council." (No explanation has ever been given of the meaning of the last clause.) The Foreword continues:

> The translation of the biblical text itself could clearly not be made from the French. In the case of a few books the initial draft was made from the French and was then compared word for word with the Hebrew or Aramaic [we are therefore speaking of at least the books of Daniel and Ezra?] by the General Editor and amended where necessary to ensure complete conformity with the ancient text. [Amending an incorrect translation of the French? Or a translation of the French that had incorrectly rendered the originals?] For the much greater part, the initial drafts were made from the Hebrew or Greek and simultaneously compared with the French when questions of variant reading or interpretation arose. Whichever system was used, therefore, the same intended result was achieved, that is, an entirely faithful version of the ancient texts which, in doubtful points, preserves the text established and (for the most part)

the interpretation adopted by the French scholars in the light of the most recent researches in the fields of history, archaeology and literary criticism.

There follow some rather sensible words on the Englishing of the Bible in general and the defense of an editorial decision to reproduce the tetragrammaton throughout as "Yahweh," even in the Psalms which were translated with an eye to Catholic liturgical use. It might be noted, incidentally, that only in this respect did The Jerusalem Bible depart from its sensible decision to stick to the proper names that had become conventional in English. In contrast, in the French original "traditional" French forms like Sédécias, Josias, and Nabuchodonosor rub shoulders with exotica like Hilqiyyahu, Miçrayim, Çeboyim, and Shéneaççar, which must be as perplexing to a French reader as they are to any other.

What is not clear from the unsigned note combined with Alexander Jones' Foreword is the extent to which The Jerusalem Bible admits to being a translation of the 1956 French archetype and where it claims to have depended on an improved text. Much more controllable in this regard are the pretensions of another satellite of the French text, the so-called Jerusalem Bible in German.[8] In this case there was an already existing German translation for most of the biblical books (the translation for the Herders Bibelkommentar plus the Beuron translation of the Psalter); only the books of Joshua, Judges, and Ruth were done afresh by the German translators. The translation was simply changed, where necessary, to conform with the reconstruction of the text presupposed by the French notes and introductions, which were reproduced quite faithfully.

The question of the independence of the English Jerusalem Bible from the French translation is, of course, very important, as is the question of the extent to which the English translators "revised and brought up to date" and otherwise improved on the French of 1956. As has already been mentioned the fascicule edition of the French Bible continued in multiple revisions after 1956, culminating in another one-volume *nouvelle édition revue et augmentée* in 1974, by which time *La Bible de Jérusalem* was at last accepted as the official and not merely the popular title of the translation. The 1974 one-volume edition not only incorporated but went beyond the fascicule editions subsequent to 1956 and therefore there is no point in comparing its text with that of The Jerusalem Bible of 1966 as a standard of the improvements that should have been registered by the English. Nevertheless, there were fascicule changes, sometimes in rather important areas, which were in existence when The Jerusalem Bible was being prepared, and which it obviously chose to ignore in favor of sticking to the 1956 version.

Thus, for example, the fascicule of Matthew's Gospel had passed through two subsequent revisions in French before The Jerusalem Bible appeared. "Je ne parle pas de la fornication" was the way the "Matthean exception" had first appeared in the translation of Matthew 19:9, and "I am not speaking of fornication" is the way it runs in The Jerusalem Bible (along with a note to match, which is a verbatim translation of the French). Meanwhile a second edition of the French had substituted "concubinage" for "fornication," and in turn this yielded to "prostitution," which also is the reading of the 1974 version—"pas pour prostitution"—along with a new note that reflects a quite different interpretation of the text. The 1968 German "Jerusalem Bible" also has a form of the 1956 French ("ausser wegen Unzucht") and the same note. Other random examples where both English and German have followed the 1956 text without regard to second thoughts which had been already expressed in the fascicules are the episode which begins with Joshua 7:2 and the translation of 1 Samuel 1:23. In the first instance, beginning the narrative of the conquest of Ai, the two derived versions reproduce the footnote of 1956 acknowledging that the site was uninhabited in the time of Joshua but suggesting that it could have served as a refuge for the people of the Bethel region. As early as 1958, however, this attempt to salvage history from the story had been abandoned by *La Bible de Jérusalem* and the note had been radically altered. 1 Samuel 1:23 in the French of 1956, the German, and the English has the possessive pronoun in the second person, justified by "versions" (the German also noted the agreement of 4QSam[a]). But the later editions of the French have restored to the text the third person pronoun of the Masoretic Text.

It is instructive to compare Isaiah 2:2-3, first in the French of 1956 and 1974, and then with the English of 1966.

1956	*1974*
Il adviendra dans l'avenir	Il arrivera dans la suite des temps
que le mont du Temple de Yahvé	que la montagne de la maison de Yahvé
sera établi au sommet des montagnes	sera établie en tête des montagnes
et s'élèvera plus haut que les collines.	et s'élèvera au-dessus des collines.
Toutes les nations y afflueront,	Alors toutes les nations afflueront vers elle,
des peuples nombreux s'y rendront et diront:	alors viendront des peuples nombreux qui diront:
"Venez, montons à la montagne de Yahvé,	"Venez, montons à la montagne de Yahvé,
allons au Temple du Dieu de Jacob,	à la maison du Dieu de Jacob,
pour qu'il nous enseigne ses voies	qu'il nous enseigne ses voies
et que nous suivions ses sentiers.	et que nous suivions ses sentiers."
Car de Sion viendra la Loi	Car de Sion vient la Loi
et de Jérusalem l'oracle de Yahvé."	et de Jérusalem la parole de Yahvé.

These are, rather obviously, different translations of Isaiah 2:2-3. The 1974 *Bible de Jérusalem* acknowledges that its translation of Isaiah has been "entièrement retraduit." More precisely, there has been an effort to make the translations of Isaiah 2:2-3 and Micah 4:1-2, which differ very little in the Masoretic Text, agree correspondingly in the French, though there remain some subtle differences even in the 1974 version which could be of interest to us if we were concerned with the French rather than the English. We are concerned with the French only to point out that both in words and in punctuation the translations represent separate interpretations of the original text. Only to this extent are we involved with the French text, not to suggest in any way that the English Jersualem Bible should have anticipated a revision of *La Bible de Jérusalem* that did not then exist.

What The Jerusalem Bible has, however, for Isaiah 2:2-3 is this:

> In the days to come
> the mountain of the Temple of Yahweh
> shall tower above the mountains
> and be lifted higher than the hills.
> All the nations will stream to it,
> peoples without number will come to it; and they will say:
> 'Come, let us go up to the mountain of Yahweh,
> to the Temple of the God of Jacob
> that he may teach us his ways
> so that we may walk in his paths;
> since the Law will go out from Zion,
> and the oracle of Yahweh from Jerusalem.'

It would be difficult, I think, to conclude that The Jerusalem Bible here is anything other than a translation—admittedly a translation into very idiomatic English—of the French of 1956. Word choices, verb tenses, punctuational and other interpretations, all agree, far and beyond the need to adjust the translation to any significant footnote, which in this instance does not exist. The German *Jerusalemer Bibel* can serve as a control, providing a translation of its own for the same commentary:

> In der Folge der Tage wird es geschehen: Da wird der Berg des Hauses Jahwes festgegründet stehen an der Spitze der Berge und erhaben sein über die Hügel. Zu ihm strömen alle Völker. Dorthin pilgern viele Nationen und sprechen:
> "Auf, lasst uns hinaufziehen zum Berge Jahwes, zum Hause des Gottes Jakobs! Er lehre uns seine Wege, und wir wollen auf seinen Pfaden wandeln. Denn von Zion wird ausgehen das Gesetz und das Wort Jahwes von Jerusalem."

Here is where The Jersualem Bible is most vulnerable from the critical standpoint. There is no doubt that an exhaustive investigation would show that is has gone its own way in various instances independently of the French. (An example is present in this very passage, as a matter of fact, since it chose to harmonize its translation of Isaiah 2:2-3 with Micah 4:1-2 by reading *dĕbar Yhwh* in both cases as "the oracle of Yahweh," whereas the latter text in the 1956 French had "la parole de Yahvé"—the formula which of course was chosen for Isaiah and Micah in 1974.) For the most part, however, and quite understandably in view of the limitations imposed by its times, it has reproduced accurately and in creditable English a work of French scholarship of the middle '50s. And while the French scholarship of the middle '50s, particularly the French Catholic scholarship represented by the École Biblique, was as critical as any that then existed, it continued to develop not only from its association with other scholarly groups but also from its own internal development and growth.[9] To take another random example: The initial note on Genesis 14 in the English Jerusalem Bible, acknowledging that it "does not belong to any of the three great sources of Genesis," maintains that "behind it lies a document of great age" and that "all we can say is that the narrative finds its most natural setting in the conditions of the nineteenth century B.C." This is a faithful translation of the note in the 1956 French Bible. In the 1974 *Bible de Jérusalem,* however, all that is left of the note is the negative part: The passage is neither J, E, nor P. Further, it seems to be "a late composition making a pastiche of ancient material"—much of which is "historically impossible." While the earlier judgment in this matter might be held equally as respectable as the later, that is hardly the point. The point is that The Jerusalem Bible has frozen *La Bible de Jérusalem* at a stage of its development which did not represent the maturest thinking of those responsible for it.

Both the actual translation as well as the annotation given it differ from 1956 to 1974, as we have seen. Nor do these, of course, affect only matters of detail. In Genesis 1:2 "God's spirit hovered over the water" according to The Jerusalem Bible, here faithfully echoing the French of 1956 and translating the note referring to Deuteronomy 32:11 to justify this understanding of the verb *mĕraḥepet.* But by 1974 *La Bible de Jérusalem* was expressing what is probably the prevailing interpretation today: "un vent de Dieu tournoyait sur les eaux" ("a wind of God was swirling over the waters") and in a footnote explicitly denied that there is any mention here of the "spirit" of God. The French of Genesis 3:22 is the same in 1956 and 1974 and is faithfully rendered in English by The Jerusalem Bible. But while the note in 1956 had it that "immortality was a pure gift of God which man's disobedience forfeited," the 1974 note says no such thing, rather that the earthly paradise is an image of the immortality to which man aspires. The difference is considerable. The earlier edition reflects a period of apologetics in Catholic biblical studies when there was still a felt obligation to defend a traditional exegesis that had gone into dogmatics regarding the "preternatural gifts" possessed by our "first parents" prior to their fall from grace. In the later edition the attempt has been abandoned in favor of a more relaxed and objective exegesis.[10]

Although the explanatory notes and introduction were a decisive factor in the initial acceptance and success of The Jerusalem Bible, it is undoubtedly in its status as a good readable version of the Scripture that its continuing reputation stands. This is apparently the status on which the editors themselves wished their version to stand or fall. In 1968 a "Reader's Edition" was published, doubtless the edition now known to most of those who use it in this country. The notes and introductions were reduced to a bare minimum, in view of an announced intention to impede the ordinary reader with as little as possible of the marginalia that are of interest to the more professional student. At the same time, in this edition, the spelling was Americanized: "honour," "labour" "favourable," and the like, became "honor," "labor," and "favorable"; "gaol" and "gaoler" became "jail" and "jailer." However, whatever was the grain (*bar* or *šěber*) that Joseph's brethren brought from Egypt to Canaan, this edition is more British than American when it has them bring it in "corn-sacks" (Gen. 42:28).

Among the collaborators acknowledged in the original edition of The Jerusalem Bible are several whose area of competence was obviously that of sensitivity to the best resonances of the English language, such as Robert Speaight and J. R. R. Tolkien. There is no doubt that they and the rest of the editors and translators in this respect performed their task with distinction. The Jerusalem Bible is in English what *La Sainte Bible de Jérusalem* is in French, a credit to the challenging capabilities of the language. It is particularly good in its narrative passages and reporting of familiar dialogue: stories are told the way good stories should be, and conversations sound like real people talking together. "Today God has put your enemy in your power," says Abishai to David. "So now let me pin him to the ground with his own spear. Just one stroke! I will not need to strike him twice" (2 Sam. 26:8). "To Job they spoke never a word," goes the old folktale about Job's friends in 2:13, "so sad a sight he made." The Jerusalem Bible has made a clean break with "Bible English" while at the same time avoiding folksiness and respecting the genre of the text it is translating. "Better a poor man living an honest life than the adept at double-talk who is a fool" (Prov. 19:1). This is not only better than other English versions earlier and later, it is also superior, to the extent that I can judge, to its French prototype. "In fact, this seems to be the rule, that every single time I want to do good it is something evil that comes to hand. In my inmost self I dearly love God's Law, but I can see that my body follows a different law that battles against the law which my reason dictates. This is what makes me a prisoner of that law of sin which lives inside my body" (Rom. 7:21-23). There is a temptation to multiply the examples of translations which are just right. Nor is it necessary to temper this praise by acknowledging the presence here and there, as in any other version of the Bible, of the odd word or phrase or idiom that could have been better handled.

We have already noted the excellent cross-referencing system reproduced in the margins (omitted, however, in the "Reader's Edition"). This, together with the system of headings, subheadings, and paragraphing—an important interpretive device, surely—has been borrowed from the French along with the other more overt notations. A further decision of format marked a definite improvement on the French, namely the relegation of verse numbers to the unobtrusive inside margins (when the division falls within a printed line it is marked in the text by a large dot). While chapter numbers are noted, they are also similarly set apart as the items of convenience they were originally meant to be and not hindrances to the sequence of the text. Also, perhaps alone of modern English versions, The Jerusalem Bible notes marginally the variant chapter-and-verse indications that occasionally occur among the versions ancient and modern (in Job 39—40, for example, or in Hos. 1—3, in much of Ecclesiasticus, etc.), which can easily confuse the reader attempting to consult more than one translation at a time. The only serious exception to this rule—and here there has been a noteworthy deviation from the French—has been the decision to follow in the Psalms the verse enumeration as it occurs in what is called "the English Bible." In this acceptation "the English Bible," I suppose, means what simply "the Bible" meant to Henry Higgins when he counted it along with Shakespeare as one of the noblest products of the English tongue, that is to say therefore, the King James Version. It seems that practically every modern English version of the Bible, even those which have consciously broken with the Authorised Version translation-tradition (such as the New English Bible and Today's English Version, both of which omit the Psalm titles in the bargain), have elected to perpetuate this eccentric system which can hardly matter much to the casual reader but which continually frustrates anyone trying to follow a commentary or work of reference written in any other language than English. One must always remember that the English text is one verse out of kilter, even as Roman Catholic commentaries on the Psalms in a bygone age were usually a whole Psalm out of kilter when they followed the Septuagint/Vulgate enumeration rather than that of the Hebrew. Only the New American Bible in recent days has refused to perpetuate this parochial "English" enumeration of Psalm verses.

In his *Trials of a Translator* Ronald Knox insisted that good translation required a better knowledge of the receptor than of the donor language, and he confessed to having had more recourse in his own work to Fowler and the Oxford Dictionary than to the standard lexica and concordances of the biblical languages. He was probably right in every respect. The Jerusalem Bible, by this test, needs no apology. No one would want to take from it the credit that is its due for having so capably filled a void that then existed in 1966 in the English-speaking Catholic world, hungry for reasonable access to the word of God. It is a monument.

As long, however, as it bears the name The Jerusalem Bible, explicitly borrowed from *La Bible de Jérusalem,* it is a monument to a biblical tradition that no longer exists. That biblical tradition has been done away with effectively through the later development of *La Bible de Jérusalem* in fascicule and in the one-volume edition of 1974, a Bible which is in many essentials altogether different from the French archetype of 1956.

If, on the other hand, The Jerusalem Bible wishes to declare itself free of the French archetype and to persist in its own right as an English version on the plane of the New English Bible, the New American Bible, the Revised Standard Version, or the like, then it seems that something must be done for which there is no evidence that anything has been done. That is to say, there is no possibility of achieving ever what a publisher's blurb in 1966 claimed for The Jerusalem Bible: "This is *the* Bible for the twentieth century." Ronald Knox insisted, again quite correctly, that the Bible should be translated afresh for every succeeding generation—and in these days of geometric evolution we know that generations overtake one another with increasing frequency in even the small portion of the twentieth century we are destined to experience. There is no such thing as a perfect translation of the Bible in any language that is destined to have a responsible life for more than a decade or so. Every existing version that has a claim to responsibility has already built into itself the machinery of future revision. Is there such a machinery built into the continuing existence of The Jerusalem Bible? If there is not—and all the indications are that there is not—then The Jerusalem Bible is destined to remain the monument that it is, a faithful reproduction of some of the best biblical scholarship of the late 1950s. It would be doubly unfortunate if the casual reader, invited to adopt The Jerusalem Bible, were led to believe that nothing of significance had occurred in the past generation to constitute it a less acceptable option in response to the perennial question, "Which Bible is best?"

Participants in the Jerusalem Bible Translation Project

GENERAL EDITOR: Alexander Jones

PRINCIPAL COLLABORATORS IN TRANSLATION AND LITERARY REVISION: Joseph Leo Alston, Florence M. Bennett, Joseph Blenkinsopp, David Joseph Bourke, Douglas Carter, Aldhelm Dean, Illtud Evans, Kenelm Foster, Ernest Graf, Prospero Grech, Edmund Hill, Sylvester Houédard, Leonard Johnston, Anthony J. Kenny, D. O. Lloyd James, James McAuley, Hubert Richards, Edward Sackville-West, Ronald Senator, Walter Shewring, Robert Speaight, J. R. R. Tolkien, R. F. Trevett, Thomas Worden, John Wright, Basil Wrighton

7
Today's English Version (The Good News Bible)

W. F. Stinespring

It was with considerable pleasure that I received the offer to contribute to this symposium on new English versions of the Bible, since I have had a strong interest in this subject for many years, and have expressed this interest in writing on several occasions.[1] It is especially gratifying to be able to comment on TEV (GNB) since I have not hitherto had that opportunity.

Already in my hands as I begin to write are two copies of TEV: the regular edition, a gift of Keith Crim, a participant in this symposium; and a "Giant Print" edition, a gracious gift from my wife to aid my declining eyesight, and without which I might not have been able to undertake this assignment. These two editions are much the same, except that the regular edition is decorated here and there with some intriguing pen sketches of the events and characters in the text nearby, while the very useful Subject Index at the end of the book is omitted from the Giant Print edition, and the latter has the "Words of Christ in Red" (like some of the older editions of KJV, though this principle is not applied to the Old Testament as it was in the older so-called red-letter Bibles).

This translation was produced by the American Bible Society in 1976 at the request of the United Bible Societies and with the help of a consultant from the British and Foreign Bible Society. A British edition is being prepared to take account of the differences in spelling and vocabulary on the two sides of the Atlantic. Perhaps this is the more necessary, since the language in the edition which is being considered here might perhaps be characterized as American colloquial, called in the Foreword a "standard, everyday, natural form of English."

Not only is the language innovative, but other features also. Formerly, the ABS (and its affiliated societies) were so conservative that they would publish in English only the KJV, and that "without note or comment." But when RSV was completed in 1952, ABS began to publish portions of it. Then in 1962 came the Oxford Annotated Bible, using the text of RSV, with notes, comments, introductions, and explanations galore. This was a great success. The addition of the Apocrypha came in 1957, and a whole new edition in 1973. In the meantime came JB in 1966 with numerous notes, comments, and other explanatory material. Being of Roman Catholic origin, it also of course included the Apocrypha. JB sold well and was read by many American Protestants. In 1970 NEB came, with introductions to the Old Testament, the Apocrypha, and the New Testament, plus a considerable number of footnotes. Though British Protestant in origin it has sold well in the U.S.A. Recently an American Study Edition has appeared, with many more notes and comments. Shortly after NEB came NAB, an American Catholic version, containing not only the Apocrypha but also an introduction to each book, many explanatory footnotes, and a section at the end on biblical theology and geography with a set of maps. About the same time there appeared the so-called Living Bible, a paraphrased version with footnotes on nearly every page in addition to explanatory expansions in the text itself. Though this version emanated from conservative circles, perhaps as a foil to the supposed radicalism of such Bibles as RSV and NEB, it sold and was read widely. Finally, there is NIV, of which I have no knowledge, though it is included in this symposium.

Great changes have taken place in the last quarter of a century. More ministers have been going to seminaries and more church members have been going to college. To more and more Bible-reading people, even the most devout, the KJV was becoming more and more unintelligible, though still revered as a precious monument of English literature, like the works of Chaucer and Shakespeare. But because the Bible is also the basic document of their religion, its readers wanted easier access to its meaning and message. Thus they welcomed new translations with notes, comments, introductions, explanatory articles, maps, and the like. Such translations began to flood the market and were bought in millions of copies, with consequent decline in sales of ABS offerings.

This of course is not the full story, but it will give an idea of what was happening. Another point to be kept in mind is that KJV is not only obsolete in its English idiom, but also obsolete in scholarship. The translators of 1611 did a remarkably good job in their day, but the fact remains that the greatest advances in archaeological discovery in the Near and Middle East and in scholarly understandings of the ancient Greek, Hebrew, and Aramaic languages have taken place during the present century, and indeed one might say, in the last half-century. These discoveries have provided scholars and publishers with strong motivation to produce new translations and new commentaries in the field of biblical studies.

At any rate, ABS came out in 1966 with its TEV of the New Testament, as a sort of trial balloon, like RSV in 1946 and NEB in 1961. This New

Testament was a great success, and so it was decided to undertake the much more difficult task of producing a new Old Testament. The task took ten years, and the product is now before us.

So we begin by looking at the format. There is a Foreword, a Preface, a table of Contents, and an Abbreviations List. Every book has an Introduction; there are chapter headings, section headings and footnotes, with various comments. At the end we find a Word List (a lexicon of words and phrases not easily understood), a list of New Testament Passages Quoted or Paraphrased from the Septuagint (to aid readers who try to look up an Old Testament passage quoted in the New Testament and find that the passage in their Old Testament, translated from the Hebrew, does not agree with the New Testament passage taken from the Septuagint or Greek Old Testament; no other Bible has this commendable feature), a table of the Chronology of the Bible (replacing Archbishop Ussher's ridiculous chronology found in some old Bibles), several pages of Maps, a Map Index, and a useful Subject Index (omitted in the Giant Print edition as noted above).

We turn now to the translation itself, beginning with the Old Testament. It so happened that I was preparing a lecture on the book of Ecclesiastes for a literary club when the first copy of TEV came into my hands. I was using as a text the Anchor Bible edition of Proverbs and Ecclesiastes prepared by my old friend R. B. Y. Scott of Princeton University.[2] Scott's translation, I thought, had gone about as far as possible in freedom of translation and modernity of idiom, with the possible exception of James Moffatt.[3]

Somewhat to my surprise, TEV on Ecclesiastes turned out to be a very free translation—freer than RSV, NEB, or even Moffatt or Scott. In fact, it seemed almost as free as LB, which claims only to be a paraphrase, not a translation in the strict sense of the word. Indeed, it reminded me of LB's flippant rendering of 5:1. "As you enter the Temple, keep your ears open and your mouth shut! Don't be a fool who doesn't even realize it is sinful to make rash promises to God." So perhaps here is a clue to the literary style of TEV: use a colloquial, conversational idiom, but offer a real translation rather than a paraphrase, by avoiding excessive expansions; if something more is needed to make the meaning clear, put it into a footnote. The most literal modern translation of this verse is in RSV, as follows: "Guard your steps when you go to the house of God; to draw near to listen is better than to offer the sacrifice of fools; for they do not know that they are doing evil." TEV renders thus: "Be careful about going to the Temple. It is better to go there to learn than to offer sacrifices like foolish people who don't know right from wrong." We note immediately that TEV uses less words than the other versions: "Be careful" instead of "Guard your steps"; "Temple" instead of "house of God"; "who don't know right from wrong" instead of "for they do not know right from wrong." We also note the colloquial form "don't," reducing two words to one and creating a sort of folksy atmosphere, as also in LB.

Before passing to other biblical books, let us look at the beginning and end of Ecclesiastes. Verse 1: KJV and RSV have "The words of the Preacher, the son of David, king in Jerusalem." The problem is how to translate the Hebrew word *Qoheleth,* rendered in Greek *Ecclesiastes* and traditionally in English "the Preacher." Scott[4] in his introduction says the word means "schoolmaster," or "teacher," definitely not "preacher" in the modern sense of that word. Scott also says that this book "is primarily a philosophical work rather than a book of religion." He also has a section on "Qoheleth's Philosophy," yet he refrains from using the word "philosopher" or any other translation, simply transliterating the Hebrew, Qoheleth, all the way. Moffatt and NEB avoid the erroneous "the Preacher" by substituting "the Speaker," as though the writer of our book presided over an assembly, which he probably did not. So what did the TEV translator do? He apparently read Scott, took to heart the hints that had been thrown out, and translated *Qoheleth* into "the Philosopher." After all, had not Scott said that the book was a "philosophical work"? So why exercise Scott's caution about using a word that most ordinary people could easily understand in a popular sense?

Well, what about verse 2, in RSV: "Vanity of vanities, says the Preacher, vanity of vanities! All is vanity." Of course the translators have tried to avoid this "vain" repetition and we have had "utterly vain is everything," "futility of futilities," "vapor of vapors," "thinnest of vapors," "nothing is worthwhile," etc., etc. TEV puts it thus: "It is useless, useless, said the Philosopher. Life is useless, all useless." You can pay your money and take your choice. I want simply to say that I think TEV is right in using the past tense in the phrase "said the Philosopher" instead of "says the Preacher" as in KJV and RSV. It is not a great point, but it does indicate that the translator was looking carefully at his Hebrew text.

Perhaps another example of careful attention to the Hebrew may be found at 3:2 in the famous "time-to" passage. Practically every previous version had said: "a time to be born, and a time to die," yet the Hebrew verb *YLD* is not passive, but active, meaning "to bear." In other words, the implication is that there is a time for your mother to bear you and another time for you to die. Scott acknowledges this in an explanatory note, but lets the traditional translation stand. TEV cleverly changes the construction from infinitive to noun and so avoids the problem of the active verb, thus: "He [meaning God] sets the time for birth and the time for death." But notice that "He sets" is an expansion, as is the article "the," in the fashion of LB.

In this connection notice also the radical rewriting of the preceding verse (3:1). The very literal RSV renders thus:

> For everything there is a season,
> and a time for every matter under heaven.

This is of course in Hebrew poetic style, with chiastic synonymous parallelism (repeating the thought in different words and in reverse order). TEV renders it in prose, eliminates the parallelism, and gratuitously adds a reference to God: "Everything that happens in this world happens at the time God chooses." This of course is paraphrase—saying what you think is or ought to be the general meaning without much regard for the style of the original, or for any style at all.

Turning now to the end of the book, we fix our attention on 10:20. This is a beautifully poetic verse consisting of two pairs of lines, each pair in parallelism. RSV translates quite literally, thus:

> Even in your thought do not curse the king,
> nor in your bedchamber curse the rich;
> for a bird of the air will carry your voice,
> or some winged creature tell the matter.

TEV puts the whole verse into prose thus: "Don't criticize the king, even silently, and don't criticize the rich, even in the privacy of your bedroom. A bird might carry the message and tell them what you said." Here we see something that is too frequently done by TEV, namely two lines of poetic parallelism turned into a single prosy sentence.

In TEV 11:1 goes this way: "Invest your money in foreign trade, and one of these days you will make a profit." This sounds a bit like an enterprising twentieth-century stockbroker, somewhat more colloquial than *The Wall Street Journal.* Traditional Bible readers will hardly recognize that they are dealing with a favorite verse, beautifully poetic, yet somewhat obscure in meaning, as translated in RSV:

> Cast your bread upon the waters,
> for you will find it after many days.

Actually, the "foreign-trade" interpretation is not new. Moffatt had it in 1925, but managed to keep his translation somewhat poetic thus:

> Trust your goods far and wide at sea,
> till you get good returns after a while.

Other translators have been more cautious, though some have suggested a reference to foreign trade in a footnote. Much depends on one's interpretation of the following verse (11:2), which reads in RSV thus:

> Give a portion to seven, or even to eight,
> for you know not what evil may happen on earth.

Since this verse begins with the word "give," many exegetes take both verses as references to the desirability of giving charity lavishly. Not so the TEV translators. They come right out and have "the Philosopher" tell us how to play the stock market, thus:

> Put your investments in several places—many places even—because you never know what kind of bad luck you are going to have in this world.

Perhaps the translators of TEV were warned by the conservative management of the ABS to avoid the implications of higher criticism. This may be the reason why the last sentence of 11:9, "But remember that God is going to judge you for whatever you do," is not enclosed in brackets or provided with a footnote to say that it is an editorial addition. It is completely out of harmony with Qoheleth's repeated insistence that often good people suffer while evil people prosper (e.g., 8:11-14), and most modern editions take note of this.

By contrast, notice the treatment of the familiar line, "Remember also your Creator in the days of your youth," in 12:1. TEV renders thus, quite accurately: "So remember your Creator while you are still young." It also has this note on the word "Creator": "The Hebrew expression for 'your Creator' sounds like the Hebrew for 'your grave.' " The TEV translator did not substitute "your grave" for "your Creator," as Scott did, but he was able and willing to alert the reader to this possibility, perhaps because such a change would be a matter only of textual or lower criticism, which is more tolerated by conservative exegetes.

The first eight verses of chapter 12 constitute a poetic meditation on aging; it is a pity that here there is no attempt to indicate this poetic structure in the phrasing and the printing, as most translators are now doing. It is very obvious that the words of Qoheleth end with verse 8 and that the final verses (9 to 14) are by another person, who was a friendly critic, but more on the orthodox side. He also may have inserted 11:9, mentioned above; compare 11:9 and 12:14. Again, it is a pity that this possibility could not have been pointed out in a brief footnote, since at least some readers will be puzzled by the lack of literary skill and greater conformity to tradition in this addition, in contrast to nearly all that precedes.

Finally, in the last sentence of verse 11, something has been put into the text that should have been relegated to a footnote. In Hebrew this sentence simply says, "They have been given by one shepherd." TEV has expanded it, thus: "They have been given by God, the one Shepherd of us all." The identity of this shepherd is much in debate, with many interpreters against the idea that God is meant. The translator should have expressed his or her preference in a footnote instead of creating a paraphrase in the style of LB.

In my opinion, the outstanding recent event in biblical publication is the Anchor Bible edition of the Song of Songs (Song of Solomon) by Marvin H. Pope.[5] He has produced a very large commentary (743 pp.) on a very small biblical book, because that small book is one of the most difficult in the entire Bible to understand and interpret. Even after Pope's Herculean effort there still remain for him and for others many unsolved problems and questions. Even Pope's translation, undoubtedly the most accurate yet produced, is not easy reading, and requires constant reference to the extensive commentary that follows.

By contrast, TEV on Song of Songs is about the easiest reading in the entire work. It is just a simple, clear, straightforward, sweet little love story. True, eight times the notes tell us that the Hebrew is unclear, but the English is abundantly clear and the story flows on without interruption. In other words, one gets the impression that the translator substituted for the unclear Hebrew what he would have liked the text to say and what he knew the readers would like to read. So, good friends, pay your money (TEV is cheap, AB is not) and take your choice. If you want it cheap and easy and pleasant, take TEV; if you want it costly and difficult and deep and serious, take Pope, for that is the real Song of Songs.

Now, we should have a look at Genesis. The very first verse presents a problem, for the conventional translation, "In the beginning God created the heavens and the earth," assumes *creatio ex nihilo* (creation out of nothing), a theological doctrine dear to many conservatives. Most modern translations, however, including even LB, with greater regard for Hebrew grammar, render essentially thus: "When God began to create the heavens and the earth, the earth was without form and void," adding the first clause of verse 2 to make a complete sentence. According to this translation, the earth was already there, but in a formless condition when God began to work on it, and readers can choose or guess for themselves how it got there. TEV seems to try to straddle the fence between these two interpretations by beginning in the traditional manner, then putting the "when" in the wrong place, thus: "In the beginning when God created the universe, the earth was formless and desolate." From this, it would be difficult to say whether creation was *ex nihilo* or not. Fortunately, a footnote gives the reader the choice of either of the other two translations.

At the end of verse 2, what is traditionally called "the Spirit of God" is rendered as "the power of God," with a footnote giving "the spirit of God" or "a wind from God" or "an awesome wind" as alternatives. The last alternative may be the best, since the phrase "of God" or "to God" is sometimes used in Hebrew merely as an intensifying adverb; e.g., in Jonah 3:3 "a city great to God" is properly translated "an exceedingly great city." In the present instance, NEB's "a mighty wind" is an excellent choice of wording. In the same verse, TEV renders "and darkness was upon the face of the deep" with this imaginative overtranslation in the style of LB: "The raging ocean that covered everything was engulfed in total darkness." TEV and LB dislike leaving anything to the imagination, and that may be why they sometimes spoil poetical passages.

But we must hurry on to the Garden of Eden story. TEV makes the proper division in the middle of verse 4 of chapter 2 without explaining why (that would be to confess the use of higher criticism), but does begin the second story of creation with a new heading, "The Garden of Eden." Whenever there is a paronomasia (play on words), it is indicated in a footnote; e.g., in verse 7, when man is made from soil of the ground the note reads: "MAN: The Hebrew words for 'man' and 'ground' have rather similar sounds." In verse 17, God's ban on the tree of knowledge is expressed thus: "You must not eat the fruit of that tree; if you do, you will die the same day." Now everybody knows that they did eat the fruit of the tree, and did not die that very day, but much later (Gen. 5:5). So what is wrong here? Once again we must invoke Hebrew grammar (semantics, really).

Frequently in Hebrew, the idiom *b^{e}yom . . .*, "on the day that . . . ," followed by an infinitive does not mean exactly twenty-four hours or the daylight hours, as in English, but simply means an indefinite period of time. Since there is no specific word for "when" in Hebrew, the expression "on the day that" is often used. This is usually best translated as "when." E.g., the very beginning of this story (vs. 4b) says literally, "On the day that the Lord God made the earth and the heavens," etc. TEV translates correctly thus: "When the LORD God made the universe," etc. Likewise the passage which we are considering, the end of verse 17, has the same idiom, saying literally: "for on the day that you eat of it you will surely die," but more correctly, "when you eat of it you will surely die." "When" is very close here to meaning "if"; hence "if you eat of it you will surely die" is probably the best rendering. Actually TEV did use "if"—"if you do [eat], you will die the same day." TEV had a good translation, but added the three fatal words, "the same day," and thus made God out to be a liar, agreeing with "the snake" in 3:4. This may be the worst blunder in the entire work.

The tendency to oversimplification may be seen in the blessing on Abraham in 12:3:

> I will bless those who bless you,
> But I will curse those who curse you.
> And through you I will bless all the nations.

The first two lines are clear enough in the Hebrew and in the various versions, though TEV spurns the chiastic arrangement that puts the object first in the second line in the Hebrew and in practically all other translations. The third line, however, is different; translated literally as a passive, it says:

> And through you all the families of the earth will be blessed.

By use of the passive voice, God seems to avoid saying that he will do the blessing. A very similar statement occurs in 18:18. There is considerable controversy about the interpretation. Some consider the verb a reflexive and read in effect: "Through you all the families of the earth shall (or will) bless themselves," as in NJV. Others (e.g., NEB) suggest a reciprocal sense, such as "all the families of the earth will ask to be blessed like you." In other words, in the Hebrew the third line is not so simple, clear, or easy as is the TEV rendering. Recognizing this, the TEV translator put in a footnote suggesting at least the possibility of the reciprocal interpretation. But the question arises: Should the Bible in English be made so simple and easy even where it is not simple and easy in the original?

A surprising oversight occurs in chapter 38, in the story of Judah's affair with his daughter-in-law Tamar. In verse 15 it is said that when Judah saw Tamar in disguise by the wayside, he thought she was a *zonah,* meaning a common prostitute or whore. TEV translates simply "a prostitute." But when Judah sent his friend Hirah to find the supposed prostitute and pay her off, Hirah, no doubt at the suggestion of Judah, inquires about the *qedeshah* who had been at that place; but nobody knows anything about such a person. In Hebrew *qedeshah* means temple prostitute, and in the Canaanite area where Judah was living at that time it was quite respectable to visit a temple prostitute. TEV uses the single word prostitute both times, and thus obscures Judah's little trick to save his reputation, although most translators, beginning with Moffatt in 1924, have made the distinction.

It is not surprising to see the ease with which the very enigmatic verse, 49:10, is treated by TEV. This verse is a stanza or strophe, consisting of four lines from that part of the Blessing of Jacob addressed to Judah. Somewhat literally translated it goes as follows:

> The sceptre shall not turn away from Judah,
> Nor the ruler's staff from between his feet,
> Until Shiloh comes [or, until he comes to Shiloh],
> And to him [shall be] the obedience of peoples.

It is the third line which has caused so much argument and conjecture. "Shiloh" makes no sense as the name of a person, and the city could hardly be meant, since it was located in the territory of Ephraim. Some interpreters have tried to give it a messianic meaning ("until the Messiah comes and all peoples or nations obey him and pay him homage," etc.). In 1962 NJV interpreted "Shiloh" as *shai loh,* meaning "tribute to him" and translated the last two lines thus:

> So that tribute shall come to him
> And the homage of peoples be his.

In 1970 NEB adopted this idea thus:

> so long as tribute is brought to him
> and the obedience of the nations is his.

And now TEV (1976) has fallen in line, rendering the whole verse very freely, thus:

> Judah will hold the royal sceptre,
> And his descendants will always rule.
> Nations will bring him tribute
> And bow in obedience before him.

Of course TEV in the second line should not have used the word "always," since it is not in the Hebrew. Incidentally, the interpretation of "between his feet" as "his descendants" also probably came from NEB. It is correct. My former students in Hebrew know that in the Old Testament the word "feet" is sometimes a euphemism for sex organs. And of course from sex organs come descendants.

Coming to the book of Exodus, we recall that the unfortunate term "the Red Sea" first occurs in that book in various English versions, but never in the Hebrew anywhere. The Hebrew term is *yam suph,* meaning literally "sea of reeds," which is the translation used by NJV throughout. Moffatt used "Reed Sea," which is clever, since it sounds good in English and is so similar in sound and sight to the familiar "Red Sea" that readers will recognize it as a substitute.

The term "Red Sea" got into English Bibles because KJV and other early English versions followed in this instance the Septuagint or Greek version instead of the Hebrew. Apparently, to the Greek-speaking Egyptians of about 200 B.C. "Red Sea" was a rather indefinite term for any body of water, large or small, east of Egypt; hence the Septuagint translators used that term to translate *yam suph.* In modern cartography, however, the Red Sea is a clearly defined entity, nearly three hundred miles south of Lower Egypt (where the Hebrews were), more than 1200 miles long, about 125 miles wide, and nearly a mile and a half deep. To be sure, the whole story of the Exodus is in a miraculous context, but there are limitations, and even Yahweh might hesitate to lead his small band of people through such a tremendous body of water.

Leaving the Red Sea aside, let us see what *yam suph* or the Reed Sea or the Sea of Reeds, or the Reedy Swamp really seems to mean when we look at a map while examining the passages containing this term. The answer seems to be threefold: (1) any one of a series of small lakes and marshes along the route of the present-day Suez Canal between the Gulf of Suez and the Mediterranean Sea; (2) the Gulf of Suez; (3) the Gulf of Aqaba. This series of meanings was adopted by TEV translators in their Word List under the heading "Red Sea," where they refer to (1) as "the region generally regarded as the site of the events described in Exodus 13." They also say that "Red Sea" is "in Hebrew literally 'Sea of Reeds.' " Unfortunately, they add to their three definitions a fourth, "the Red Sea proper," which is completely wrong. It was deleted in later printings.

Still, progress has been made. Hitherto, new translators have been content to find one new rendering of *yam suph,* such as "Reed Sea" or "Sea of Reeds" and to use it in all occurrences. Now it would appear that TEV is about to use different translations for the different meanings of *yam suph* to make the puzzling moves in Exodus and Numbers more understandable. But let us see what actually appears.

The first occurrence is in Exodus 10:19, translated in TEV as follows:

> And the LORD changed the east wind into a very strong west wind, which picked up the locusts and blew them into the Gulf of Suez. Not one locust was left in all of Egypt.

If the locusts were blown from "all of Egypt," most of them indeed would have gone into the Gulf of Suez, though some of them from Lower Egypt (where the Israelites and the king were) would have gone into "the Sea of Reeds" north of the Gulf of Suez, where the Suez Canal now is. But this translation is more than half right and it should be rated "Good."

The verse has a footnote referring to the next occurrence of *yam suph* in 13:18. I was hoping that this verse would have the translation "the Sea of Reeds," with a footnote to the effect that meaning (1) should be taken. Alas and alack! the translation in the text is "the Red Sea"—not really a translation of the Hebrew at all—with a footnote repeating the four meanings of "Red Sea" as given in the Word List. In effect, this is putting a wrong translation in the text, then adding a footnote saying that the translation is wrong. NAB did precisely the same thing with the very same text. So hard does the Red Sea blunder die! It is the same story in 15:4 and 22, but this time there is no footnote to warn the hapless reader. Later printings delete the fourth meaning.

The next three occurrences in Exodus 23:31; Numbers 14:25; and Numbers 21:4 all use meaning (3), the Gulf of Aqaba, probably correctly.

In Numbers 33:8, 10, 11 the situation is very confused even in the Hebrew text, and even more so in TEV. It seems to me that the place of crossing is meant in all three verses; hence the translation should be "the Sea of Reeds." But TEV has "the Red Sea" in verse 8, "the Gulf of Suez" in verse 10, and verse 11 simply omits the first clause, which reads: "and they departed from the Sea of Reeds." Thus is confusion worse compounded. The first two occurrences in Deuteronomy, 1:40 and 2:1, are translated correctly as "the Gulf of Aqaba." But in 11:4 the reference is to the place of crossing in Egypt; again the translation is "the Red Sea," with a footnote referring to the Word List, which ambiguously explains that this translation is wrong. The same is true of the three occurrences in Joshua, 2:10; 4:23; and 24:6; but no warning footnote is given in these instances. In Judges 11:16 we have "the Gulf of Aqaba," correctly; likewise in 1 Kings 9:26. In Nehemiah 9:9 and Psalms 106:7, 9, 22; 136:13, the reference is to the miraculous crossing and the translation is "the Red Sea," wrongly and with no footnotes. In Psalms 136:15 the phrase "in the Sea of Reeds" is simply omitted. Finally, in Jeremiah 49:21, where it says, "When Edom falls, . . . the cries of alarm will be heard as far away as the Gulf of Aqaba," the translation is obviously correct.

TEV's handling of this problem represents a good beginning and a missed opportunity. No other translation that I know of has attempted to work out all the meanings of *yam suph* and then use each meaning in its proper context, though several have rid themselves of "the Red Sea." TEV failed to do this, and also failed to capitalize on its own realization that *yam suph* means "the Sea of Reeds," which primarily refers to "a series of lakes and marshes between the Gulf of Suez and the Mediterranean." So I must rate this effort at about a D.

With a comparable geographic problem, I feel that TEV had better success. The words *Cush* and/or *Cushi* occur nearly thirty times in the Hebrew text. Formerly, these words have been translated "Ethiopia" and "Ethiopian" respectively, or in a few cases simply transliterated when the reference was uncertain or *Cushi* appeared to be a personal name. Modern historical research has discovered that there were two areas called *Cush* in ancient times, one in Africa, formerly called Ethiopia, the other in Mesopotamia, where the Kassites (or Cushites) lived.

Two problems then arise for the modern translator: (1) to distinguish between the two areas called Cush; (2) to deal with the change in meaning of the geographical term *Ethiopia,* which in ancient times meant the territory immediately south of Egypt, sometimes even including Nubia or Upper Egypt, whereas now Ethiopia is used as a synonym for Abyssinia, far to the south of Egypt, with the huge territory of Sudan in between. So, the only thing to do in most of these cases is to translate *Cush* as "Sudan" and *Cushi* as "Sudanese," and TEV has done it correctly, with perhaps two exceptions.

Genesis 2:13 is translated thus: "The second river is the Gihon; it flows around the country of Cush." This is an accurate rendering; but there is a footnote saying: "Cush (of Mesopotamia); or Sudan." Since this passage is in the Garden of Eden story and the Garden of Eden is by common consent depicted in Mesopotamia, this Cush must be the Mesopotamian one. The second part of the note is erroneous and should be dropped. The second instance is in Genesis 10, the so-called Table of Nations. It seems to me that we are dealing with the two Cushes in this chapter. In verses 6 and 7 Cush is connected with Egypt, Libya, Canaan, and South Arabia; in verses 8 to 12 Cush is connected with Nimrod, a heroic figure of Babylonia and Assyria. Surely the former is the African Cush, the latter the Mesopotamian. A footnote to this effect would have been helpful.

It will now be apparent to the reader that the present writer feels that the term "Red Sea" should not appear anywhere in an English Old Testament. The same is true of such phrases as "the daughter of Zion," "the daughter of Jerusalem," "the daughter of Judah," "the virgin daughter of Zion," "the daughter of Egypt," "the daughter of Babylon," "the daughter of my people," etc., occurring about fifty times, mostly in the books of the prophets. All of these phrases are wrong on two counts: (1) the Hebrew word *bath* in these context does not mean "daughter" but "girl" or "maiden," with an affectionate coloring; (2) the following word is not a possessive genitive but an appositional genitive, like "the city *of Durham*" or "she goes by the name *of Mary*" in English; in other words, Jerusalem did not *have* a daughter, Jerusalem *was* a maiden loved by Yahweh.

Thus we can translate "the daughter of Zion" literally as "maiden Zion," but the affectionate coloring is still not there; it would be better to say something like "dear Zion" or "beloved Zion." Likewise, in the book of Ruth, when Naomi calls Ruth *bitti,* the proper translation is "my daughter"; but when Boaz in 2:8 uses the same expression, it obviously does not mean "my daughter"; something like "my dear" would be closer to the mark.

In my article "Zion, Daugher of" in IDBS,[6] TEV is listed as one of the few English versions that have got rid of the nonexistent Daughter of Zion. Let us see how TEV has done this, and observe the affectionate coloring if any.

The book of Lamentations has the largest number of occurrences of this idiom—seven. The first is in 1:6a, literally translated by KJV thus: "And from the daughter of Zion all her beauty is departed." TEV renders: "The splendor of Jerusalem is a thing of the past." Alas, here we have only the single word "Jerusalem," a prosaic substitute for something laden with pathos, such as "ravished maiden Zion." And why not say "Zion" when the Hebrew says "Zion" and "Jerusalem" when the Hebrew says "Jerusalem"?

Passing on to 1:15c we find the same idiom with the word "virgin" prefixed. RSV translates:

> "the Lord has trodden as in a wine press the virgin daughter of Judah."

The meaning: The Lord has trodden the poor little ravished maiden Judah like a wine press. TEV has it this way:

> "He crushed my people
> like grapes in a wine press."

The verse began in the first person, with Jerusalem speaking. In the last third of the verse which we are considering, the Hebrew changes to the third person, such a change being characteristic of Hebrew poetry. TEV erases this change and translates "maiden Judah" as "my people," thus doing away with the poetic change of person and the even more poetic picture of Judah as a ravished maiden. Are such drastic changes really necessary to make the Bible more understandable to less sophisticated readers?

Anyhow, they are there: plain place names without overtones of affection, omissions of whole lines, combinations of two poetic lines into one. The daughter of Zion is gone completely, and that is good riddance; but there is nothing to take her place, and that is bad. All of which, widely applied, leads to intriguing poetry turned into dull prose. Is this new biblical prose sufficiently intriguing in its own way? Perhaps the years ahead will answer that question.

Before we pass on, another complaint must be registered. The traditional (KJV) translation of Isaiah 1:18 is dead wrong when it says:

> Though your sins be as scarlet, they shall be as white as snow; though they be red like crimson, they shall be as wool.

This unconditional promise of salvation is of course theologically, exegetically, and historically wrong, as the very next two verses so plainly show:

> If ye be willing and obedient, ye shall eat the good of the land. But if ye refuse and rebel, ye shall be devoured with the sword.

Everyone knows that in the teaching of the prophets there is no forgiveness or salvation without repentance. So, beginning with Moffatt in 1924 most modern translations (but not RSV) have made sense out of nonsense by simply substituting a modal auxiliary, such as "may," "can," "might," or "could" for the emphatic future form "shall" in the two lines "they shall be as white as snow" and "they shall be as wool." The *American Translation* (AT) put these two lines in the form of a question. All this is not only in accord with sensible theology but also with Hebrew grammar; for the so-called imperfect form in Hebrew functions not only as a future indicative tense, but as a mood of uncertainty, corresponding to the subjunctive in Latin and Greek. This usage is called "the modal imperfect," and thus appropriately calls for a modal auxiliary in English.

So how do the TEV translators deal with this rather important matter? First of all, they introduce the first person (God speaking) and the verb "wash," neither of which is in the Hebrew. Then they proceed to translate wrongly, making the promise of forgiveness and reconciliation unconditional and also turning poetry into prose thus: "You are stained red with sin, but I will wash you as clean as snow.[a] Although your stains are deep red, you will be as white as wool.[b]" Having realized that something was not quite right here, they added note *a*, which suggests that the second clause of the first sentence may be read: "do you think I will wash you as clean as snow?" and note *b*, which suggests that the whole second sentence may be read: "Although your stains are deep red, do you think you will be as white as wool?" Not only is this a confused and awkward translation, but it seems to go to the other theological extreme by implying utter damnation without hope of reconciliation.

Perhaps all this is a bit confusing, and it may be well to translate in the simplest, yet poetic, terms what the Lord said through Isaiah on this occasion:

> Though your sins be as scarlet,
> they could be as white as snow.
> Though they be red like crimson,
> they could be like wool.
> If you become willing and obedient,
> you shall eat the good of the land.
> But if you refuse and rebel,
> you shall be devoured by the sword.

In concluding my review of the Old Testament, let me mention some instances in which TEV has done well. First, there is the 23rd psalm. This psalm, as most people have heard it from KJV and RSV, is mainly an affirmation of immortality or at least some meaningful existence after death—ideas that did not come into Judaism until the Greek period, beginning about 300 B.C., and the psalm was written long before that. So somewhere along the way, the psalm came to be interpreted as support for such ideas as immortality, resurrection, and everlasting life, and thus became a favorite piece to be read at funeral services. Really, the first four verses give a picture of God as a shepherd leading his people or an individual worshiper through perilous ways and times, while the last two verses show God prospering his true worshiper at the expense of his enemies for a whole lifetime. There is nothing about a future life; in fact, there is very little about that anywhere in the Old Testament. Christians can look for that in the New Testament.

How was this change brought about? Simply by misinterpreting and mistranslating two tiny phrases, one near the beginning of verse 4 and the other at the end of verse 6. Practically every modern translation except RSV has made the necessary correction. RSV has the old, incorrect readings in the text and the correct readings in the footnotes, thus: verse 4 "the valley of the shadow of death," note, "Or, *the valley of deep darkness*"; verse 6 "for ever," note, "Or *as long as I live.*" Probably RSV put the wrong readings in the text to give the average readers what they want to hear, and put the right readings in the footnotes to throw a sop to the scholars. But the RSV Committee continues to meet to make further "improvements," and who knows what might come forth?

Pardon the long preamble merely to give TEV a pat on the back, but it seemed necessary. TEV in some other spots seemed to be relegating the right reading to mere "footnote status" (e.g., "Sea of Reeds" for "Red Sea") out of deference to traditionalism. But not in the 23rd psalm!

vs. 4, Even if I go through the deepest darkness,
I will not be afraid, LORD,
for you are with me.

vs. 6, I know that your goodness and love will be with me all my life;
and your house will be my home as long as I live.

Good! Now I wish to commend TEV for following Moffatt, AT, RSV, JB, and NAB (not NEB) for retaining the word "again" in that line in Hosea 11:9 which properly reads, "I will not *again* destroy Ephraim." The "again" is there in the Hebrew, but some exegetes try to get rid of it because it makes plain that Ephraim (i.e., Israel) will be or has been destroyed once. These exegetes try to make out Hosea to be such a prophet of love that he believed God would never punish Israel, regardless of her sins. Nonsense! There is no such prophet or God in the Old Testament.

Also to be commended is TEV's rendering of Isaiah 40:9:

Jerusalem, go up on a high mountain
and proclaim the good news!
Call out with a loud voice, Zion;
announce the good news!

This translation is free, but it does preserve the idea that Jerusalem is in this instance proclaiming the good news. Unfortunately there is a footnote saying that another possibility is to say that someone, presumably the prophet, is to rise up and proclaim the good news *to* Jerusalem. This is contrary to the Hebrew and would necessitate about nine alterations of the text. KJV has the right reading. RSV follows suit, but also adds the erroneous footnote. Moffatt has it wrong, NEB has it wrong, with a footnote giving the right reading. AT was wrong in its first edition (1927), but changed in a later edition (1948). This drastic change in the text was probably due to a mistaken sense of consistency. In 41:27 and 52:7 the good news is indeed being given *to* Jerusalem. But according to the Second Isaiah Jerusalem was both a transmitter and a receiver of the good news. So I give credit to TEV for giving preference to the correct reading.

Finally, a few words should be said about two tricky passages in the book of Job. In KJV, Job 13:15 reads thus: "Though he slay me, yet will I trust in him: but I will maintain mine own ways before him." A glance at the Hebrew will show that something is wrong here. Not only so, but the whole context shows Job doubting, questioning, and complaining against God's treatment of him. RSV turns full circle, translating the first sentence flatly thus: "Behold, he will slay me; I have no hope." Actually, this is a little too strong. It would have been better to take the first verb as a present subjunctive (modal imperfect as described above) and say, "Behold, he *may* slay me," as does Pope in AB.[7] TEV gets the sense very well by inverting the sentence and turning it into a question: "I've lost all hope, so what if God kills me?" TEV does equally well in the next verse (16), where again KJV has managed to turn doubt into a nonexistent faith.

Perhaps the most difficult passage in the Old Testament is Job 19:25-27. All are familiar with verse 25 in KJV: "For I know that my Redeemer liveth, and that he shall stand at the latter day upon the earth." The big problem is the identity of the person called *goali* in Hebrew, perhaps best translated "my defender." Here in KJV the translation, "Redeemer" with a capital R, implies that it is God, and some Christians even see a prediction of Jesus Christ (as in Handel's oratorio, "The Messiah"). But most modern interpreters, noting that throughout the dialogue God is the adversary and not the defender, take *goali* to be a human defender. TEV compounds the ambiguity by translating, "But I know there is someone in heaven who will come at last to my defense." There is no reference to heaven in the original, and we are left in doubt by the TEV translator as to the identity of this heavenly figure and where his defending will be done. The expression "upon the earth" in KJV really says in Hebrew "upon the dust." "Dust" in Hebrew is often used as a characteristic of Sheol, the place of the dead under the earth; hence it can be argued that the defending will be done in the underworld after Job's death.

The problem of where or when Job will be exonerated becomes more acute in the very problematical verse 26. No one claims to be able to render this verse as it stands, but RSV has tried to follow the Hebrew as closely as possible:

> "And after my skin has been thus destroyed,
> then from my flesh [note: or "without my flesh"] I shall see God."

The main difficulty here is the Hebrew expression "from my flesh," i.e., before death, or "without my flesh," i.e., after death. TEV sees the difficulty clearly thus:

> Even after my skin is eaten by disease,
> while still in this body [note: or "although not in this body"] I will see God.

A further note states truly: "Verse 26 in Hebrew is unclear."

Verse 27 attempts to show how or under what conditions Job will see God. It says, not too clearly, "whom [i.e., God] I shall see for myself, and my eyes shall behold, and not a stranger [or, "but not as a stranger (or adversary)"]." The ambiguity here is whether Job and not a stranger will see God, or whether Job will see God as no longer a stranger or adversary. TEV opts for the latter, correctly, I think:

> I will see him with my own eyes,
> and he will not be a stranger.

To summarize, here is one man's opinion. Job in 19:25-27 does not suddenly change from doubt and resentment to conventional faith in a conventional God. Rather, he reasserts his faith in his own innocence, and believes that eventually, perhaps after his own death, he will find a strong human (or angelic?) defender who will prove his innocence so clearly that even God will acknowledge it and cease to be his enemy.

To be sure, at the end of the book as it now stands, God personally rebukes Job, Job recants, and his health and prosperity are restored with interest right here on earth, in agreement with the conventional theology of that day. But the Job of the Dialogue has no inkling of such an outcome.

The books of the Apocrypha have recently been translated and are now available in an edition of TEV. The ABS is to be warmly commended for this change in policy.

As was mentioned near the beginning of this paper, the TEV New Testament appeared in 1966 and was widely read. It was also reviewed and commented on in many places, and hence there is no need to spend much time and space on it here. In general it seems to read more smoothly and be more accurate than its Old Testament counterpart. After all, Greek is easier and better understood than the Semitic languages, Hebrew and Aramaic, while the textual basis of the New Testament is incomparably richer and fuller than in the case of the Old Testament.

Even so, I cannot resist the temptation to make a few remarks on a few passages. In Matthew 1:21 an angel speaks to Joseph about Mary thus, according to TEV: "She will have a son, and you will name him Jesus—because he will save his people from their sins." To be sure, this is exactly what the Greek and all the translations say. But more is needed; a play on words is involved, though it is completely lost in English as also in Greek. An explanatory footnote is needed, thus: "The Aramaic form of the name Jesus (Yeshua) sounds like the Aramaic verb meaning 'he will save.' " This is properly done in the Oxford Annotated Bible at this point, as well as many times in the Old Testament of TEV (e.g., in Gen. 32:28-30).

In Matthew 5:6 we have the famous beatitude, "Blessed are those who hunger and thirst for righteousness, for they shall be satisfied" (RSV). TEV renders thus: "Happy are those whose greatest desire is to do what God requires; God will satisfy them fully!" In spite of the fact that TEV prints the Beatitudes in poetic lines, this one has been reduced to very ordinary prose by eliminating the metaphorical "hunger and thirst." Here again, as in parts of the Old Testament, inspiring poetry has been reduced to uninspiring prose in a futile attempt to make the reading of the Bible "easier."

In the Lord's Prayer (Matt. 6:9-13; Luke 11:2-4) the most difficult line for me is the one that says: "Lead us not into temptation, but deliver us from the evil one." It seems to me to be bad theology to assume that God might deliberately lead us into temptation, or "hard testing" as TEV puts it. Temptation or hard testing is inevitable in this world. What we need is help from God to withstand the temptation. It seems to me that the Syriac versions may be translated: "Let us not succumb to temptation but deliver us from the evil one." This is to me a sensible petition, which is at least worthy of a commendatory footnote.

In Matthew 6:19 there should have been a footnote giving the possibility that it is moths and worms that destroy rather than moths and rust. Putting together two disparate things like moths and rust is not characteristic of Semitic thought, as combining moths and worms would be. The Greek word *brosis* can be taken either way, as the Arndt and Gingrich lexicon makes clear. Some other versions definitely favor "worms."

It has always seemed to me that the saying in Matthew 8:22 and Luke 9:60, "let the dead bury their dead," is not a very sensible thought, and that there may have been a confusion between the active and passive voices of the verb and hence that the original saying may have been "the dead will be buried," i.e., somebody will take care of that. TEV gives no help on this. But the volume on Matthew in the Anchor Bible series by W. F. Albright and C. S. Mann[8] does help. They translate: "Follow me, and let the dying bury their dead," explaining that "in several Semitic languages, including Hebrew/Aramaic, the word for *dead* can also mean *dying*" (p. 96). The word "dying" can then be taken literally, or metaphorically, referring to those who have not chosen to follow Jesus and hence belong to a dying cause, with no important or pressing work to do. This is a clever suggestion and should be seriously considered.

And finally, a few words about a favorite text of mine, because it is so utterly absurd and difficult as it stands. It is Mark 9:49, which reads as follows in KJV: "For every one shall be salted with fire, and every sacrifice shall be salted with salt." The second clause is not in all the best manuscripts, and is now generally regarded as a later addition from Leviticus 2:13 with intent to improve the sense. Most modern translations omit it.

Moffatt made excellent sense, as usual: "Everyone has to be consecrated by the fire of discipline," but he had to change "salted" to "consecrated" and add "discipline." Goodspeed says: "Everyone must be seasoned with fire," a very small and cautious change.[9] RSV, JB, NEB, and NAB just take the Greek straight without trying to make sense. Only C. C. Torrey in *The Four Gospels* shows a plausible way to recover the original meaning.[10] In his time Torrey was the greatest living authority on Aramaic, the language of Jesus. He put this verse (without the addition from Leviticus) back into Aramaic, found that what appears in Greek as "with fire" was in Aramaic "is going to spoil." He also knew that the word for "all" in Aramaic could mean "everything" as well as "everyone." So he read the verse as a common-sense rule in ancient living: "Everything that is going to spoil should be salted." This fits in perfectly with the following verse on the virtues of salt, literal and figurative. The fire came in erroneously from the preceding verse, with which verse 49 has no connection.

Now what does TEV do? Not much. They take both clauses from KJV, scramble them together, and come out thus: "Everyone will be purified by fire as sacrifice is purified by salt." They got rid of some of the salt, but the troublesome fire is still there. There is not much connection between what fire will do to people and what salt will do to sacrifices. Torrey's suggestion, which changes only one vowel in one small word, is much less radical than many of the changes made throughout the Bible by TEV in trying to make sense out of difficult passages.

However, let it be said to the credit of the TEV translators that they usually add those warning footnotes: "Hebrew unclear," "Aramaic has two additional words, the meaning of which is unclear," "Some manuscripts do not have verses 43-44," "Some manuscripts add verse 17," etc., etc. The reader should be careful to read all these footnotes, for they arc TEV's way of admitting that the Bible is not so simple and easy to understand after all, especially in passages where the manuscript evidence is ambiguous.

But there is no cause for despair, for in recent times much progress has been made in clarifying difficult passages. However, there are some whose original meaning may never be recovered.

Today's English Version Translators

NEW TESTAMENT: Robert G. Bratcher

OLD TESTAMENT: Robert G. Bratcher, Chair; Roger A. Bullard, Keith Crim, Herbert Grether, Barclay M. Newman, Heber F. Peacock, John A. Thompson

APOCRYPHA: Heber F. Peacock, Chair; Roger A. Bullard, Barclay M. Newman

8
The Living Bible

James D. Smart

The May 1976 issue of *The Presbyterian Record* contained an elaborate two-page advertisement for a book which calls itself *The Living Bible*. Also, the board of congregational life in its material for Family Sunday suggested readings from this book which would require purchase of it and would imply that a board of our church was recommending public use of it as a valid substitute for authentic scholarly translations of the Bible. Even the promoters of this book do not dare to call it a translation of the Bible. They call it a "paraphrase" by which they can only mean that from time to time they put into the text phrases which have no equivalents in the original text but which they think make better and easier reading. Ninety-eight percent of the time the book proceeds as though it were just another translation of the Bible in modern language.

Enthusiasts for it use it as though it were the most up-to-date version of the Bible. Recently when I was addressing a conference of Mennonite ministers and students in Indiana, the ministers complained that their people who were wedded to the King James Version until just yesterday were now carrying this book to church and demanding that readings in the service of worship should be from it. People will do well to examine it with some care before they invest in it.

First, let us look at two passages in John's Gospel. We are all familiar with the great opening verses: "In the beginning was the Word, and the Word was with God, and the Word was God. He was in the beginning with God; all things were made through him and without him was not anything made that was made" (RSV). The author of the Gospel had an important reason for beginning in this way. He wished to make clear to the church, a church in which there were serious differences about what to do with the Old Testament, that the word of God in creation, the word of God to which Israel's prophets, psalmists, wise men and historians had long borne witness and the word incarnate in Jesus Christ were one and the same word. But what words does *The Living Bible* put into the mouth of the author of this Gospel? "Before anything else existed, there was Christ, with God. He has always been alive and is himself God. He created everything there is—nothing exists that he didn't make." The purpose of the author in beginning as he did is completely frustrated.

In John 1:17 we read in RSV "For the law was given through Moses; grace and truth came through Jesus Christ." The word "law" translating the Greek *nomos* has behind it the Hebrew word *Torah,* which was the name used by the Jews for the Pentateuch and often signified the whole Old Testament. "Law" suggests "laws" to us, but *Torah* was much more than laws. Before all else it was the story of God's loving care for Israel and for humankind. A glance at John 5:46 makes clear that for the author of this Gospel the *Torah* of Moses was primarily witness to the same Word that in the fulness of time was incarnate in Jesus. But how does *The Living Bible* give us John 1:17? "For Moses gave us only the Law with its rigid demands and merciless justice, while Jesus Christ brought us loving forgiveness as well." Not only is this *not* what the author wrote but it promotes the false conception of the Old Testament as "rigid" and "merciless" in its enforcement of a legal kind of justice in contrast to a New Testament that knows only loving forgiveness. Justice in the Old Testament is never merciless. How can anyone forget that the God of the Old Testament is a God who deals with people in love and asks of them that they should respond to God and to others with a similar love?

It is startling to read in Luke 1 that this evangelist began his Gospel "Dear friend who loves God." This is not a translation—or a paraphrase of anything Luke wrote—but a fanciful playing with the name of the patron, Theophilus, to whom Luke addressed his Gospel. Even more startling is it to find the words put in Luke's mouth: "Several biographies of Christ have already been written." No reputable New Testament scholar would ever make the mistake of calling the four Gospels "biographies." That misconception makes an intelligent reading of them impossible. They do not have the first elements of either an ancient or a modern biography—which is why attempts to write a biography of Jesus are so invariably unsuccessful and have to resort so largely to imaginative reconstruction. The Gospels are not biographies but are testimonies to the decisive revelation of God in Jesus Christ.

In Luke 7:37, where Jesus is being entertained in the house of Simon the Pharisee, the RSV tells how "a woman of the city who was a sinner" precipitated a highly dramatic confrontation between Jesus and his host. But in *The Living Bible* this becomes "a woman of the streets who was a prostitute." Admittedly many preachers assume that this woman was a prostitute. But nothing in the story validates that assumption. A "sinner" in first century Judaism was anyone who for any reason refused conformity to the 613 laws which defined and guarded the life of the righteous Jew. All Gentiles were sinners. All nonconformists were sinners. Youths attracted by Greek sports or drama or philosophy were sinners. And all such sinners were excluded from the synagogue community and were treated as unbelievers. Therefore *The Living Bible* is injecting into Luke's story an interpretation for which the text itself provides no support. Another instance of this playing fast and loose with the text is the transformation of Jesus' words "the Son of Man" in Luke 9:22 and 26 into "I, the Messiah." It does not occur to the perpetrator of this folly that Jesus had his own very special reason for using the term "Son of Man." Not everyone would dare to correct Jesus!

The treatment of Mark provides further instances of this disrespect for the original text and confident attempts to improve it. Mark 1:2 in *The Living Bible* reads: "In the book written by the prophet Isaiah God announced that he would send his Son to earth." A note confesses this is only "implied" but one searches in vain in the original text of verse 2 for any trace of it. In verse 4 John the Baptist "preaching a baptism of repentance for the forgiveness of sins" becomes "taught that all should be baptized as a public announcement of their decision to turn their backs on sin, so that God could forgive them." But repentance even for John is primarily a turning round to *God* and not just a turning of one's back on sin. In verse 10 "like a dove" becomes "in the form of a dove" which seems to suggest that God the Holy Spirit took the form of a bird, a dove, at Jesus' baptism! God incarnate in a bird? In Mark 6:2 the astonishment of Jesus' fellow townspeople at his embarkation on a prophetic mission which made them say, "Is not this the carpenter?" finds a more abusive expression: "He's no better than we are. He's just a carpenter."

More serious is the attempt to improve Paul in the letter to the Galatians. Paul in the midst of a serious controversy chose his words with extreme care. Each one has to be weighed. Here in chapter 1 *The Living Bible* insists on translating Paul's word "gospel" as "way to heaven." It occurs in verse 6 and then in the crucial verse 11. Paul here is defending his gospel as a revelation of God to him in his confrontation with the risen Lord, not something taught him by the Jerusalem apostles. His own status as an apostle equal in authority with Peter and James is at stake. What was revealed to him when (verse 16) Christ was revealed *in* him and he began his lifelong life *in Christ* was the life of the new age, the life of the new creation, which began now and would come to its fulfillment in eternity. Paul's focus was not on heaven but on a kingdom of heaven that he saw breaking into time now and transforming human life.

Nothing has brought more reproach on Christianity in the past century than the representation of it as primarily "a way to heaven" that encourages people in a passivity toward the injustices and miseries of the present world. It is sad to see it at this date foisted on Paul as his gospel—pie in the sky by and by. There is also an unfortunate version of verse 15 which completely conceals the assertion of Paul that before he became a Christian he knew himself to have been marked before his birth and called to perform some special service for God.

There is space only for a glance at the Old Testament. In Isaiah's account of his visionary experience of God, his confession "I am a man of unclean lips and I dwell in the midst of a people of unclean lips" becomes in *The Living Bible,* "I am a foul-mouthed sinner, a member of a sinful, foul-mouthed race," which gives a totally false conception of Isaiah's concern. Bad language was not the problem but a total corruption of life which was poisoning the Judean community. The sin was social, economic and political.

The treatment of Isaiah 40 ff. is especially bad. For example: 40:2, "she has received of the Lord's hand double for all her sins" becomes "the Lord will give her twice as many blessings as he gave her punishment before." This simply is not what the prophet wrote. In 40:21 the prophet's magnificent arraignment of a people careless of the great traditions of its faith: "Have you not known? Have you not heard? Has it not been told you from the beginning? Have you not understood from the foundations of the earth?" becomes tamely and inaccurately: "Are you so ignorant? Are you so deaf to the words of God—the words he gave before the worlds began?" Why would the prophet point to words "before the worlds began" rather than to words that had been crucial in the history of Israel? Verse 26 of chapter 40 has to be prettied up by likening God's control of the procession of the stars to a shepherd leading his sheep, calling each by its pet name and counting them to see that none is lost or strayed!

The boldest insertions begin in chapter 41. In verse 5 we are told: "The lands beyond the sea watch in fear and wait for word of Cyrus' new campaigns." No issue in the interpretation of these chapters is more hotly debated by scholars than the identity of the mysterious figure who is to win victories for God. Some say it is the Israel of the future. Calvin saw it as Abraham. Others identify it as Cyrus who is mentioned only in 44:28 and 45:1. Still others hold those two mentions of Cyrus to be clearly later editorial intrusions into the text. *The Living Bible* settles the matter once and for all. It inserts the name of Cyrus into eight verses where it does not occur at all in the biblical text and invents whole sentences to describe his conquest of Babylon. In 43:14 where the text is so broken that no scholar can do more than speculate about the original meaning, *The Living Bible,* untouched by knowledge of the Hebrew, proceeds boldly: "I will send an invading army against Babylon that will walk in almost unscathed. The boasts of the Babylonians will turn to cries of fear." A verse such as this can only make one wonder whether the producers of this "Bible" have any knowledge of the original languages.

What is astonishing about the circulation of this book is that it is being bought mainly by people who in the past have been concerned that they should have an "infallible" Bible. The King James Version had their confidence for long years and they rejected all the modern translations which were produced by competent scholars. But now they have recognized that the language of a seventeenth-century version is a barrier to twentieth-century understanding. Exposed by the Tyndale Press to a Bible in modern language, they have embraced it enthusiastically. Some seem almost inclined to make this their "infallible" Bible of today!! But surely anyone with a tradition of respect for sound scholarship, and a sense of awe before the testimony of prophets and apostles, will look carefully before making this specious volume a substitute for those translations of the Bible that by their integrity have won the approval of the major churches of the world.

9
The New American Bible

WALTER HARRELSON

The New American Bible (NAB) has already found its place in pulpit, liturgy, study, and classroom. Within the short period of its life it has achieved remarkable success and received very wide commendation. Various study editions of the translations have been printed, some without the textual notes (regrettably), but none, I believe, without the notes at the bottom of the pages or without the introductions to the biblical books. The NAB is clearly a splendid achievement in modern English versions of the Bible. *(The New American Bible, Translated from the Original Languages with Critical Use of All the Ancient Sources by Members of the Catholic Biblical Association of America: With Textual Notes on Old Testament Readings.* Paterson, N.J.: St. Anthony Guild, 1970.)

History

This English version had its origins in the decision taken in the 1930s to do a fresh English translation of the Latin Vulgate, one that would not be bound to the English edition of Rheims-Douay. The New Testament appeared in 1941, and much work had by then also been done on the Old Testament (including what Protestants call the Apocrypha, except for 1 and 2 Esdras and the Prayer of Manasseh). However, the papal encyclical of Pius XII *Divino Afflante Spiritu* of 1943, and the Second Vatican Council that began in 1962, brought about massive changes in the Roman Catholic world. These events also led to authorization of a direct translation from the Hebrew, Aramaic, and Greek rather than from the Latin Vulgate version, and to the choice of a vernacular style of English—a style intended to be suitable at once for liturgy and pulpit, for scholarly study by clergy and laity, and for reading of the Bible in the home.

The changes from the original plans were thus considerable, and they took place over a rather long period of time. Portions of the Old Testament had in fact been issued in the translation initially made from the Vulgate. These were bound for a time with portions made directly from the Hebrew, Aramaic, and Greek. Eventually, however, the Bishops' Committee of the Confraternity of Christian Doctrine (which holds the copyright) entrusted the Catholic Biblical Association of America with the task of doing the entire Bible into a vernacular English that was translated from the original languages, on the basis of the best texts available and with the help of the ablest scholars who could be enlisted.

Joining the largely Catholic team were four non-Catholics: Frank M. Cross, Jr., David Noel Freedman, John Knox, and James A. Sanders. Forty-six other editors and translators are listed as having been involved in the work, along with quite a few others who assisted with study helps, illustrations, and the like. The first edition of the completed work appeared in 1970.

Character of the Translation

As noted above, the translation aims to be inclusive in use. It is intended to serve liturgical and pulpit uses as well as be a study Bible and a translation suitable for devotional use and for reading in the home. The recent revolutionary steps taken to encourage the reading and study of the Bible on the part of lay members of the Roman Catholic Church, along with massive reforms in liturgical life, provided the appropriate context for such an all-inclusive effort in Bible translation.

The NAB translators were able to work with great freedom. They had no English language tradition to uphold, such as the RSV translators have had. They did not work as closely with colleagues from the field of English letters as did the translators of the NEB. And they did not, apparently, work quite so closely together as a team as have some of the other translation committees. There appears to have been, at any rate, a good deal of freedom provided the translators in their individual or small-group work on particular portions of the Bible.

Some real gains result from these dimensions of freedom. It may also be the case that some of the flaws that one finds in the translation owe something to these aspects of freedom. For example, I find that the translation seems not to have a standard on the matter of word-order; that it has not successfully eliminated English words or expressions that lack a fairly widespread currency; and that it seems to follow somewhat different approaches to reliance upon the ancient versions in the different portions of the translation. The use of the LXX in the books of Samuel, for example, is remarkably large. These are, however, the kinds of matters that can easily enough be handled in revisions to come.

The NAB in most respects seems to me to resemble the RSV more than it resembles the NEB or the JB, the other two translations with which it has great affinity. It is a fresh translation marked by restraint in the use of conjecture or in departures from the Masoretic Hebrew text. While there are some instances of resort to conjecture, the translators have been conservative in this regard. They have shown much interest in calling attention to peculiarities of word-order in English when (often) the Hebrew order is not the normal one. Although not a literal or word-for-word translation by any means, the NAB still strives for the flavor of the order and the style of the ancient languages. It certainly does not operate on the principle of finding the "dynamic equivalent" of the ancient language in the "target" language.

The Form of the Edition

The NAB edition with which I am working is an inexpensive one, published with several mistakes in the introductions to the biblical books and in the notes, showing occasional indications of carelessness in the proofreading of the text itself, and lacking the textual notes on the Old Testament and Apocrypha. Despite the fact that it is an inexpensive edition and produced without adequate care, it is a superb example of readability. The more carefully published editions, on better paper, are even more easily read. Editors and technical staff are to be praised for this achievement.

The type is clear, the ink dark enough for very easy reading, and the layout of the publication is done with great care. Chapter headings are placed in the center of the columns. Subject headings are brief, lucid, and printed in heavy type and placed at the left margin. Poetry is printed as poetry, as is some rhythmic prose that may not be poetry at all. The verse numbers normally appear at the far left margin of the column, with space between them and the beginning of the text. An asterisk calls attention to the first set of notes at the bottom of the pages, which are cross-references to appropriate biblical passages. A dagger in the text indicates the presence, in the lower section at the bottom of the pages, of an explanatory note. The asterisks and daggers do not intrude badly upon the vision of the reader.

The fact that the editors have chosen not to include footnote indications of textual variations or corruptions makes the text all the more readable, of course. Whether the decision to collect all such textual notes into a single appendix has been a good thing will require further reflection, perhaps, but it certainly contributes to easy reading of the biblical translation itself.

Regarding punctuation, the translators have wisely eliminated one set of quotation marks by the decision to use a colon, rather than to enclose a following speech in quotation marks. In this way they are able to be much more sparing in the use of quotation marks within quotation marks. The result is very satisfactory, since more is gained in ease of reading than is lost in terms of possible confusion. Indeed, it may well be the case that the reader will be able the better to know who is speaking at a given time by this reduction of the frequency of use of quotation marks.

In the way that colons, semicolons, and commas are used, as well as by fairly frequent use of the dash, the translators have contributed clarity to the text and made it read easily. An example from Isaiah 3:12 will indicate this point.

> My people—a babe in arms will be their tyrant,
> and women will rule them!
> O my people, your leaders mislead,
> they destroy the paths you should follow.

Many other examples could be given, and will be reflected in materials quoted below for other purposes.

Attention is called in the notes to differences between the Hebrew versification and chapter enumerations and that of the other ancient versions. Normally, the Hebrew versification is followed, in contrast to most English versions. Occasionally there are transpositions of verses or sections, with explanations given in the notes for such relocations. For example, the translators have seen fit to relocate Hosea 1:10—2:1 (Hebrew and NAB 2:1-3) after chapter 3.

The spelling of place names and proper names breaks with the Vulgate and Rheims-Douay and follows the system found in modern English versions.

Deficiencies of Style

There is one major difficulty with the NAB, in my judgment. There are too many instances of infelicity of style, awkwardness in word order, and use of unsatisfactory or uncommon words or terms. Certainly, such matters are often ones of personal taste, and thus my own sensibilities may be of little weight. Not all of the examples given below, however, are likely to be due merely to differences between the reviewer's taste and that of the translators.

In Exodus 20:26 we read: "You must not go up by steps to my altar, on which you must not be indecently uncovered." The sense is plain, but the translators have not given enough attention to just how that expression reads or sounds.

Beginning in Genesis 8:20, the translators use "holocaust" for the Hebrew term *'ōlāh.* This Greek term has just the right meaning for the Hebrew one, of course, but to the modern English reader "holocaust" can only call to mind the horrors of Nazi Germany. The decision to employ "holocaust" seems in every way unfortunate.

In Psalm 139:1, 23 the translators have chosen to translate: "O LORD, you have probed me . . ." and "Probe me, O God. . . ." "Probe" is a good term, carrying with it the connotation of a searching out, an investigation in depth. That surely is what the Hebrew verb means. And yet, the translation grates and seems stylistically unsatisfactory. It seems to me much better to stay with "search" or "examine," which one finds in the other recent English versions.

In Ecclesiastes 12:13 NAB has: "Fear God and keep his commandments, for this is man's all." "Man's all" is too laconic and unfelicitious. Surely, a better reading is "the whole duty of man," the customary rendering, or the NEB's "there is no more to man than this."

In Psalm 46:5 (vs. 4 in most other English editions) the translators decided to handle the matter of a river whose streams make glad the city of God by translating: "There is a stream whose runlets gladden the city of God." That may be fine, but must it not be insisted that very few English readers will ever before have read or heard the word "runlet"? In the same psalm, at verse 10 (vs. 9), NAB translates: "He has stopped wars to the end of the earth." That is certainly accurate, but it feels a bit unsatisfactory. If one is to get away from "makes war cease" it might be better to translate: "He has brought war to an end throughout the earth."

Once more in the same psalm we have an uncommon use. In verse 11 (vs. 10) we have "Desist! and confess that I am God." I like the punctuation that leaves the "and" uncapitalized. But the use of "desist" seems to me unwise from the point of view of style and of English usage. "Be still!" or "Silence!" would work very well.

In my judgment, a few mistranslations occur. In Psalm 73:15 the translators have rendered: "Had I thought, 'I will speak as they do.' " It seems to me virtually certain that the poet is *not* referring to the scoffing comments of the wicked as found in verses 10 and 11. He is rather referring to the temptation he himself had faced, and overcome, of making public the sentiment found in verses 13 and 14.

Another mistranslation, much more understandable, is the rendering of Exodus 20:2 as follows: "I, the LORD, am your God." In my view, the other alternative is so much the better that it must be followed: "I am the LORD your God." Yahweh is presenting himself; the term the LORD is not simply in apposition with the personal pronoun.

In Exodus 20:17 my edition of NAB does not include the clause "You shall not covet your neighbor's house(hold)." It may be that a simple printer's error has occurred, for the textual notes do not point to a decision on the part of the translators to eliminate this opening clause. In any event, my NAB now reads for Exodus 20:17: "You shall not covet your neighbor's wife, nor his male or female slave, nor his ox or ass, nor anything else that belongs to him." It is an excellent translation, and the elimination of the opening clause may well be justified on the basis of Deuteronomy 5:21 and the judgment that Exodus' reference to "household" is well covered in the following enumeration. But some reference to this decision ought to appear in the textual notes or in the explanatory notes at the bottom of the page.

Psalm 104:26 also contains a faulty translation, I believe. We have the following translation:

> And where ships move about
> with Leviathan, which you formed to
> make sport of it.

The much more natural translation is: "and Leviathan, whom you formed to sport in it [namely, the sea]." The NEB and JB both understand Leviathan to have been created as Yahweh's plaything. That seems to me to be unlikely enough. But that Leviathan should have been formed by Yahweh in order to make sport of it or to taunt it seems to me highly implausible as a sentiment of this poet.

Several occurrences of unusual word order apparently appear because of the translators' decision to call attention to an unusual word order in the original by a similar device in English even where the resultant expression is jarringly infelicitious. This seems to me to be unnecessary and unwise. I have noted many occurrences of unusual English word order that I think are excellent. But some are poor, among them the following:

Psalm 73:23	Yet with you I shall always be.
Psalm 44:6 (vs. 5)	Our foes through you we struck down.
Psalm 48:11 (vs. 10)	Of justice your right hand is full.

In a subsequent revision it will be possible to eliminate such instances, if they should be eliminated. I do know how difficult this matter is for translators. Once again, I may be expressing only my own personal taste.

Excellent Translations

But by far the larger space belongs in this review to those instances in which the NAB has come up with memorable and apt translations. Among the many in my notes let me mention the following ones.

In Genesis 1:1 we find: "In the beginning, when God created the heavens and the earth. . . ." This translation keeps the definiteness and once-for-all character of the Hebrew word *(b^e^re'shîth)* with which the Bible opens. At the same time, it expresses the temporal dimension that opening lines of creation stories, including the ones with which the Bible opens, surely contain. It is an exactly correct solution to a problem that has troubled translators through the centuries. And it is better, I think, than the very good translation of NEB: "In the beginning of creation, when God made heaven and earth. . . ."

Another right rendering is the inclusion in Genesis 3:6 of the Hebrew expression *'immāh* which often has been omitted by translators. The NAB has: "And she gave some [of the fruit] to her husband, who was with her, and he ate." The omission of "who was with her" in RSV and NEB is a serious matter, for it eliminates clear evidence that *the narrator* understood that the man was present with the woman during the entire conversation with the snake. Both the man and the woman share, and share equally, in the act of disobedience; that is what the narrator knows and says. The traditional elimination of the preposition with its pronominal suffix has been of no small negative consequence in the history of exegesis down to the present.

Since we have criticized the use of a somewhat unusual English word order above, we should give an example of a very effective use. In Numbers 12:6-8 we have the following speech of Yahweh set out as poetry:

> Should there be a prophet among you,
> in visions will I reveal myself to him,
> in dreams will I speak to him;
> Not so with my servant Moses!
> Throughout my house he bears my trust;
> face to face I speak to him,
> plainly and not in riddles.
> The presence of the LORD he beholds.

That is a splendid translation of a quite complex set of Hebrew lines. And in the same chapter, a few verses along, we have in vss. 10-14 a fine example of the translators' skill in handling a conversation between God and the people. It is clear, the punctuation does not get out of hand, and it reads very well:

> When Aaron turned and saw her [Miriam] a leper, [11]"Ah, my lord!" he said to Moses, "please do not charge us with the sin that we have foolishly committed! [12]Let her not thus be like the stillborn babe that comes forth from its mother's womb with its flesh half consumed." [13]Then Moses cried to the LORD, "Please, not this! Pray, heal her!" [14]But the LORD answered Moses, "Suppose her father had spit in her face, would she not hide in shame for seven days? Let her be confined outside the camp for seven days; only then may she be brought back."

In 2 Samuel 1:21 we have a good translation of a line from David's lament over the death of Saul and Jonathan: "Upon you [the mountains] lie begrimed the warriors' shields." While the Hebrew simply has "for there upon the mountains was the shield of the mighty defiled," it seems entirely appropriate for the mountains to continue to be addressed in the second person, as NAB's translation assumes.

In the same poem, NAB translates in 1:19: "How can the warriors have fallen!" That too is an excellent translation; in my view, it is better than the customary apostrophe: "How are the mighty fallen!"

In a number of instances the NAB translators use colloquial English to excellent effect. In Judith 14:18 Bagoas is made to say when he sees the headless Holofernes in the tent, "The slaves have duped us!" There is frequent use of this term for deception or tricking.

In the legal materials we also find masterfully clear English translations of several of the complex laws. One that I like very much is the rendering of Exodus 21:35: "When one man's ox hurts another's ox so badly that it dies, they shall sell the live ox and divide this money as well as the dead animal equally between them." Another is the law concerning the female slave in Exodus 21:7-11:

> "When a man sells his daughter as a slave, she shall not go free as male slaves do. [8]But if her master, who had destined her for himself, dislikes her, he shall let her be redeemed. He has no right to sell her to a foreigner, since he has broken faith with her.
> [9]If he destines her for his son, he shall treat her like a daughter. [10]If he takes another wife, he shall not withhold her food, her clothing, or her conjugal rights. [11]If he does not grant her these three things, she shall be given her freedom absolutely, without cost to her."

It is difficult to imagine how such a circumstantial, lucid, and still literal translation could be made better.

Scholars have recognized in recent years that the messianic oracle on Bethlehem-Ephratha found in Micah 5:1-4 probably comes to an end with the Hebrew expression *w^{e}hāyāh zeh shālôm.* The question is how best to translate the clause. NAB has a good translation: "He shall be peace." I would prefer "And he shall be (or shall be called) Peace," capitalizing the last term as a kind of parallel to the messianic titles of Isaiah 9:1-7. But the NAB closes the oracles with the reference to the one who shall be peace, rightly identifying the remainder of verse 4 as a part of the following oracle.

This list of good translations could continue, but we will break off at this point and look at the question of how the NAB translators have made use of new textual materials and how they have informed readers of such use.

Use of the Ancient Texts and Versions

In the 124 pages of textual notes that are found at the end of some editions of the NAB, a massive amount of up-to-date textual criticism of the Hebrew Bible and the Apocryphal books is to be found. I have used these materials extensively in working on proposed revisions of the RSV translation of the books of 1 and 2 Samuel. The notes are very succinct, perhaps too succinct. They are transliterated according to a familiar and quite usable scheme. It is regrettable that the printing of the notes did not include identification, at the top of each page, of the biblical book to which the notes pertain. In later editions that might be done. Indeed, it might be wise to refer to the page numbers of the Bible to which the notes pertain, thereby facilitating the reader's use of these notes.

It might also be the case that the holders of the copyright would want to refuse to let publishers print the NAB without these notes. My own inexpensive copy of NAB lacks them. They are published separately by the St. Anthony's Guild, Paterson, N.J., but that hardly suffices. In my judgment the NAB should not exist without these notes, since the translators have seen fit to make no reference in the text itself to any of the textual problems treated in the notes.

Textual notes on the books of the Protestant Apocrypha are particularly welcome, since they reflect a great deal of fresh textual study and sum up in very brief form the results of textual scholarship on these books.

The textual materials available to the translators were rich indeed. Some of the translators were in possession of unpublished materials that could be put to use in a modern English translation for the first time. Happily, most of this material is now available to the scholarly world, as for example in the *Biblia Hebraica Stuttgartensia* (1967/77).

A few examples of good usage of the materials available now follow. In 2 Samuel 23:1 NAB reads: "The utterance of the man God raised up." The Masoretic Text has "The utterance of the one who was raised on high," or the like. The Hebrew is *huqam 'āl.* One of the Qumran manuscripts reads *hēqîm 'ēl,* "the one God raised up." That text seems to be exactly right.

We have an excellent translation in 2 Samuel 6:6: "When they came to the threshing floor of Nodan, Uzzah reached out his hand to the ark of God and steadied it, for the oxen were making it tip." The reading "Nodan" for "Nacon" is supported by the Qumran materials and by some LXX manuscripts. The reading "for the oxen were making it tip" is a fine translation based on a repointing of the Hebrew *shām'ṭû* to *sh'māṭô.* The verb thus refers to the sliding ark, not to the stumbling oxen.

The NAB encloses in brackets one expression that I would have preferred to see in the text. In 2 Samuel 11:3 we have a text that, on the basis of Qumran and Josephus, would read as follows: "She is Bathsheba, daughter of Eliam, and wife of Joab's armor-bearer Uriah the Hittite." That is NAB's translation except for the fact that the words "Joab's armor-bearer," which are found in the Qumran text and in Josephus, are placed in brackets.

Missed Opportunities

Every translator has a set of favorite renderings that have not as yet found their way into the accepted translations. I have some too. One of these occurs in Psalm 8. The NAB has an excellent translation of this hymn of praise to God the Creator. It handles the opening part of the poem perfectly, I believe:

> 2[1]O LORD, our LORD,
> how glorious is your name over all the earth!
> You have exalted your majesty above the heavens.
> 3[2]Out of the mouths of babes and sucklings
> you have fashioned praise because of your foes,
> to silence the hostile and the vengeful.

I remain convinced that what comes from the mouth of babes and infants both praises God and silences God's enemies.

But in verse nine (eight), where we have the reference to the sea monster who moves along on the paths or passages of the seas, the NAB has remained with the limp translation "whatever." The appearance of the Hebrew term *'ōbhēr* at the beginning of this laconic half-line seems to me much too weighty to justify or allow such a tame translation. I would like to read "the One who passes along the paths of the seas," thus making the reference to the sea monster, or Leviathan, the more unmistakable. Psalm 104:26 has the creature created to sport and cavort in the sea; that is its proper work. Psalm 8:9 identifies the creature as under the sway of human authority, just as are all other creatures called into being by God. And Genesis 1:21 underscores the fact that God himself created these monsters (the verb used is the special one for divine creation, *bārā'*).

In 2 Samuel 23:7 NAB follows the lead of most translations in dropping the closing Hebrew word in the poem identified as David's last words. I regret that decision. It is true that the text is difficult, but I think that the translators stopped too soon in their rendering: "He who wishes to touch them [the thorns, a simile for the wicked] must arm himself with iron and the shaft of a spear, and they must be consumed by fire." The last line is the problem. The poet, I believe, is drawing the analogy to the wicked as thorns, somewhat in the manner of Jotham in the fable of Judges 9:15. He had pointed out that one is wise to touch the wicked only with care, as one touches thorns with an iron instrument or the shaft of a spear. But the poet does not say, I believe, that they must be consumed by fire. He rather stresses how quickly thorns are consumed by fire after having been gathered up with such great difficulty. I would translate the last line as follows: "and they will be consumed by the fire in a single sitting." This is a possible rendering of the Hebrew *bashshābheth,* and it fits the customs of the ancient East very well: the use of brambles and thorns for warming oneself and for cooking when other fuel is not available, even though such fuel is very quickly consumed and hardly repays all the effort expended in gathering it.

The Explantory Notes

At the beginning of each book and at the bottom of each page the reader finds helps to understanding the text. They are very good. Occasionally readers may be put off by the explicit assertions that the faith of ancient Israel remained imperfect, finding its completion in Christ, and by the way in which this claim is supported. But I find a remarkably sensitive treatment of theological issues in these notes. The writers frequently observe that not all Catholic scholars accept the position being presented.

In the introductory notes to the individual books or to sections of the Bible a great deal of information is packed into brief paragraphs: information on the contents of the book, the types of literature found, the argument of the book, including summaries of the thought of the writer or writers in question. Theological questions are not at all ignored, but (as noted above) the authors usually avoid any suggestion of a dogmatic understanding that must be accepted.

The same kind of treatment is found in the explanatory notes. In the notes on the Psalms, which I have examined with some care, the authors identify the uses of particular psalms in the worship of the church, call attention to the ways in which certain psalms have been understood to find fulfillment in the Christian revelation, and also show the importance for certain basic theological understandings that a given psalm or passage has. These notes are far from a commentary on the Bible, of course. Space allows for only the briefest of comments. Yet, the translation would be the poorer without these fine notes.

The cross-references to other biblical passages seem to strike the right balance between reference to all possible passages that might be of interest and value and reference only to those unmistakably akin to the one in question. I find the list an excellent one, and also find that it is very easy to use.

Male-oriented Language

The translators seem to have made no attempt to reduce the dominance of masculine-oriented language in the Bible. The translators of the RSV are currently making such an attempt and have gained some experience in doing so. I suspect that in a forthcoming edition of the NAB a similar attempt will be made. I see much to be gained and little to be lost in this kind of effort.

It is certainly the case that some passages are the product of a male-dominated society and that it would be wrong to change the language. But in many instances it is also the case that the reference is to the human being, not to a man or to men. In those instances it is worthwhile to strain the English language to find a way of showing that such references are not male-oriented. One of the most difficult examples I know is Psalm 8. If the NAB were to be changed in such a way as to avoid using masculine language when the whole human community is clearly intended, it might have to read somewhat as follows (I change only the terms required to effect this change):

> 2O LORD, our LORD,
> how glorious is your name over all the earth!
> You have exalted your majesty above the heavens.
> 3Out of the mouths of babes and sucklings
> you have fashioned praise because of your foes,
> to silence the hostile and the vengeful.
> 4When I behold your heavens, the work of your fingers,
> the moon and the stars which you set in place—
> 5What are human beings that you should be mindful of them,
> or mortals that you should care for them?
> 6You have made them little less than the angels,
> and crowned them with glory and honor.
> 7You have given them rule over the works of your hands,
> putting all things under their feet:
> 8All sheep and oxen,
> yes, and the beasts of the field,
> 9The birds of the air, the fishes of the sea,
> and whatever swims the paths of the seas.
> 10O LORD, our LORD,
> how glorious is your name over all the earth!

I find such a translation to be both faithful to the Hebrew text and a better rendition of what the contemporary Christian community should wish to say, given the unmistakable distortions of language that have done harm to both men and women over the centuries. It is worth our while, therefore, to find ways to remove the masculine-dominated language that should and can be eliminated.

The NAB is in some respects the best available English translation of the Bible. I have sought to show some ways in which that is true, and some ways in which a revised edition might give it even greater right to such designation.

Participants in the New American Bible Translation Project

BISHOPS' COMMITTEE OF THE CONFRATERNITY OF CHRISTIAN DOCTRINE: Charles P. Greco (Chair), Joseph T. McGucken, Vincent S. Waters, Romeo Blanchette, Christopher J. Weldon.

EDITORIAL BOARD: Louis F. Hartman [†1970] (Chair for the Old Testament), Myles M. Bourke (Chair for the New Testament), Patrick W. Skehan (Vice-Chair), Stephen J. Hartdegen (Secretary), Gerard S. Sloyan (English Editor for the New Testament)

ASSOCIATE EDITORS AND TRANSLATORS: Edward P. Arbez [†1967], Edward J. Byrne [†1952], Edward A. Cerny [†1962], Christian P. Ceroke, John J. Collins, M. Emmanuel Collins, Frank M. Cross, Jr., Patrick Cummins [†1968], Antonine A. DeGuglielmo, Alexander A. Di Lella, John J. Dougherty, William A. Dowd, Joseph A. Fitzmyer, David Noel Freedman, Michael J. Gruenthaner [†1962], Thomas P. Halton, Hilary Hayden, Maurice A. Hofer, John Knox, Justin Trellner [†1949], Richard Kugelman, Joseph L. Lilly [†1952], Roderick F. MacKenzie, Edward A. Mangan [†1955], Daniel W. Martin, William H. McClellan [†1951], James M. McGlinchey [†1961], Frederick Moriarty, Richard T. Murphy, Roland E. Murphy, William L. Newton, Eberhard Olinger [†1967], Charles H. Pickar, Jerome D. Quinn, Christopher Rehwinkel, John F. Rowan [†1953], James A. Sanders, Raymond Schoeder, Edward F. Siegman [†1967], David M. Stanley, Matthew P. Stapleton, John E. Steinmueller, John Ujlaki [†1964], Bruce Vawter, John P. Weisengoff

† deceased

10
The New International Version

Robert G. Bratcher

The publication of the New International Version of the Bible in October 1978 was the culmination of a process that began in the '50s, after the publication of the Revised Standard Version in 1952. At this late date it is hard to remember the abusive and arrogant language that was heaped on the RSV. It was denounced as "liberal," "modernistic," "blasphemous," and "communist-inspired." It was repudiated by nearly all conservatives and fundamentalists as a perversion of the Word of God, which was, of course, taken to be the King James Version.

In 1956 the Christian Reformed Church appointed a committee to study the possibility of a new translation, and the National Association of Evangelicals did the same in 1957. In 1967 the New York Bible Society assumed responsibility for the project and appointed a committee of fifteen scholars to direct it. In 1968 Dr. Edwin H. Palmer became the fulltime Executive Secretary of the project, and work on the new translation began. The Gospel of John was published in 1969 and the entire New Testament appeared in 1973. Isaiah was published in 1975, Daniel in 1976, and Proverbs and Ecclesiastes in 1977.

During this time other Bibles were appearing, sponsored or published by conservative groups. *The Amplified Bible* was published in 1965, *The Modern Language Bible* in 1969, and the *New American Standard Version* in 1971. Kenneth Taylor's paraphrase, *The Living Bible* (1971), outdid them all in popular favor. Although these versions enjoyed, and still enjoy, varying degrees of popularity, none of them has succeeded in becoming *the* Bible of conservative Protestants in this country.

The NIV bids fair to establish itself as the Bible for evangelicals. Its reception has been nothing short of spectacular. By December 1978 over 1,200,000 copies had been sold, and it seems reasonable to assume that in time this translation will replace the King James Bible in private and church usage among evangelical conservatives.

The total cost of the NIV has been reported at two and a quarter million dollars. One hundred and fifteen scholars from more than a dozen evangelical denominations took part in the work (see the Preface, p. vii, and the Appendix at the end of this article). They were divided into twenty teams composed of four or five persons on each team: two co-translators, two consultants, and one English stylist. Each team's work was submitted to an Intermediate Editorial Committee (either of the Old Testament or of the New Testament), and then went on to the General Editorial Committee and finally to the fifteen-member Committee on Bible Translation. It is reported that 200,000 hours were spent on the preparation of this translation.

The publicity released with the publication of the NIV stresses the interdenominational and international character of the work. The Preface (p. vii) names thirteen different denominations represented, in addition to "other churches," not named. This interdenominational aspect of the work "helped to safeguard the translation from sectarian bias" (p. vii). As for the countries represented, a pamphlet entitled "The Version of Our Time" gives a "partial list" of 97 scholars, of whom 87 are Americans. The other ten include three each from Canada and England, and two each from Australia and New Zealand. Evangelical seminaries were strongly represented; seven scholars are listed from the Trinity Evangelical Divinity School of Chicago.

Heavy emphasis is placed on the translators' "high view of Scripture." The Preface to the New Testament (1973) states that they were all committed to "the full authority and complete trustworthiness of the Scriptures, which they believe is God's Word in written form." The Preface to the Bible includes the following statement: "The translators were united in their commitment to the authority and infallibility of the Bible as God's Word in written form." And, as quoted by the publisher, Zondervan, the translators believe that "the Bible alone, in its entirety, is the Word of God written and is therefore inerrant in the autographs."

The following principles guided the translators in their work:

1. Begin with and be faithful to the original text in Hebrew, Greek and Aramaic languages.
2. Clearly reflect the unity and harmony of the Spirit-inspired Writings.
3. Retain only what the original languages say—not inject additional elements of unwarranted paraphrasing.
4. Communicate God's revelation in the language of the people—to do for our time what the King James Version did for its day.
5. Be equally effective for public worship (pulpit and pew), for private study and devotional reading.
6. Establish universal acceptance by creating an ecclesiastical team of 100 scholars who hold to a high view of Scripture as set forth in the Westminster Confession of Faith, the Belgic Confession, and the Statement of Faith of the National Association of Evangelicals.

All these principles are commendable and, by and large, unexceptionable. Some comments may, however, be appropriate.

Principle number 1 states what every translation of the Bible claims to do. In addition it characterizes this Bible as a fresh translation of the original texts and not a revision of any existing translation. The translators were conscious, however, of the force of tradition, and they reveal this awareness in the statement in the Preface (p. viii): "The Committee also sought to preserve some measure of continuity with the long tradition of translating the Scriptures into English."

Principle number 2 assumes that "the unity and harmony" of the biblical books is a given fact. However, any straightforward reading of the texts shows that complete unity and harmony do not exist. Hence, no translation which actually followed principle number 1 could hope to exhibit a complete "unity and harmony" that does not exist. For example, the Bible opens with two different creation accounts (Gen. 1:1—2:4a and 2:4b-25), which cannot be harmonized in any honest representation of available scholarly knowledge. (Contrary to the weight of previous commentary, the NIV includes 2:4a in the second account, not the first one.) Again, the writer of 2 Samuel 24:1 says that Yahweh incited David to take a census of the people; the writer of 1 Chronicles 21:1 says that Satan incited David to take the census. In 1 Samuel 17:1-51 we read the account of how David killed Goliath; 2 Samuel 21:19 says that Elhanan killed Goliath. Matthew 8:5-13 says that the Roman centurion in Capernaum personally requested Jesus to heal his servant; Luke 7:1-10 says that the centurion sent Jewish elders and friends, but never spoke personally to Jesus. Genuine biblical scholarship, which pays attention to the clear evidence of the biblical texts, has long known of these and many other examples of disharmony. A faithful translation (principle number 1) would not try to camouflage these differences. It would reflect the unity and harmony of the biblical books wherever they really exist, and disunity and disharmony wherever they exist.

Has the NIV attempted to impose an artificial unity and harmony upon the biblical text? Certainly it has not done so in any of the passages cited above. But the translation of Isaiah 7:14 may be considered an exception to the rule. The NIV text reads: "Therefore the Lord himself will give you[a] a sign: The virgin will be with child and will give birth to a son, and [b] will call him Immanuel.[c]" The footnotes read: *a* "The Hebrew is plural." *b* "Masoretic Text; Dead Sea Scrolls *and he* or *and they*." *c* "*Immanuel* means *God with us*." (It is difficult to see how the NIV translators can say that the Dead Sea Scrolls text can be understood as "and they." The reading of IQIsa[a] means either "and he will call" or else—if vocalized as a *pu'al*—"and his name will be called." There is no Hebrew or Versional text which has "and they will call," as in Matt. 1:23.)

The quotation of this verse in Matthew 1:23 reads as follows: "The virgin will be with child and will give birth to a son, and they will call him Immanuel." In an interview printed in the Houghton College Bulletin (*Milieu*, December 1978), Dr. Stephen W. Paine, retired president of Houghton College and one of the members of The Committee on Bible Translation, made some comments about the work: "We said we must all believe in the inerrancy of Scripture. This was a lifesaver because it wiped out a lot of nitpicking." He then referred specifically to the translation of *hā'almāh* in Isaiah 7:14, saying that the Hebrew word itself may be understood to mean "young woman" or "virgin." But when this passage is quoted in Matthew 1:23, he said, "if you believe in the inerrancy of Scripture, you have to believe that Matthew correctly reproduced Isaiah and came out with the Greek word which means only virgin." So if the translator really believes that "Matthew is inerrant as well as Isaiah . . . there's only one way the translation can come out to make them both correct."

The same kind of reasoning seems to have been operative in the translation of Psalm 16:10 and Acts 2:27. In the Acts passage Peter quotes Psalm 16:8-11 and says that David was talking about Christ (vs. 31). So verse 27 reads: "because you will not abandon me to the grave, / nor will you let your Holy One see decay." This is *ipsis litteris* the NIV translation of Psalm 16:10: "because you will not abandon me to the grave,[b] / nor will you let your Holy One[c] see decay." (The footnotes read: *b* "Hebrew *Sheol.*" *c* "Or *your faithful one.*") The use of the capital letters in "your Holy One" indicates that the NIV translators believe that the Hebrew psalmist was talking about the resurrection of Jesus Christ. And it should be noted that although "your holy one" qualifies as a defensible translation of the Greek text of Acts 2:27, it would hardly seem to qualify as a good translation of the Hebrew text of Psalm 16:10; the alternative "your faithful one" is much better.

Such a criterion for translating OT passages quoted by NT writers is impossible to apply. Of the (more or less) 275 direct quotations of OT passages in the NT, there are almost 100 which agree neither with the Masoretic Text nor with the present Septuagint. Where is the "inerrant" New Testament (or Old Testament) writer to be found?

Principle number 3 accords quite well with number 1. There may be differences of opinion, however, as to what constitutes "unwarranted paraphrasing." Would "We're going to drown" in Matthew 8:25 be considered an unwarranted paraphrasing of *apollumetha*? Or "will take their places at the feast" in Matthew 8:11 be thought an unwarranted paraphrasing of *anaklithēsontai*? Not in this reviewer's opinion, but others might want to differ.

Principle number 4 reflects the idea that the King James Version of

1611 was written in the language of the people. However, the language of the King James Version was not the popular language of the day. It already had some archaic and obsolete expressions, as a carry-over from the Bishops' Bible (and even from Tyndale), which it was intended to replace. And the language of the NIV can hardly qualify in every place as being "the language of the people," as will be seen below.

Principle number 5 is ambitious, and indeed expresses the goal of every serious attempt at translating the Bible.

It is to be doubted that the aim of principle number 6 ("universal acceptance") could ever be reached. No one translation will ever again become the *textus receptus* of the English-speaking world, as did the King James Version in its long and illustrious reign.

The reference to the various Confessions is worth examining. The Westminster Confession of Faith (1647), in article 4 of chapter 1 declares that God is the Author of holy Scripture "and therefore it is to be received, because it is the Word of God." Article 8 states that the Hebrew Old Testament and the Greek New Testament "being immediately inspired by God, and by his singular care and providence kept pure in all ages, are therefore authentical." The Belgic Confession of Faith (1561; revised 1619) declares in article 3 that God commanded the prophets and apostles "to commit his revealed Word to writing; and he himself wrote with his own finger the two tables of the law. Therefore we call such writings holy and divine Scriptures." And article 1 of the Statement of Faith of the National Association of Evangelicals states: "We believe the Bible to be the inspired, the only infallible authoritative Word of God."

Principle number 6, then, declares that all the scholars who worked on this translation subscribe to the statements made in these Confessions.

It is to be assumed that the Apocrypha will not be translated, if the NIV translators adhere to the spirit and the letter of the Confessions cited.

The mechanical part has been superbly executed. The book is a manageable 4 centimeters thick (15.5 cms. wide, 23 cms. long), the paper is of top quality, thin enough to make for a reasonably sized book yet opaque enough to keep the print from showing through to the opposite side of the leaf. The text is printed in one column, and the use of poetic structure is frequent and effective. The text is divided into sections, with brief section headings. The psalms do not have headings. In Job the speakers are identified in the margin, as are the speakers in the Song of Songs. Meticulous attention has been paid to punctuation: compare Matthew 21:16: "praise'[d]?"; Mark 4:12: "forgiven!'[a]"; Luke 20:17: "capstone[c]'[d]?" I have caught only one typographical error: Psalm 40:5e (Hebrew: 40:6e): "were I to speak and tell f them."

At the end of the volume there is a page-long Table of Weights and

Measures, followed by fourteen maps (eight for the Old Testament and six for the New Testament); the color of the maps may not command universal approval.

The Preface provides useful information on several aspects of the work, and should be carefully read by all who intend to use this Bible.

Text

In making textual decisions the translators were guided by standard textual principles. For the Old Testament their basic text was "the standard Hebrew text, the Masoretic Text as published in the latest editions of *Biblia Hebraica*" (Preface, p. viii). Use was made of the Dead Sea Scrolls, the Samaritan Pentateuch, "and the ancient scribal traditions relating to textual changes." The ancient Versions were also pressed into use. Standard procedures are followed throughout, and frequently the NIV departs from the Masoretic Text where Hebrew manuscripts, the Samaritan Pentateuch, or the Versions preserve what seemed to be a preferable reading. In Genesis 4:8, for example, with the Samaritan Pentateuch and some of the Versions, NIV adds "Let's go out to the field," which is lacking in the MT. In Genesis 4:15, where the MT reads *lākēn* ("thus, therefore"), some of the Versions read the equivalent of *lō' kēn* "Not so," which NIV follows. In Psalm 19:4 (Hebrew: vs. 5) MT has *qawwām* "their line"; some of the Versions attest "their voice," which seems preferable, and which NIV adopts. In Psalm 49:11a (Hebrew: vs. 12a) MT has "their thoughts *(qirbām)* are their homes forever"; the reading of Septuagint and Syriac seems preferable, "their tombs *(qibrām)* are their homes forever." See also Psalm 22:16 (Hebrew: vs. 17); 24:6b.

But one looks in vain for anything that is *labeled* a conjecture. 1 Samuel 13:1 for example, appears as follows:

> Saul was ⌊thirty⌋[a] years old when he became king, and he reigned over Israel ⌊forty-⌋[b] two years.
>
> [a]1 A few late manuscripts of the Septuagint; Hebrew does not have *thirty*.
> [b]1 See the round number in Acts 13:21; Hebrew does not have *forty-*.

In this passage the Hebrew text is defective; MT says that Saul was one year old when he became king and he ruled over Israel two years. The Targum explains: "Saul was innocent as a child a year old when he began to reign." The Hebrew text says that Saul reigned two years; the NIV text "forty-two years" is clearly a conjecture, and the reference to the "forty years" in Acts 13:21 as a "round number" is curious.

The use of lower half-brackets is explained in the Preface (p. x): "To achieve clarity the translators supplied words not in the original texts but required by the context. If there was uncertainty about such material, it is enclosed in brackets." But this definition does not square with the use of the half-brackets in 1 Samuel 13:1.

Another such example is to be found in 2 Kings 6:33, where the MT reads "the messenger arrived and said"; the words that follow, however, are manifestly spoken by the king of Israel, not by the messenger himself. NIV has ". . . the messenger came down to him [that is, Elijah]. And ⌊the king⌋ said. . . ."

In most instances the half-brackets seem quite unnecessary. Some examples may be given: "the wings of ⌊my⌋ dove" (Ps. 68:13 [Hebrew: vs. 14]); "will possess ⌊the land⌋ as far as Zarephath" (Obad. 20); "I will not turn back ⌊my wrath⌋" (Amos 1:3, 6, 9, 11, 13; 2:1, 4, 6); "to alienate you ⌊from us⌋" (Gal. 4:17); "for ⌊that day will not come⌋ until" (2 Thess. 2:3); "⌊This matter arose⌋ because" (Gal. 2:4). This is a needless and distracting device, of interest only to scholars, who by definition are able to assess such matters on their own. It resembles the King James Version habit of printing in italics the words for which there were no lexical equivalents in the original text.

In some places the NIV takes into account the *tiqqune sopherim* ("corrections of the scribes"). (Reliable information concerning this phenomenon can be found in Carmel McCarthy's article, "Emendations of the Scribes," in *The Interpreter's Dictionary of the Bible,* Supplementary Volume, pp. 263-264.—Ed.) In Job 32:3, for example, the MT is translated in the NIV text: "they had found no way to refute Job, and yet they had condemned him"; the footnote reads: "Masoretic Text; an ancient Hebrew scribal tradition, *Job, and so had condemned God.*" According to an ancient scribal tradition Genesis 18:22 had once read "Yahweh remained standing before Abraham." This was changed by the Masoretic scribes (a *tiqqun*) to "Abraham remained standing before Yahweh." NIV translates the MT, which reflects the scribal change, and cites the tradition of an earlier reading in a footnote, again as "an ancient Hebrew scribal tradition." In Hosea 4:7 the earlier text had read, according to tradition, "they changed my glory into shame"; this was changed by the Masoretic scribes to "I will change their glory into shame." Here NIV retains "they exchanged" from the uncorrected pre-Masoretic text but combines this phrase with "their glory" from the scribally corrected MT.

The translators' Greek text of the New Testament was an eclectic one, and the Preface (p. ix) states that they used "the best current printed texts of the Greek New Testament." Mark 16:9-20 is separated from 16:8 by a space and a line, with the information: "the two most reliable early manuscripts do not have Mark 16:9-20." John 7:53—8:11 is set off from the rest of the text by a space and a line, with a note at the top: "The earliest and most reliable manuscripts do not have John 7:53—8:11." John 5:3b-4 is omitted from the text, as are most other *Textus Receptus* scribal additions, even where complete verses are involved (see Luke 23:16; Acts 8:36). The doxology of the Lord's prayer (Matt. 6:13) is given in a footnote (identified as being in "some late manuscripts"). The *Textus Receptus* addition in 1 John 5:7-8 is given in a footnote as appearing in "late manuscripts of the Vulgate."

In John 7:8 the NIV translators prefer the easier reading *oupō* "not yet," instead of the harder reading *ouk* "not," assigning the latter to a footnote. In Matthew 27:16-17 not even in footnote does the NIV indicate that according to some witnesses Barabbas' given name was Jesus. And in Luke 10:1, 17 the number 72 is preferred, with the number 70 appearing in footnote as an alternate reading.

Exegesis

The exegesis of the text is essentially conservative, that is, there is no determined attempt to break new ground in understanding and representing the meaning of the original text. The beginning of the Bible reads in a familiar fashion (in contrast to other recent translations such as NJV):

> In the beginning God created the heavens and the earth. [2]Now the earth was[a] formless and empty, darkness was over the surface of the deep, and the Spirit of God was hovering over the waters.
>
> [a]2 Or possibly *became*

Genesis 3:15 differs little from what has become traditional (in contrast to other recent translations such as NEB):

> And I will put enmity
> between you and the woman,
> and between your offspring[a] and hers;
> he will crush[b] your head,
> and you will strike his heel.
>
> [a]15 Or *seed* [b]15 Or *strike*

Psalm 2:12 is translated: "Kiss the Son, lest he be angry / and you be destroyed in your way, / for his wrath can flare up in a moment. / Blessed are all who take refuge in him." The use of initial capital letters in "the Son," "his Anointed One" (vs. 2), "my King" (vs. 6), and "my Son" (vs. 7), clearly reflects Christian bias in the interpretation of this Hebrew psalm, as also "your Holy One" in Psalm 16:10, seen above.

The problematic third line in Genesis 49:10 is not translated according to traditional exegesis. NIV has "until he comes to whom it belongs," with the traditional "until Shiloh comes" in a footnote. In Psalm 105:28b the MT reads "for they did not rebel against his words." This is difficult to understand, since the subject of the verb is the Egyptians. Some have conjectured that instead of *mārû* "rebelled," *shām*ʿ*rû* should be read: "they did not keep his commands." But there is no manuscript witness for this reading. The Versions offer a different text: Septuagint and Syriac omit the negative *lō'*, which results in "for they rebelled against his words," the text favored by the majority of modern translations (e.g., RSV). NIV stays with the MT, but interprets it as a rhetorical question: "for had they not rebelled against his words?" This may be possible, but seems highly unlikely. This is also how the New Jewish Version translates this passage, but it does add in a footnote: "Meaning of Hebrew uncertain."

Where the meaning of the text was considered uncertain, a footnote may indicate this: "The meaning of the Hebrew for this word [or "sentence" or "phrase"] is uncertain" (see, for example, Eccles. 2:5; Jer. 8:13, 18; Amos 3:12; 9:6).

In the genealogical list from Shem to Abraham, in Genesis 11:10-27, NIV suggests that the Hebrew "father" in verses 10-25 may be understood to mean "ancestor." But it seems highly unlikely that men at the age of 35, 34, 32, 30, and 29 years could have been ancestors; perhaps grandfathers, but hardly ancestors.

In the New Testament the problems of determining the meaning of the original text are not nearly so great as they are in the Old Testament. The Greek *sarx* in Romans 7—8 and Galatians 5—6 is translated "sinful nature," with "flesh" as an alternative in footnotes. Glossolalia in 1 Corinthians 12—14 is represented by "speak in (a) tongue(s)" in the text, with footnotes giving the alternative "other/another language(s)." The same is done for the manifestation of the Spirit at Pentecost, in Acts 2:4: "speak in other tongues" appears in the text, with a footnote: "Or *languages.*"

The family of words *hilasmos, hilaskomai,* and *hilastērion* (Rom. 3:25; 1 John 2:2; 4:10; Heb. 2:17) is translated "an atoning sacrifice," with an alternative in footnote, "turn aside God's wrath, taking away our sins."

When applied to Christ, *monogenēs* is translated "one and only Son," with a footnote: "only begotten Son" (John 1:14; 3:16, 18; 1 John 4:9). In the case of Isaac (Heb. 11:17), he is Abraham's "one and only son," with no alternative in a footnote.

One rather unusual device is the use of quotation marks to set off a word or phrase which the translators judge is being used in a sense different from the normal one. In Matthew 9:10, 11 (and parallels) the text reads:

> [10]While Jesus was having dinner at Matthew's house, many tax collectors and "sinners" came and ate with him and his disciples. [11]When the Pharisees saw this, they asked his disciples, "Why does your teacher eat with tax collectors and 'sinners'?"

Surely a footnote is required explaining what is meant by "sinners" in quotation marks, since, in English, the use of such marks indicates either that the writer is being facetious, not really meaning what he writes, or else that the word so marked is regularly used in a different sense. If the Greek *hamartōloi* does not mean what the English word *sinners* means, then a faithful translation should use another word.

Similarly Matthew 6:1 has: "Be careful not to do your 'acts of righteousness' before men, to be seen by them." In the same way "gods" appears in quotation marks in Psalm 82:1, 6 as well as in the quotation of Psalm 82:6 in John 10:34. One curious instance is the use of quotation marks with "seven(s)" in Daniel 9:24-27. In Revelation 1:13; 14:14 "like a son of man" appears within quotation marks.

Cultural Features

For terms of distances and measures, NIV sometimes provides the American equivalent in the text and in a footnote gives the Hebrew or Greek form and the metric equivalent. This is done in Genesis 6:15-16 for measurements of Noah's ark. In Luke 24:13 the text has "about seven miles" as the distance from Jerusalem to Emmaus; the footnote reads: "Greek *sixty stadia* (about 11 kilometers)." John 2:5 has "from twenty to thirty gallons" in the text, and the footnote has "Greek *two to three metretes* (probably about 75 to 115 liters)."

But sometimes the Greek or Hebrew term is given in the text, with the modern equivalents appearing in footnotes. Acts 1:12 gives the distance from the Mount of Olives to Jerusalem as "a Sabbath day's walk," with the modern equivalent in a footnote. In Revelation 14:20; 21:16, 17 the text has the Greek terms: 1,600 stadia, 12,000 stadia, and 144 cubits. The measurements for the tabernacle, the ark of the covenant, and the furnishings for the tabernacle in Exodus 25—27, 36—38 are all given in terms of cubits, as are the measurements for Solomon's temple and palace in 1 Kings 6—7 (and parallel 2 Chron. 3—4) and the measurements of the new Temple and land in Ezekiel 40—48.

In the New Testament, except for the passages noted above, measurements of length, distance, capacity and weight are all given their modern equivalents in the text. Modern equivalents, however, are not used for hours of the day or days of the week. The days always appear in the New Testament as "Preparation day," "Sabbath," and "the first day of the week." And the hours are always in terms of the Greek divisions: "tenth hour" (John 1:39), "third hour," "sixth hour," and "ninth hour" (Mark 15:25, 33, 34). The same is done in the parable of the workers in the vineyard (Matt. 20:1-16).

In some instances modern names are given for areas and countries, but this is not consistently done. "Cush" appears in the OT with a footnote: "the upper Nile region" (and see Acts 8:27); in Genesis 2:13, however, the footnote reads "Possibly southeast Mesopotamia." In the NT the traditional "the Sea of Galilee" is used as a name, but when that body of water is referred to it is called a lake.

Yam suph in the OT is always translated "the Red Sea," accompanied by a footnote: "Hebrew *Yam Suph;* that is, Sea of Reeds" (and see also Acts 7:36; Heb. 11:29).

The use of the nonce word "kinsman-redeemer" to translate *gō'ēl* in Ruth (see 2:20; 3:8,12; 4:1,3,8) does not seem a happy decision. In Job 19:25 it is translated "my Redeemer." (Cf. the discussion of "your Holy One" in Ps. 16:10, above.) The sacrifices known as *sh^elāmîm* are translated "fellowship offerings," with the traditional term "peace offerings" given in footnote (see 1 Kings 8:63,64). The Hebrew *ḥerem* is translated "devoted thing(s)," accompanied by a good explanatory footnote (see Josh. 7:1; 8:26).

It would seem that "prayer shawls" in Matthew 23:5 is an anachronism. For some reason "Mary Magdalene" is used in the Synoptics, but in John she appears as "Mary of Magdala."

Translation

The NIV translators did not see their task as that of trying to reproduce the Hebrew (and Aramaic) and Greek texts by a literal rendition. "They have striven for more than word-for-word translation. Because thought patterns and syntax differ from language to language, faithful communication of the meaning of the writers of the Bible demands frequent modifications in sentence structure and constant regard for the contextual meaning of words" (Preface, p. viii).

The NIV is certainly less literal than the RSV. A comparison of the translation of Galatians 3:2-5 in both versions will make this evident:

RSV	*NIV*
Let me ask you only this: Did you receive the Spirit by works of the law, or by hearing with faith? Are you so foolish? Having begun with the Spirit, are you now ending with the flesh? Did you experience so many things in vain?—if it really is in vain? Does he who supplies the Spirit to you and works miracles among you do so by works of the law, or by hearing with faith?	I would like to learn just one thing from you: Did you receive the Spirit by observing the law, or by believing what you heard? Are you so foolish? After beginning with the Spirit, are you trying to attain your goal by human effort? Have you suffered so much for nothing—if it really was for nothing? Does God give you his Spirit and work miracles among you because you observe the law, or because you believe what you heard?

But literalism still appears in the NIV, such as the titles "Daughter of Tarshish" (Isa. 23:10), "Virgin Daughter of Sidon" (Isa. 23:12), "The Daughter of Tyre" (Ps. 45:12 [Hebrew: vs. 13]), "Daughter of the Babylonians" (Isa. 47:1). The literal "horn" continues to show up: "by your favor exalt our horn" (Ps. 89:17 [Hebrew: vs. 18]; see also 89:24 [Hebrew: vs. 25]; 112:9; 132:17; 148:14; Luke 1:69). This translation gets rid of "gird up your loins" (see 2 Kings 4:29, "Tuck your cloak into your belt"; see also 1 Kings 18:46), for which it is to be congratulated. Surely it would have been advisable to get rid also of "horn(s)." "Anointing you with the oil of joy" (Ps. 45:7 [Hebrew: vs. 8]; Heb. 1:8) is translationese, as is "the firstfruits of all their manhood" in Psalm 105:36.

Some passages are painfully literal. Romans 3:18 (quoting Ps. 36:1 [Hebrew: vs. 2]) reads, "There is no fear of God before their eyes." The structure and form of the underlying Hebrew appear quite plainly. Ephesians 1:18 has "the riches of his glorious inheritance in the saints." Romans 3:25 reads: "God presented him as a sacrifice of atonement, through faith in his blood." The structure of the English sentence misleadingly requires that "faith" have God as subject. Luke 9:55-56 translates the Greek literally: "But Jesus turned and rebuked them, and they went to another village." In English this can only mean that "they" are the same ones referred to by "them," that is, James and John; the meaning that comes from the English text is that Jesus rebuked James and John and so only these two went off to another village.

Psalm 147:10 is needlessly literal: "His pleasure is not in the strength of the horse, / nor his delight in the legs of a man." The chiasmus in Matthew 7:6 is disregarded, so that pigs continue to attack people and tear them to pieces.

1 Samuel 14 reports a battle that the Israelites, under the command of Saul, waged against the Philistines. In verse 3 we read that the priest Ahijah was wearing (or carrying) an ephod—the means for obtaining an oracle from Yahweh. At the appropriate time (vs. 18) Saul told Ahijah to bring it to him. (There the MT has "the ark of God" instead of "ephod." There are various explanations for the change in vocabulary; LXX has "ephod.") Just as Ahijah was preparing to seek divine direction by means of the Urim and Thummim, the noise from the Philistine camp indicated that they were ready to attack. So Saul told Ahijah to desist from seeking the divine guidance. In the Hebrew text Saul's words are, "Take away your hand." The literal translation in the NIV will leave all readers, except scholars, quite perplexed. "While Saul was talking to the priest, the tumult in the Philistine camp increased more and more. So Saul said to the priest, 'Withdraw your hand.' " The reader is left to wonder what Ahjah was grabbing at. This is a literal translation that conveys no meaning to the modern reader.

Galatians 3:16, 29 speak of Abraham's "seed" (and "the Seed" in 3:19), but in the OT passages the Hebrew word is translated "offspring" (see Gen. 12:7; 13:15; 24:7).

As is to be expected, the translation represents a conservative point of view. Few passages will cause much difficulty with conservatives, and in some instances it appears that a special effort has been made to avoid any controversy. Such seems the case in Isaiah 7:14 and Psalm 16:10, seen above. But not always does NIV represent such a tendency. The quotation of (part of) Micah 5:2 in Matthew 2:6 as a messianic prophecy has led many to read Micah 5:2 as a specific reference to Christ, so that the last two lines (not quoted in Matt.) of the verse are read in that light. The King James Version translates: "whose goings forth *have been* from of old, from everlasting," and this has been taken to refer to the eternal preexistence of Christ. The RSV was strongly criticized for translating "whose origin is from of old, from ancient days." NIV has translated, "whose origins[d] are from of old, from ancient times.[e]" (Footnotes: *d* "Hebrew *goings out.*" *e* "Or *from days of eternity.*")

It is rather surprising that the NIV, at this late date, is apparently quite insensitive to the change that has been taking place in American English concerning what some choose to call male-oriented language. No longer are "man" and "men" seen by many persons to be generic terms, including people of both sexes, but as referring exclusively to people of the male sex. The same is true of "he" and "him." At times the NIV seems to be aware of the changed situation, but in too many places "man" and "men" occur where it would have been a more faithful translation to use expressions and terms which include both sexes. Psalm 1:1 begins "Blessed is the man who . . ." and Isaiah 40:6 reads "All men are like grass. . . ." In the Sermon on the Mount the disciples are enjoined, "let your light shine before men" (Matt. 5:16); see also "trampled by men" (5:13); "do your 'acts of righteousness' before men" (6:1); "honored by men" (6:2); "to be seen by men" (6:5); "if you forgive men" (6:14); "if you do not forgive men" (6:15); "to show men they are fasting" (6:16); "it will not be obvious to men" (6:18); "all men will hate you" (10:22); "acknowledges me before men" (10:32); "disowns me before men" (10:33).

It is significant that the RSV committee has already announced it will attempt to eliminate all unnecessary male-oriented language in the forthcoming revision of the text. Surely the NIV committee should resolve to do the same.

Style

The translators stated that in matters of style their purpose was that the English should be "clear and natural . . . idiomatic but not idiosyncratic, contemporary but not dated." The archaic "thou," "thee" and "thine" have been discarded, along with corresponding archaic forms of the verbs. Given the differences between American and British English, a British edition has been prepared which "reflects the comparatively few differences of significant idiom and spelling" (Preface, p. viii).

The language is not always today's English, and the style is not always that of current usage, and presumably the translators were aware of this. But in general the language is appropriate to the kind of translation aimed at, that is a translation that seeks to preserve "some measure of continuity with the long tradition of translating the Scriptures into English." For those who are used to the Bible in the King James Version or the Revised Standard Version, this translation sounds like the Bible.

The NIV is closer in style and form to the RSV than to any other English version. It is an irony worth pondering: this Bible came into being as the result of the repudiation of the RSV by the majority of conservative Protestants in this country, and now that it has appeared it closely resembles the RSV. The principles that guided it in textual, exegetical, linguistic and stylistic matters are hardly distinguishable from those which guided the RSV. The average Bible reader, hearing the reading of Psalm 46, would not be able to tell whether it was the RSV or the NIV, so much alike are the two. And except for the "thous" and "thys" in verses 4-5, Psalm 23 is practically the same in the two versions.

To sum up one's impression after spending some time with this translation: The NIV is the product of careful and conscientious scholarship; while still too closely tied in form to the underlying Hebrew and Greek structures, it is nonetheless a significant achievement, and its appearance is an occasion for rejoicing. It is to be hoped that at long last the NIV will once and for all lay to final rest the still widespread belief that the King James Version is the original Word of God and that any translation that differs from it is a perversion, a devil's masterpiece produced by people with a low view of Scripture.

Participants in the New International Version Translation Project

Edwin H. Palmer, Executive Secretary and Coordinator

COMMITTEE ON BIBLE TRANSLATION: Kenneth L. Barker (Dallas Theol. Sem.), Ralph Earle (Nazarene Theol. Sem.), Burton L. Goddard (Gordon-Conwell Theol. Sem.), R. Laird Harris (Covenant Theol. Sem.), Earl S. Kalland (Conserv. Bapt. Theol. Sem.), Youngve R. Kindberg (President, New York International Bible Society), Richard N. Longenecker (Wycliffe Coll., Univ. of Toronto), William J. Martin (Regent Coll., Vancouver), Stephen W. Paine (Houghton Coll.), Robert Preus (Concordia Theol. Sem.), John H. Stek (Calvin Theol. Sem.), Larry L. Walker (Southw. Bapt. Theol. Sem.), J. C. Wenger (Goshen Bibl. Sem.), Marten H. Woudstra (Calvin Theol. Sem.)

OTHER TRANSLATORS AND EDITORS: Robert L. Alden (Conserv. Bapt. Theol. Sem.), Gleason L. Archer (Trin.Evangel. Div. Sch.), Glenn W.Barker (Fuller Theol. Sem.), James Battenfield (Grace Theol. Sem.), S. Herbert Bess (Grace Theol. Sem.), Harvey J. S. Blaney (Asbury Theol. Sem.), W. Gordon Brown (Central Bapt. Sem., Toronto), Donald W. Burdick (Conserv. Bapt. Theol. Sem.), Frederic W. Bush (Fuller Theol. Sem.), E. Leslie Carlson (Southw. Bapt. Theol. Sem.), Philip S. Clapp (West. Evangel. Sem.), Edmund Clowney (Westmin. Theol. Sem.), Ralph R. Covell (Conserv. Bapt. Theol. Sem.), John J. Davis (Grace Theol. Sem.), Wilber T. Dayton (Wesley Bibl. Sem.), Raymond Dillard (Westmin. Theol. Sem.), David Englehard (Calvin Theol. Sem.), Milton Fisher (Ref. Episc. Sem.), Lewis A. Foster (Cincinnati Bible Sem.), Francis Foulkes (Bible Coll. of New Zealand), Richard B. Gaffin (Westmin. Theol. Sem.), Wesley L. Gerig (Fort Wayne Bible Coll.), Donald Glenn (Dallas Theol. Sem.), Louis Goldberg (Moody Bible Inst.), David Gooding (Queens Coll., Belfast, Ire.), Clarence B. Hale (Wheaton Coll.), Murray J. Harris (Trin. Evangel. Div. Sch.), Everett Harrison (Fuller Theol. Sem.), Roland K. Harrison (Wycliffe Coll., Toronto), Gerald F. Hawthorne (Wheaton Coll.), Roy E. Hayden (Oral Roberts Univ.), William Hendriksen (Boca Raton, Fla.), D. Edmond Hiebert (Mennonite Brethren Bibl. Sem.), Mark E. Hillmer (Northw. Luth. Theol. Sem.), F. B. Huey (Southw. Bapt. Theol. Sem.), John C. Jeske (Wis. Luth. Sem.), S. Lewis Johnson (Dallas, Tex.), Walter C. Kaiser (Trin. Evangel. Div. Sch.), Kenneth S. Kantzer (Trin. Evangel. Div. Sch.), Homer A. Kent (Grace Theol. Sem.), F. Derek Kidner (Tyndale House, Cambridge, Eng.), Simon Kistemaker (Ref. Theol. Sem.), Meredith G. Kline (Gordon-Conwell Theol. Sem.), Fred C. Kuehner* (Ref. Episc. Sem.), William L. Lane (West. Ky. Univ.), G. Irvin Lehman (East. Mennonite Coll.), Paul E. Leonard (Trin. Evangel. Div. Sch.), Arthur H. Lewis (Bethel Theol. Sem.), Jack P. Lewis (Harding Grad. Sch. of Relig.), Walter L. Liefield (Trin. Evangel. Div. Sch.), G. Herbert Livingston (Asbury Theol. Sem.), Allan A. MacRae (Bibl. Sch. of Theol.), Donald H. Madvig (Bethel Theol. Sem.), W. Harold Mare (Covenant Theol. Sem.), Thomas E. McComiskey (Trin. Evangel. Div. Sch.), J. Ramsey Michaels (Gordon-Conwell Theol. Sem.), A. R. Millard (Univ. of Liverpool, Eng.), Leon Morris (Ridley Coll., Melbourne, Aus.), Robert Mounce (West. Ky. Univ.), Roger Nicole (Gordon-Conwell Theol. Sem.), John Oswalt (Asbury Theol. Sem.), J. Barton Payne (Covenant Theol. Sem.), Stephen Reynolds (Glenside, Pa.), Charles Pfeiffer* (Central Mich. Univ.), Robert P. Roth (Northw. Luth. Sem.), Charles Ryrie (Dallas Theol. Sem.), Jack B. Scott (Ref. Theol. Sem.), Elmer B. Smick (Gordon-Conwell Theol. Sem.), Francis Steele (Upper Darby, Pa.), Harold G. Stigers (Covenant Theol. Sem.), Marvin E. Tate (South. Bapt. Theol. Sem.), G. Aiken Taylor (Asheville, N.C.), Merrill C. Tenney (Wheaton Coll.), Gerard Van Groningen (Ref. Theol. Sem.), Wilbur B. Wallis (Covenant Theol. Sem.), Bruce K. Waltke (Regent Coll., Vancouver), Rowland Ward (Australia), G. Henry Waterman* (Wheaton Coll.), John Werner (International Linguistics Center), Walter W. Wessel (Bethel

Coll.), David J. Williams (South Calif. Coll.), Marvin R. Wilson (Gordon Coll.), Donald J. Wiseman (Univ. of London, Eng.), Herbert M. Wolf (Wheaton Coll.), Leon J. Wood* (Grand Rapids Bapt. Bible Sem.), Ronald Youngblood (Bethel Theol. Sem.), John M. Zinkand (Dordt Coll.)

*deceased

LITERARY CRITICS AND OTHER CONSULTANTS: Edward M. Blaiklock (Univ. of Aukland, New Zealand), Frank E. Gaebelein (Headmaster Emeritus, The Stony Brook School), Charles Hummel (Intervarsity Christian Fellowship), Dennis F. Kinlaw (Asbury Theol. Sem.), Elisabeth E. Leith (South Hamilton, Mass.), Calvin Linton (George Wash. Univ.), Kathryn Ludwigson (Grand Rapids Bapt. Bible Coll.), Alvin Martin (Fuller Theol. Sem.), Virginia Mollenkott (William Patterson Coll.), W. T. Purkiser (Kansas City, Mo.), Palmer Robertson (Westmin. Theol. Sem.), Walter R. Roehrs (Concordia Theol. Sem.), Samuel J. Schultz (Wheaton Coll.), Margaret Nicholson Smith (Editor, *American-English Usage*), John J. Timmerman (Calvin Coll.), Richard F. Wevers (Calvin Coll.)

(Information above provided by the New York International Bible Society)

11
Study Bibles

Robert G. Bratcher

Most English translations of the Bible are provided with footnotes of various kinds: textual variations, alternative renderings, and sometimes a few cultural and historical notes. Many Bibles also have references to other passages in the Scriptures which bear upon a particular verse or statement. An increasing number of Bibles have more extensive helps for the reader, and these are usually called "Study Bibles" or "Annotated Bibles." This chapter will look at some of the Study Bibles most widely used today.

The New Oxford Annotated Bible with the Apocrypha
Revised Standard Version
(New York: Oxford University Press, 1977)

This Study Bible provides two introductory articles, one on the Old Testament (including a separate brief introduction to the Pentateuch), the other on the New Testament. In addition, at the end of the New Testament there are six special articles, all of them written by well-known biblical scholars, whose names are given in "The Editors' Preface" (p. ix).

It should be explained that in this volume the sixty-six book Bible and all the editoral material pertaining to it appear as a unit, pp. i-xxviii and 1-1564. Then, as a separate work in the same volume, comes "The Apocrypha, Expanded Edition, Revised Standard Version," pp. i-xxiv and 1-340. In this volume "The Bible" and "The Apocrypha" are two separate collections of books. At the very end of the volume appear two sets of maps, "The New Oxford Bible Maps" and its index, and "The New Oxford Apocrypha Maps" and its index.

H. H. Rowley's article on "How to Read the Bible with Understanding" is a model of valuable guidance lucidly and succinctly presented. Any reader who takes the time to ponder what he says will read the Bible with a much greater degree of understanding and profit. As the subtitle of the article indicates ("The Diversity and the Unity of the Scriptures"), Rowley is at pains to point out that there are certain themes in the Bible which, notwithstanding all its diversity, give it unity. "In both Testaments it is the same God who is revealed, and this above all else gives unity to the Bible."

Roland E. Murphy's article "Modern Approaches to Biblical Study" explains the various ways in which the biblical material can be studied by means of literary criticism, form criticism, redaction criticism, and transmission (or tradition) history.

The other articles, "Characteristics of Hebrew Poetry" by George W. Anderson, "Literary Forms in the Gospels" by Bruce M. Metzger, and "Survey of the Geography, History, and Archaeology of the Bible Lands" by Georges A. Barrois, provide an admirable summary of an immense amount of technical information. The last article, "English Versions of the Bible," was written by Luther A. Weigle, who was the general chair of the Revised Standard Version Committee. He traces the history of the translation of the Bible into English from the earliest Anglo-Saxon paraphrases in the seventh century to modern times. A table of "Measures and Weights in the Bible" and a "Chronological Table of Rulers" are the last special articles. A useful "Index to the Annotations" and twelve maps bring the volume to a close.

For the section "The Apocrypha" there is an introductory article by the editor, Bruce M. Metzger, which deals not only with the apocrypha (or the deuterocanonical books, as Catholics prefer to call them) but also with some pseudepigraphical writings. There is a "Chronological Table of Rulers," a useful tabulation of the titles given to books associated with Ezra and Nehemiah, and an Index to the Annotations. One fascinating bit of information concerns Christopher Columbus. 2 Esdras 6:42 states that the land surface of the globe is six-sevenths of its total area, while the seas cover only one-seventh of the surface. On the basis of this information Columbus figured that it would take only a few days of good sailing weather for him to reach the Indies, by sailing west. "It was partly by quoting this verse from what was regarded as an authoritative book that Columbus managed to persuade Ferdinand and Isabella of Spain to provide the necessary financial support for his voyage" (*Apocrypha,* p. 22).

Every book is provided with an introduction, all of which are about the same length (half a page). For many books the space provided for the introduction is adequate, but for others it is quite insufficient. It would appear that considerations of space were uppermost, and the various writers were strictly limited on the length of the introductions.

The introduction to Daniel explains that the book is not actual history. It appears under the name of an ancient worthy, Daniel or Dan'el, twice referred to in Ezekiel (14:14; 28:3). The author is a pious Jew who lived at the time of Antiochus Epiphanes, 167-165 B.C. The notes for the text reflect this understanding of the book, and explain the various figures and time periods in terms of the sufferings and hopes of pious Jews in a time of persecution and suffering.

For the purpose of this survey, the annotations which appear at the bottom of the pages are of greater interest. The reader may judge the quantity and the quality of this material by looking at one passage, Mark 1:14-39. The entire section is entitled "Beginnings of Jesus' Activity in Galilee." Although the Matthaean and Lucan parallels of the various smaller units in this section are given, no mention is made of Matthew 14:12-25 as a parallel to the whole section. The notes are as follows: (1) For *verses 14-15* the parallel passages Matthew 4:12-17 and Luke 4:14-15 are cited. Nothing is said about verse 14, not even the phrase "the gospel of God." Verse 15 is explained as the summary of Jesus' message, and *Repent* is explained; "return to God's way"; *believe the gospel* is defined as "accept the message," and reference is made to the note at Matthew 4:17, which gives an excellent brief explanation of the phrase "the kingdom of heaven" in Matthew (equivalent to "the kingdom of God" in Mark). The reader who fails to turn back to the note at Matthew 4:17 will be deprived of valuable information on the scope of Jesus' message, especially in terms of the temporal element of the kingdom of God. (2) For *verses 16-20* the parallels in the other Gospels are given. Actually only the passage in Matthew is strictly parallel; the passages in Luke (5:1-11) and John (1:35-42) recount the call of the first disciples, but under quite different circumstances. (3) *Verses 21-22* are separated from verses 23-28, which at first seems odd, since 21-22 set the stage for the encounter with the demon-possessed man in the Capernaum synagogue. The reason for this is that there is a parallel to these verses in Matthew 7:28-29, although in a different setting, namely, the conclusion of the Sermon on the Mount. (4) For *verses 23-28* the parallel in Luke 4:33-37 is given, and there is a note on *unclean spirit,* stating that it was so called because its effect was "to separate man from the worship of God." One wonders whether the average reader will fully understand the implication of the explanation. A note on the explanation seems needed. Verse 27 refers the reader to the note at Matthew 7:29, which speaks of Jesus' authority in teaching. In light of the previous reference to Matthew 7:28-29 this seems rather otiose. (5) *Verses 29-34* give references to the parallels in Matthew and Luke, and at verse 32 it is explained: "The sabbath ended at sunset." What this intends to communicate is that the Sabbath laws prohibited people from bringing their sick friends and relatives to Jesus on that day; after sundown, when the Sabbath ended, they could do so. Again one wonders if the average reader understands what the note is intended to say. Verse 34 refers to the note at verses 43-44. (6) *Verses 35-39* give the parallels in Matthew and Luke. Verse 35 refers to a note at Luke 3:21, which lists other occasions when Jesus prayed. A note at verse 38 explains "I came out" as a reference to Jesus' departure from Capernaum.

For this short paragraph, then, quite a bit of information is supplied. Two of the notes are so brief as to be of little use for the average reader. And notes are missing for the following: "The time is fulfilled" and "(the kingdom of God) is at hand" in verse 14; "What have you to do with us?," "us" and "the Holy One of God" in verse 24.

Rarely will a note disagree with the exegesis followed in the text. But at Galatians 4:3 the note on "the elemental spirits of the universe" observes: "a better translation is 'rudimentary notions of the world,' referring to elementary religious observances (vss. 9-10; Col. 2:8, 20)."

The New English Bible with the Apocrypha
Oxford Study Edition
(New York: Oxford University Press, 1976)

The arrangement for this volume is somewhat different from that of the Revised Standard Version Annotated Edition. The Old Testament is numbered pp. 1-1033; then come the Apocrypha, pp. 1-257; then the New Testament, pp. 1-333; and finally the Special Articles, pp. 1-62.

There are Introductory articles to the Old Testament (G. R. Driver), the Pentateuch (Lloyd R. Bailey), and the Apocrypha (W. D. McHardy); "The Place of the Apocrypha" (Arnold J. Tkacik); and an Introduction to the New Testament (C. H. Dodd).

In their essay on "Reading the Bible," the three editors (Samuel Sandmel, M. Jack Suggs, and Tkacik) try to help today's readers cross the barriers of time and culture which separate them from the biblical writers. To achieve this a lively and creative imagination is needed. But there is also some basic knowledge about the Bible without which a reader can easily misunderstand the text. The writers define inspiration both as the divine influence on the biblical writer and the quality of genius which may be manifested in works of art or architecture or space travel. Both senses of inspiration apply to the biblical literature.

"Literary Forms of the Bible" by Gene M. Tucker and Leander E. Keck considers the Bible as a whole, including the canon, the order of books in the Old Testament and the New Testament, and the kinds of literature in the Bible. In a brief consideration of authorship, the point is made that for most of the books of the Bible we should not think in terms of creative writing but "of creative editing done within the context of communities of faith" (p. 10). There are five kinds of books in the Bible: narrative works, poetic books, prophetic books, letters (in the New Testament) and apocalypses.

The writers then turn their attention to the various genres within books: narratives; prophetic genres; legal genres; widsom and instruction, including parables, sermons (which are not what we call sermons but "extended religious discourses"), prayers, hymns, and rituals. The writers conclude: "Posing these literary questions—What kind of text is it? Where did it come from? How was it used?—enables the texts to speak to us, and not simply to reflect our own expectations of them. By looking at the Bible in this way our appreciation and understanding of it should be both broadened and deepened" (p. 24).

The article by John J. Dreese, "A Sketch of the History and Geography of the Lands of the Bible," is quite brief (ten pages). What is missing, and is greatly to be desired, is the inclusion, preferably in tabular form, of the dates of the apperance of the canonical literature, or books, into the chronological record of people and events. Every now and then a hint is given. For example, in describing the exile and restoration, the writer says: "Out of the successively collected records of Israel's past and the writings of the scribes, the book we now know as the Bible began to take shape" (p. 31). Of course the introduction to each separate book gives the date of its appearance; but it would be very helpful if such data were included in the outline of the history of Israel and of the Church.

"Reckoning Time" (by Tkacik) and a "Selected Index to People, Places, and Themes of the Bible" (by Richard V. Bergren) are the last two special articles. Nine maps, preceded by an Index, bring the volume to a close.

Let us examine some of the notes in Genesis 1—3, as a sample. The introduction to Genesis refers to the introduction to the Pentateuch, where the reader is given a brief account of the various literary strands, beginning with J in the tenth century B.C., which were drawn into the making of the Torah, which was given its final written shape "after the Babylonian Exile," that is, after 538 B.C. The book of Genesis has two main parts: the primeval history (1—11) and the history of the patriarchs (12—50). The latter "can be placed in the context of the known history of the Ancient Near East (2000–1500 B.C.)."

(1) *1:1—2:4: The creation account, composed by priests. 1:* The usual explanation of this verse is that it implies creation *ex nihilo*—and reference is made to 2 Maccabees 7:28 (could not Heb. 11:3 also be cited?). *2: Abyss, Wind:* these are "portrayed as creations, subject to God." That they are subject to God seems evident; it is not so evident that they are portrayed as having been created by God.

(2) *2:5—3:24: A second account of primeval time.* Explanations (in 2:5-9) are given for *LORD God, Flood, Dust, Living creature; Eden, garden;* and *Tree of Life.* One misses a note on "the tree of the knowledge of good and evil," especially since it figures prominently in the story of the Fall in chapter 3 (also 2:17). What does it mean to "be like gods knowing both good and evil" (3:5; see 3:22)? Most readers will assume that only by eating the fruit

of the tree of the knowledge of good and evil was the human creature enabled to distinguish between right and wrong; before that he was an innocent child, so far as moral distinctions are concerned. Is that the point of the story? *Certainly die* (vs. 17) is explained as "become mortal." This seems to imply that the man and the woman were created immortal. What, then, is the meaning of 3:22? Here it is said that by eating the fruit of the tree of life they would become immortal.

In chapter 3, verses 14-19 are of the greatest interest and call for careful explanation. To be told that these are etiological tales, explaining why human beings and snakes are enemies, why childbirth is painful, and so forth, is most helpful. One wishes more, however, especially at verse 15, which speaks of the enmity between the serpent's "brood" and the woman's "brood" (to use the NEB language, which here is singularly infelicitous). In 3:21, under *Adam* it is said: "the word 'man' occurs here for the first time without a definite article, becoming a name." But what about the occurrence of the word without the article at 3:17?

Some notes do not seem very relevant for the average reader, such as the one at 2:7 where it is said that the idea of *dust* results from "observation of bones in the tomb." In 2:14 we are told that the headwaters of the Tigris and the Euphrates "were sacred to the Assyrians," and at 2:29 we read that *Rib* represents perhaps the borrowing of a pun from the Sumerian, where the same word means "rib" and "to make alive." In 3:1 we are referred to an ancient extrabiblical story about the serpent, and mention is made of the significance attached to a snake's shedding of its skin. How is the reader helped by being told that there is a pun on the Hebrew words for "crafty" (3:1) and "naked" (2:25)? Is this pun intentional, or is it merely a case of accidental assonance? One would like to have a note on "partner" (in 2:18). To American ears, at least, "partner" sounds too much like "buddy."

We may take a brief look at another section, the Psalms. There are excellent headings for all the psalms, generally drawn from the text itself; and each one is identified according to the classification given in the Introduction to the Psalms. Psalm 2 is identified as a "Royal Psalm used at the time of coronation. . . . Because the emperor-king was considered to be chosen by God, for subjects to *conspire* against him was to conspire against the LORD." At verse 7: *You are my son:* "a formula apparently used at the time of the coronation (see 2 Sam. 7:14; Ps. 89:26-27)."

Psalm 23 is classified as a hymn or a psalm of pilgrimage to the Temple. In verse 1 *want* is explained as "lack." In verse 3 *name's sake* is explained: "the 'name' gives the nature of a person or a god." Does this help the reader to understand the meaning of "for his name's sake he guides me in the right path"? In verse 5 *table* is explained as "probably when a sacrifice was eaten in the Temple." The ending of the psalm ("my whole life long") is explained as follows: "The poet will continue to *dwell* in the Temple in desire and in worship."

Psalm 29 is considered by many to be an Israelite adaptation of an ancient Canaanite poem written in honor of the storm god Baal. It describes a raging storm sweeping in from the Mediterranean and blowing itself out in the desert. The *mighty waters* (vs. 3) are the Mediterranean Sea; *the voice of the LORD* (vs. 4) is the thunder (and, it should have been added, *flames of fire* in verse 7 are lightning). In verse 10 *the flood* is the reservoir of waters above the heavenly dome.

It is interesting to compare the notes in the RSV and the NEB. In both Bibles the notes are generally of high quality; there seem to be more notes in RSV than in NEB. Sometimes this is due to the fact that RSV notes must explain the text; in Ephesians 2:20, for example, the note explains "the foundation of the apostles and prophets" in the text as the foundation laid by them; NEB needs no note, for its translation of the passage is "the foundation laid by the apostles and prophets." But at Ephesians 4:8 RSV says only: "Ps. 68:18." NEB explains more helpfully: "In the manner of rabbinic exegesis, the wording of Ps. 68:18 is altered to accomodate it to its new interpretation; the 'ascent' is applied to Christ and is understood as implying a prior 'descent' in the incarnation."

In critical matters RSV tends to be more conservative than NEB. RSV considers Ephesians to be Pauline; NEB takes it to be non-Pauline. Both consider the Pastorals to be deuteropauline, and 2 Peter is regarded by both as pseudonymous. RSV thinks the Letters of John were written by the author of the Gospel of John; NEB does not think this very likely. RSV goes along with tradition for the authorship of Jude; NEB referring to "most scholars," is inclined to doubt tradition.

The Jerusalem Bible
(Garden City, New York: Doubleday & Co., 1966)

It takes only a glance at the Table of Contents (pp. viii-ix) for the serious student of the Bible to discover the amount of information that is packed into this volume of over 2,000 pages. There are introductions for all the books of the Bible; sometimes several books are dealt with in one article, as is the case with the Pentateuch (pp. 5-14). The writers were given plenty of room, so these are substantial introductions, which deal not only with historical and literary matters but with religious factors as well.

The religious lesson of the Pentateuch is made clear: "the golden threads, the warp and woof of the Pentateuch," are the Promise, the Choice, the Covenant, the Law.

The lesson of the book of Job is stated concisely: "faith must remain even when understanding fails."

For Protestants, in particular, the individual introductions to the deuterocanonical books are especially valuable.

It should be noted that some significant changes in editorial content have been made in a new edition of the French original of this Bible (*Nouvelle édition entièrement revue et augmentée,* 1973). In dealing with Genesis 1—11, for example, the article "Introduction to the Pentateuch" refers to the truths revealed therein, such as Creation, the unity of the human race, the fall and its permanent consequences. And then the writer adds: "All these are truths which have their bearing upon thological doctrine and which are guaranteed by the authority of scripture; *but they are also facts, and the certainty of the truths implies the reality of the facts. It is in this sense that the first chapters of Genesis are called historical*" (italics added). In the new French edition, in place of what is underlined above, the following is said: "they are also facts, and if the truths are certain, they imply real facts, even though we are unable to perceive their shapes under the mythical garment in which they are dressed, in keeping with the mentality of that time and that milieu."

Significant changes have been made also in the new French edition in the Introduction and the notes to Song of Songs, which is defined as "a collection of songs which celebrate the mutual and faithful love which binds marriage." It is to be hoped that a translation of the new edition will be made into English.

In the Introduction to the Prophets (pp. 1115-1141), general matters are considered before the individual books are dealt with. Such questions are discussed as the nature of prophecy, the history of the prophetic movement, and the teachings of the prophets. It is a pity that the introductions to the individual books of the prophets are all grouped together (pp. 1124-1141); it would have been better if each introduction had been placed at the beginning of the book itself. The serious student of Jonah, for example, would be helped by reviewing such earlier comments on the nature and purpose of this delightful story as: "The use of the story of Jonah [in the Gospels] should not be invoked as a proof of its history. Jesus employs the Old Testament story as Christian preachers use the New Testament parables; to teach by means of well-known illustrations, without implying any opinion as to the historical reality of the facts."

In the New Testament, Ephesians is regarded as Pauline, and so are the Pastorals. Hebrews, although reflecting Pauline thought, was not written by Paul; it is anonymous.

The Supplements (pp. 455-498, after the New Testament), include a Chronological Table (pp. 455-473) which goes from the beginning of biblical history to the time of the Emperor Hadrian of Rome (A.D. 135) and the Second Jewish rebellion, under Simon bar Cochba. Here all the biblical writings are entered at the appropriate place. There is also a Calendar, a table of Measures and Money, an Index of the biblical themes dealt with in the footnotes, and nine maps.

Of the greatest value of all are the footnotes and the references on the outside margins of the pages. These marginal references are elaborate, and at times provide an almost complete concordance of many important words and themes.

The notes are excellent, supplying information of all kinds. For example, at Isaiah 11:2 (p. 1161) one sees a long note on "spirit of Yahweh," which recounts the use and meaning of the Hebrew *ruah* throughout the Old Testament, and further developments in the New Testament. There is also a note on the Messianic age, the kingdom of peace (11:6: "The wolf lives with the lamb"): "Here the messianic age is symbolically described as a return to the peace of Eden."

At Acts 11:27 the note on "prophets" is a short excursus on prophets and prophetism in the Early Church. And one has only to turn the pages of Romans to see the long notes that take up as much as four-fifths of a page (the notes for every two facing pages are all on the right hand page). On 1:16-17 there are notes on *faith, Jews first, the justice of God,* and *faith leads to faith.* On this last phrase the note reads: "The expression probably means that faith is the one necessary condition to ensure this revelation." The note on *grace* (at Romans 3:24) is perhaps the longest one of all.

Another excellent feature of the Jerusalem Bible is the outline provided for each book, which gives the major divisions and smaller sections within each division. For such a short book as Joel, for example, the outline is:

- I. The Plague of Locusts
  - A. A Liturgy of Mourning and Entreaty
    - a. Lamentation over the ruin of the country
    - b. A call to repentance and prayer
    - c. The day of Yahweh and the present calamity
    - d. A call to repentance
  - B. The Prayer Answered
- II. The New Age and the Day of Yahweh
  - A. The Outpouring of the Spirit
  - B. The Judgement of the Nations
  - C. The Glorious Future of Israel

(There are further subdivisions, with section headings, under some divisions.)

The New Scofield Reference Bible
King James Version Text
(New York: Oxford University Press, 1967)

The Scofield Bible was first issued in 1909. A revised edition, prepared by the editor himself, appeared in 1917. In 1967 a new edition was published, the work of an editorial committee of nine men, with E. Schuyler English serving as chair. The introduction to this edition (pp. v-viii) sets out the different changes that have been made, but stresses the fact that on such matters as the plenary inspiration and inerrancy of the Scriptures and other doctrines all members of the revision committee share Scofield's views. This includes Scofield's position "about our Lord's return and related events in the realm of Bible prophecy" (p. vii).

The text is that of the King James Version (referred to as the Authorized King James Version). There are some changes in the text at the following points: (1) obsolete and archaic words; (2) words whose meaning has changed; (3) indelicate words or expressions; (4) relative pronouns, that is, from "which" to "who" when persons are referred to; (5) proper names of Old Testment people cited in the New Testament, to make them conform to Old Testament spelling (e.g., Elias to "Elijah"); and (6) "in some few instances incorrect translations have been clarified." Most of the changes are identified by a vertical bar on either side of a word; the change is in the text, the King James word is in the margin. At 2 Kings 18:27, for example, one is to read "eat their own *refuse,* and drink their own *water,*" instead of "dung" and "piss." An example of change number 6 ("incorrect translations . . . clarified") is found at Proverbs 19:24 and 26:15, where the King James "bosom" is changed to "dish."

Scofield's approach to the Bible was governed by what is called dispensationalism. A dispensation is defined as "a period of time during which man is tested in respect to his obedience to some specific revelation of the will of God. . . . The dispensations are a progressive and connected revelation of God's dealings with man" (footnote 3, Gen. 1:28). According to Scofield there are seven dispensations revealed in the Bible: Innocence; Conscience (or Moral Responsibility); Human Government; Promise; Law; Church; and Kingdom. There are also eight covenants. A covenant is defined as "a sovereign pronouncement of God by which He establishes a relationship of responsibility" between God and an individual or group (footnote 1, Gen. 2:16). Scofield sees eight covenants: Edenic, Adamic, Noahic, Abrahamic, Mosaic, Palestinian, Davidic, and the New Covenant. The dispensational system goes back to the time of John N. Darby, an Irish Anglican priest who was active during the first third of the nineteenth century. (A good summary of dispensationalism and its presuppositions is available in Dewey Beegle, *Prophecy and Prediction* [Ann Arbor: Pryor Pettengill, 1978], chapters 12-13.)

Closely allied with the dispensational system is an elaborate eschatology, some of which is briefly set forth in the note to 2 Thessalonians 2:3: (1) the working of the mystery of lawlessness, which has been expanding throughout the Church Age; (2) the removal of that which restrains it, that is, the Holy Spirit; (3) the manifestation of the lawless one, the man of sin, with the resulting apostasy; and (4) the return of Christ to the earth to overthrow the man of sin and to establish the millennial kingdom.

The whole system is informed by a fantastic allegorical hermeneutic which transforms Old Testament figures and incidents into types. The "coats of skins" in Genesis 3:21, for example, are "a type of Christ, made unto our righteousness (1 Cor. 1:30)." All the festivals in Leviticus 23 are treated as types of Christian beliefs. The Feast of Weeks (Lev. 23:15-22) is a type of "the descent of the Holy Spirit to form the Church. For this reason leaven is present, because there is evil in the Church (Matt. 13:33; Acts 5:1-10; 15:1). Observe, it is now loaves, not a sheaf of separate growths loosely bound together, but a real union of particles making one homogeneous body." The unleavened bread (Lev. 23:6-8) represents Christ: "With the wave sheaf no leaven was offered, for there was no evil in Christ; but the wave loaves, typifying the Church, are 'baked with leaven,' for in the Church there is still evil" (footnote on Lev. 23:17).

The Devil occupies a prominent place in the scheme. Isaiah 14:12-14 "evidently refer to Satan . . . Lucifer, 'day-star' can be none other than Satan. This significant passage points back to the beginning of sin in the universe. When Lucifer said 'I will,' sin began" (footnote to Isa. 14:12). Ezekiel 28:11-17 also describes Satan, in his "unfallen state." And the note on Genesis 3:1 explains the relation between Satan and the serpent, the creature "which lent itself to Satan."

Care is taken to smooth over or eliminate any discrepancies or contradictions. In 2 Samuel 24:24, for example, it is said that David paid 50 silver shekels for Araunah's threshing floor and oxen, but 1 Chronicles 21:25 says David paid 600 gold shekels. A footnote at 1 Chronicles 21:25 explains that the discrepancy is imaginary, for the passage in 2 Samuel speaks of the price of the threshing floor alone, while the Chronicles passage speaks of the price of "the place (Heb. *maqom*) or area on which afterward the Temple, with its spacious courts, was built." This explanation conveniently overlooks the fact that "place" in 1 Chronicles 21:25 is "the place of the threshing floor" (vs. 22), no more and no less.

But some discrepancies will not yield to such facile "explanations." In a longish note at 1 Chronicles 11:11 the editor speaks of the differences in numbers between the accounts in Samuel and Kings and those in Chronicles. "Actually, out of the approximately 150 instances of parallel numbers in these books, fewer than one-sixth disagree." Well, that's not such a bad average, and apparently can be easily accommodated by Scofield to a belief in the plenary inspiration and inerrancy of the Scriptures.

The volume closes with an Index to Subject Chain References and an Index to the Annotations. The is a 188-page Concordance, and there are maps.

The New Chain-Reference Bible, Fourth Improved Edition
(Indianapolis: B. B. Kirkbride Bible, Inc., 1964)

This 1625 page volume (King James text) is the result of some thirty years of work on the part of Frank Charles Thompson and his wife Laura Broughton Thompson. It was first copyrighted in 1908. The subtitle provides a fairly complete description of the contents of this Bible: "Containing Thompson's original and complete system of Bible Study, including a complete numerical system of chain references, analyses of books, outline studies of characters, and unique charts; to which has been added a new and valuable series of pictorial maps, archaeological discoveries, together with many other features."

The system devised by the Thompsons enables the reader to follow throughout the Bible the successive occurrences of a word, phrase, or theme. Practically all verses in the Scriptures are classified and catalogued. The Preface claims that "the one hundred thousand references connected directly, or indirectly, with this system [that is, of groupings into chains of references] make this Bible the most unique and complete topical reference Bible in print." The General Index after the New Testament (pp. i-xxvi) lists in small type, four columns per page, what seem to be at least 7,500 different topics, places, persons and subjects which are to be found in the Bible. It is mind-boggling to think of the amount of tedious and persistent toil that went into the preparation of this compendium.

"The New Comprehensive Bible Helps" (365 pages in all) are a mélange of all sorts of charts, tables, lists, and studies. The "Condensed Cyclopaedia of Topics and Texts," together with Special Bible Readings, Analyses of the Books, and Character Studies (pp. 1-238), constitute the heart of the matter. Here, under 4,300 different headings, the various topics and texts, identified by numbers in the margins of the text itself, are listed, classified, and subdivided. In many instances biblical verses are cited in full. To take one example: "Battle of Life" (pp. 8-9, items 356-374) includes the following: (a) Ancient Heroes, (b) The Spiritual Conflict, (c) The Soul's Enemies, (d) Weapons and Armor, (e) Divine Protection, (f) Divine Protector, (g) The Victory.

There are also Prominent Bible Characters, Bible Harmonies and Illustrated Studies, and an Archaeological Supplement (pp. 308-365) by G. Frederick Owen, which is relatively up to date. It includes the findings at Qumram, Wadi Murabba'at, and Kirbet Mird, up to 1959. Twelve maps, with Index (no pagination), complete the volume.

The charts and tables reflect highly idiosyncratic tastes, and unusual, not to say bizarre, ways of handling the biblical material. There is, for example, a chart entitled "Seven Editions of Divine Law" (p. 178), as follows: (1) Written on Nature (Ps. 19:1), (2) Written on Conscience (Rom. 2:15), (3) Written on Tables of Stone (Exod. 24:12), (4) The Entire Scriptures (Rom. 15:4), (5) Christ the Illustrated Edition (John 1:14), (6) Written on the Heart (Heb. 8:10), (7) The Outward Christian Life Living Epistles (2 Cor. 3:2, 3).

The dates ("Periods of Old Testament History," p. 186) are according to the reckoning of Archbishop Ussher (1581-1656) "but they are used only as a working basis, and are not regarded as accurate." The Fall is dated 4004 B.C.; the Flood, 2348 B.C.; and the dispersion of the races (Babel), 2234 B.C.

As is to be expected, much of the Old Testament material is treated in an allegorical and typological manner. Song of Songs and Psalm 45, for example, are seen as portraits of Christ and his attributes.

This volume will be used by those who share the editor's presupposition that the Bible is a huge collection, a jumbled hodgepodge of statements, facts, notions and beliefs which need to be sorted out, catalogued and classified, in order to make sense to the reader.

The Ryrie Study Bible
New American Standard Translation
(Chicago: Moody Press, 1978; also available in other versions)

This Bible does not contain the kind of material found in the Scofield Bible and the Thompson Chain-Reference Bible. It is more like the RSV and NEB editions examined above. Its editor, Charles Caldwell Ryrie, of the Dallas Theological Seminary, provides notes and comments of a strongly conservative bent.

As might be expected, Genesis 1—11 is dealt with as history. In Genesis 1:5 and following, "day" is a twenty-four hour period, not an age. The light created on the first day was not the sun "but some fixed light source outside the earth," which was replaced by the sun and moon on the fourth day. The waters above the dome (second day) are explained as "a vast body of water in vapor form over the earth, making a canopy that caused conditions on the earth to resemble those inside a greenhouse. This may account for the longevity of human life (Gen. 5) and for the tremendous amount of water involved in the worldwide flood (Gen. 6—9)."

In Genesis 3:21 the garments of skin were "God's provision for restoring Adam's and Eve's fellowship with Himself and imply slaying of an animal in order to provide them." Cain's wife (Gen. 4:17) may have been his "sister, niece, or even grand-niece. Since Adam's and Eve's genetic systems had no mutant genes in them, such a marriage would not be dangerous as it is today." The capacity of Noah's ark (Gen. 6:15) is calculated to have been equal to that of "522 standard railroad stock cars (each of which can hold 120 sheep). Only 188 cars would be required to hold 45,000 sheep-sized animals, leaving three trains of 104 cars each for food, Noah's family, and 'range' for the animals. Today it is estimated that there are 17,600 species of animals, making 45,000 a likely approximation of the number Noah might have taken into the ark."

The size of Nineveh is given in Jonah 3:3: "Now Nineveh was an exceedingly great city, a three days' walk." The text means that the diameter of the city was the length of a three days' walk; this is made abundantly clear in the expression "one day's walk" in the next verse. On a conservative basis, this would be something like forty-five miles. But Ryrie's note takes the phrase to mean the circumference of the city, and says: "The circumference of the city, including some surrounding land, was about 60 miles." This makes for a diameter of nineteen miles; in any case quite a lot of "surrounding land" would have to be included for Nineveh to measure up to the size ascribed to it in this passage.

Song of Songs is taken to be a love song, by Solomon, and the comment is made about this determined philanderer: "The experiences recorded in this book may reflect the only (or virtually the only) pure romance he had."

In Matthew 24:34 (and parallel Mark 13:30), "this generation" does not refer to the contemporaries of Jesus, but to "race" or "family," that is: "the Jewish race will be preserved . . . until the Lord comes." And in Matthew 16:28 (and parallel Mark 9:1), "the Son of Man coming in His kingdom" is explained as the transfiguration, which took place a week later. This means that Jesus was only saying that "some of those who are standing here" would be alive a week later.

Some notes do not conform to the kind of interpretation that one might anticipate. At Isaiah 7:14, for example, "the virgin" is explained as probably "the woman, a virgin at the time, whom Isaiah took later as his second wife . . . a type of the virgin Mary." And there is a sensible textual note on the longer ending of Mark: "The doubtful genuineness of verses 9-20 makes it unwise to build a doctrine or base an experience on this (especially vss. 16-18)."

There are a number of Helps at the end of the volume, such as a Harmony of the Gospels, A Synopsis of Bible Doctrine, Archaeology and the Bible (by Howard V. Fos, from the *Wycliffe Bible Encyclopaedia),* a Topical Index of Scripture, and the New American Standard Concordance. Maps and an Index conclude the volume.

Of the Study Bibles examined in this survey, the Jerusalem Bible provides more valuable helps for the reader than any of the others. The study editions of the Revised Standard Version and the New English Bible are extremely useful; no person should read the Bible without the minimum helps provided by these two editions. As for the other Bibles, it is clear that each one has certain features which are useful and helpful, particularly for preachers. But the overall attitude toward the biblical literature is so dominated by theological and philosophical biases as to nullify much of the good qualities that these editions possess. In this reviewer's opinion they certainly do not provide an adequate guide for a person who wants to learn what the Bible really means.

APPENDIX 1
Zeal to Promote the Common Good

(The King James Version)

Roger A. Bullard

That robust and rotund Defender of the Faith, His Royal Majesty Henry VIII, he of the six wives, left to the English-speaking world a legacy of at least six Bibles. He had the translator of the first, William Tyndale, burned at the stake in what is now Belgium. At the same time he was commissioning another and less gifted scholar, Miles Coverdale, to revise Tyndale's work for publication with royal license. This in turn was later revised as Matthew's Bible. (Matthew was a pseudonym for John Rogers, the ill-fated Tyndale's literary executor.) This was revised as the Great Bible, which came to be used widely in the Church of England and whose readings were incorporated into the Prayer Book during the reign of Henry's son, Edward VI. Two other versions appearing during Henry's time were less important. These four are significant, however, because of their genealogy: Tyndale, the first in the line; Coverdale, his reviser; "Matthew," his reviser; and the Great Bible, Coverdale's own revision of "Matthew."

Her Catholic Majesty Mary Tudor, who followed Edward to the throne, sent swarms of English Protestants fleeing to the continent to escape the persecution she presided over. One group of English scholars of the Puritan persuasion emigrated to Geneva, which was then dominated by the Reformers of Calvinist stripe. They produced there a remarkable version of Scripture, the Geneva Bible, actually published in England in 1560, soon after the accession of Elizabeth to the monarch's position as head of the Church of England. This became the beloved Bible of English-speaking Protestantism. Associated primarily with the Puritans, it was not read from the pulpits of the Church of England (though it was from the Reformed pulpits of Scotland). It was fairly inexpensive; it was in Roman type and easy to read; it had helpful diagrams, tables, and illustrations; and it was a good translation. It also had margins heavily laden with doctrinal notes, far more consonant with the Presbyterian and Puritan persuasions than with the High Church episcopacy.[1] This was the Bible of Shakespeare and Milton and John Bunyan, the Bible of the Pilgrim Fathers. For generations it was to be *the* Bible to most people who spoke English.

But the bishops were not content to let the Geneva win in the field. In 1568, a select committee of churchmen, most of them bishops of the Church of England, published a revision of the Great Bible, known as the Bishops' Bible. While the Geneva Bible was being read by the people at home, the Bishops' Bible was read from the pulpits in England; it also provided the scriptural readings of the Prayer Book used in the church's liturgy.

But when the Virgin Queen died without issue and James VI of Scotland was summoned to be James I of Engand, the Puritans thought they saw their chance. Here was a monarch of their own persuasion, from Presbyterian Scotland, where the Geneva Bible was read even in services of worship. But they were deceived. They were soon to discover that kings were not easily dissociated from the power foci of the episcopacy.

This first of the Stuart kings had hardly arrived in London before he was presented with a massive petition urging redress of Puritan grievances. Toward a resolution of this internal struggle in the Church of England, a conference was held in 1604 at Hampton Court with representatives of both wings of the church arguing their case to the king. Not a great deal came of this conference, but there was a resolution passed, "That a translation be made of the whole Bible, as consonant as can be to the original Hebrew and Greek; and this to be set out and printed, without any marginal notes, and [it] only to be used in all Churches of England in time of divine service."

The suggestion that a new Bible be made was offered by the learned Puritan divine John Reynolds, and it was not well received. Richard Bancroft, then Bishop of London, said, "if every man's humour were followed, there would be no end of translating." The Puritan point was that they could not swallow the version then in use in the churches: the Bishops' Bible. The church establishment obviously was content. But James saw an opportunity to win himself a place in history. He took to the idea, but must have startled the Puritans when he began to run down, not the Bishops' Bible, but the Geneva Bible. Lying through his teeth, he claimed that he had just recently been presented a copy of that Bible, with which he was unfamiliar, (he had in fact been raised on it) and that he thought it the very worst of all English Bibles.[2] The argument went on; minutes were taken of the meeting and later published, with all expletives deleted. James was a rather foul-mouthed character, and the man who wrote up the record did not want to offend the sensibilities of Christian readers with some of His Majesty's riper expressions.[3]

Bancroft could see where the argument was going, and proposed to the king that if a new translation were to be made, it should be without any notes. In the resolution as passed, each side got a point. The Puritans, that it should be a new translation, and the bishops, that it should be without notes. (It was really the notes of the Geneva version rather than the translation, which alienated the high church faction.)

The meeting broke up, and it soon became evident that the church was willing to let the whole matter die a quiet and natural death. When Convocation of the Church of England was held that year, not a word was said about a new Bible. But James was determined that it should come about. The King James Version, as it is known in America, is well named, for without the crown's pushing, the reluctant bishops would never have gotten the project moving.

It appears that James, sometime during the spring of 1604, took matters into his own hands and sought out nominations for a panel of translators. We do not know exactly how this was done, but probably he asked the universities for their advice. During the summer the king informed Bishop Bancroft that he had made his appointments, "fifty-four learned men." Some of the work began about this time, but there was another problem that loomed large: money. This was going to be an expensive project, and James was never the wealthiest monarch in Christendom. He proposed that the church foot the bill, and instructed the reluctant Bancroft to circulate two letters among the bishops. One suggested that whenever some position in the church should become open by virtue of the death of the holder, consideration should be given to the appointment of one of the translators, so that each man should have a compensation of at least £20 a year for his labors. The second suggested voluntary contributions be made, with each bishop being responsible for raising part of the cost. The attitude of the church toward the project can easily be seen in the results gotten from these circulars. From the first, there was very little action arising; from the second, none at all. Money was apparently a sore point among the translators during the work, and may have been part of the reason that work on the Bible did not immediately begin in earnest.[4]

The idea of a new Bible had been first suggested by the Puritans, but James soon turned it into a weapon against them. This was his intention from the start, as can be seen from a letter he wrote back to Scotland soon after Hampton Court: "We have kept such a revel with the Puritans . . . as was never heard the like . . . I have peppered them . . . soundly."[5] When the king finally managed to get the project moving, it was clear that the cards were heavily stacked against the Puritans. Of the forty-seven men who actually did the work, four can be clearly identified as Puritans. Moreover, a list of fifteen principles were drawn up to guide the work, actually a wise move, but close examination of them shows how intent the king was on putting down the Puritans.[6]

The very first rule shows how thoroughly the concept had changed since the motion was made at Hampton Court for "a new translation." It was now determined that the new Bible is to be a *revision* of the Bishops' Bible, altered as little as fidelity to the original will permit—hardly the Puritans' goal. The second was a good rule, that the proper names of the text should be spelled as in common English usage, rather than using a scholarly transliteration of the Hebrew or Greek. In effect, this was a strike against the Geneva Bible, which had been very careful to employ scholarly phonetic equivalents of the names in the original languages.[7] The third rule established that the "old ecclesiastical terms" were to be maintained. It was the Puritans' intention, in proposing a new translation, to get away from this. It was one of their chief objections to the Great and Bishops' Bibles. Specific mention is made of one case: "congregation" is not (as in Geneva) to be used instead of "church." This had become for the Puritans a test case, a kind of litmus indicator to determine the extent to which a translation veered toward the catholicizing tendencies of the bishops. The fourth rule was specifically formulated to keep the new Bible in line with the ancient catholic tradition treasured in the Church of England: that when a word had several meanings, that word was to be followed which was most commonly used by the ancient church fathers. The fifth rule laid down that the division of the chapters was to be altered as little as possible—another sideswipe at the Geneva version. The sixth was a broadside against the Puritans and their Bible, that there were to be no doctrinal notes attached, but only textual notes of a scholarly nature. This had been Bancroft's point in the discussions at Hampton Court.

The translators were divided into six committees, called "companies" at the time, two at Oxford, two in London at Westminster, and two at Cambridge. Three of the groups were responsible for the Old Testament, two for the New, and one for the Apocrypha.[8]

The first Westminster committee, which prepared Genesis—2 Kings, was chaired by Lancelot Andrewes, probably the best known today of all the scholars. He was a high churchman, who strove for a reasonable and catholic theology. Famous for his linguistic abilities, he would spend vacations learning new languages. A colleague referred to him as the Interpreter General at Babel. He was secular and wordly in his interests, often in the company of the king at the horse races and bloodier sports of the day, but today he is best remembered for writing one of the all-time classics of Christian spirituality: the *Private Devotions,* published posthumously. T. S. Eliot regarded him as his spiritual mentor.[9]

John Overall was Dean of St. Paul's, and a secret political radical. Opposing the divine right of kings, he believed that revolution was justified when kings acted against justice. His writings were unpublished until 1690. Just before the work began, he married one of the most famous and beautiful women in England, whose conduct would occasion a great deal of gossip before the project was completed.

Hadrian a Saravia, of Hispano-Flemish background and "a most terrible High Churchman," came from the Continent where he had been active in anti-Calvinist causes. His writings were spirited defenses of episcopacy. He is otherwise known as one of the first figures of the Protestant Reformation to insist on the Christian duty to preach the gospel in non-Christian lands.

John Layfield was the traveler among the translators. He made a voyage to the New World, and published an account of his adventures in Puerto Rico. He was an amateur architect, and was relied on for advice in passages dealing with the construction of the Tabernacle and the Temple.

Richard Thompson, better known as "Dutch" Thompson, was a confirmed anti-Calvinist, and was noted for two things: his consummate skill with languages and his bouts with the bottle. It was said of him that he never went to bed sober.

William Bedwell was an Arabic scholar who had published dictionaries of both Arabic and Persian. He was one of the first scholars to draw attention to the importance of Arabic for the understanding of Hebrew, although we might question his skill in this regard when we notice that in one of his writings he attempts to connect the Arabic name *Sahara* with the Spanish *sierra,* and explain the meaning on the basis of that connection.

1 Chronicles—Ecclesiastes was prepared by one of the Cambridge committees, chaired at first by Edward Lively, one of the best Hebrew scholars in England. His colleagues were much concerned about his financial state, and went to some trouble to find him a small parish to help him support his family, but he died very early in the work, leaving eleven children in poverty.

John Richardson was a member of this group. A jolly, popular, fat man, he had been a friend of Dutch Thompson's during student days. He was Professor of Theology at Cambridge, a rigorous anti-Calvinist, but bold enough on one occasion, in the presence of the king, to argue for the right of the church to excommunicate kings.

Lawrence Chadderton was one of the few Puritans on the panel. Although at Hampton Court, which he had attended as a Puritan representative, he was vigorously opposed by Bishop Bancroft, the two men were old friends. He had once saved Bancroft's life during a college brawl. He had been disowned by his father when he left the Catholic Church. The older man gave his son one shilling with which to buy a beggar's purse. In later years he was President of Emmanuel College, Cambridge, a post which he resigned in order to make sure that the man who succeeded him would be one who shared his views. He could have waited; he lived to be 103, still reading Greek without glasses.

Francis Dillingham, an especially good Greek scholar, was the most noted male chauvinist on the panel. A vigorous defender of the married clergy, a subject then disputed in England, he wrote quite a bit on the subject, including a book called, *A Golden Key Opening the Lock to Eternal Happiness,* a kind of marriage manual in which he passed on to husbands advice on how to keep their wives in check. He was a bachelor himself. (Actually, few of the translators were married.)

Thomas Harrison, a Puritan, was a much respected man, loved for his humility and tolerant attitudes to those holding different opinions. On learning that a student had made a speech attacking his theology, he charitably suggested that the young man had him confused with somebody else. He was something of a poet, and his work was said to have been of excellent quality, although none of it has survived. He had a reputation as a Hebrew scholar.

Roger Andrewes, Lancelot's brother, served with this committee, along with Andrew Bing, a tall young man of sunny disposition. The latter was only thirty when the work began, and he outlived most of his colleagues.

The books of Isaiah—Malachi were prepared by an Oxford committee chaired by John Harding, Regius Professor of Hebrew at Oxford University. During the course of the work he was involved in a political scramble for the presidency of Magdalen College, which he managed to obtain. He died the year before the Bible was published.

Also on this group was John Reynolds, upon whose initial suggestion the King James Version was conceived. One of the most noted Puritan leaders of his day, he was a famous Greek scholar specializing in Aristotle, and as good a Hebraist as any of his colleagues. Those who knew him well insisted that he was not as thoroughgoing a Puritan as his reputation suggested, and they pointed out that he often wore a surplice and that he knelt in chapel. Reynolds devoted himself unremittingly to the translation. He became quite ill, and his colleagues vainly begged him not to throw his life away, even for the Bible. The committee often met at his house during his illness. He died at the age of fifty-eight, while the work was still in progress.

A colleague on this committee was Thomas Holland, one of the older members, and something of a non-conformist in doctrine and lifestyle. He opposed the idea that bishops were of a different order from elders, but the bishops seemed to have treated him as a harmless "old codger whom all Oxford loved." He was a pious man, learned in the church fathers, and gave increasing amount of time to prayer. Whenever he would take leave of his fellows, his parting words would be: "I commend you to the love of God and the hatred of popery and superstition." These are supposed to have been his dying words. He died the year after the translation appeared.

Richard Kilbye, a fellow of humble origins, was a close friend of Izaac Walton, the compleat angler. He was also known as a grammatical stickler and pedant.

Miles Smith, a Puritan with a dislike for ceremony, ended, in a sense, this work that John Reynolds began. He was one of the final editors of the Bible, and the author of the Preface. He was given much credit for the translation, though he never claimed any himself.

In the New Testament, the Gospels, Acts, and Revelation were prepared by the second Oxford committee, chaired by a rather unlikely character, Thomas Ravis. He was a violent anti-Puritan, with an intolerance accented by a gruff, surly manner. While Bishop of London, he declared of the Puritans, "By the help of Jesus, I will not leave one preacher in my diocese who does not subscribe and conform!" He compelled those under him to make certain changes in their personal finances, expelling or imprisoning any who resisted. However, he had a reputation for lavish spending on social affairs, and for use of church funds to improve his episcopal properties.

George Abbot held political opinions that were contrary to James, but in spite of this he managed to stay on the king's good side by traveling to Scotland in an attempt to persuade the Church of Scotland to accept the episcopacy. His moderate success seems to have gone far to making up, in the royal eyes, for his other, non-conforming ideas. In fact, in 1611, he was promoted to Archbishop of Canterbury, as much by his flattery of the king as anything. He later was involved in an unfortunate accident, which made him the only one of the translators to kill a man. While he was hunting, one of his arrows glanced off a tree and killed a game warden. He never forgave himself for this and personally gave the widow a generous annual payment, but he was temporarily suspended from office as being "a man of blood." Opinion of the bishops was divided as to whether he could continue in office, but James ruled in his favor.

Sir Henry Saville, a handsome but humorless Greek scholar, mathematician, historian, and bibliophile, was one of the most impressive intellects among the translators. He traveled in Europe collecting manuscripts and books which he donated to the Bodleian library. He founded the chairs of astronomy and geometry at Oxford and he was tutor to Queen Elizabeth. He made it his life's work to edit for publication the complete works of St. John Chrysostom, a point which caused him considerable difficulty in his marriage. His wife, who shared none of his education, was intensely jealous of the time that her husband devoted to these labors, and at one time threatened to burn his notes on Chrysostom, dissuaded only by the intervention of one of her husband's colleagues. It was said that he was driven to such force of study over the death of a young son. Obviously a wealthy man, he eventually published Chrysostom at the staggering expense of £8000.

The second Westminster committee, which translated the Epistles, had few notables. The second Cambridge committee, responsible for the Apocrypha, boasted a few interesting characters. There was Samuel Ward, a nervous young man, youngest of all his colleagues, and a moderate Puritan. He kept a diary in which he constantly carped against his own sin of gluttony: "Today I drank too much, today I ate too many plums, today I ate too much cheese, today I slept too late." He stuttered, perhaps part of the reason for his shyness, but others referred to him as a Moses, not only for his difficulty of speech, but for his gentle nature.

Ward must have been thoroughly cowed by his intensely aggressive colleague Andrew Downes, a distinguished classicist, expert in Demosthenes. A ruddy-faced man with steely blue eyes, exceptionally intolerant, he would talk to people while arrogantly leaning back in a chair, legs propped up on a table. He was an incessant quarreler on the committee, and his standing among his colleagues was not helped when it was found that of all the translators, he alone had managed to finagle some money out of King James.[10]

John Bois, a prodigy of sorts who was reading Hebrew at the age of six, kept a work schedule running from four in the morning to eight at night. He had started school as a medical student. He later decided that the more one knows about medicine, the more given to hypochondria one is, so he gave it up and went into biblical scholarship. He was a pleasant, humble man, well respected, but with an unhappy marriage. When the Apocrypha project ended, he and Downes went over to the Epistles committee. Bois kept notes on these discussions and they have survived. They are the only notes from committee work left by any of the translators and are valuable for the insight they provide on the reasoning, the scholarship, and method of the panel.[11] Bois and Downes later had a falling-out over the question of how much help the two of them had provided to Sir Henry in his edition of Chrysostom.

These scholars worked pretty much as committees on translation have always proceeded. Each man provided a draft translation of assigned material, and this was then reviewed in session by the local committee. As revised after this discussion, it was sent to the other committees for examination and comment.

The Hebrew text used by the committees preparing the Old Testament was the most up-to-date available at the time, including a 1572 edition unavailable to previous translators. It was based on the 1525 Rabbinic Bible published in Venice and edited by Arias Montanus, a Benedictine scholar in Spain.[12] In the work of translation the scholars could consult translations into the modern languages, largely early products of the Reformation, such as Luther's Bible, including of course, all the previous English translations. There were also commentaries: the ancient church fathers, the medieval rabbis, and the recent biblical scholarship of the continental reformers. The KJV is the first English Bible openly to acknowledge its debt, as in the preface it does, to Jewish scholarship. The writings of many of the medieval Jewish exegetes were coming to be well known among Christian scholars of the time, and several of the translators were fairly well at home in rabbinics. The interpretations of David Kimchi and Isaac Luria are especially noteworthy. David Kimchi was especially highly regarded by Christian scholars of the day. In a great many difficult passages, the authority of his name seems to have been sufficient to establish his interpretation in the KJV text.[13]

The New Testament translators had Beza's fifth edition (sometimes called the ninth, but four of these were simply reprintings). It was an atrociously bad text, with an unfortunate history, but it was commonly received in those days when textual criticism was still in its embryonic stage. The New Testament panel made use of a recent Roman Catholic translation, the Rheims New Testament (the corresponding Old Testament had not yet appeared). It seems to have contributed a good bit to the Latinate vocabulary of the King James New Testament. Neither the principles nor the preface make specific reference to the Rheims, but it is known to have been used.[14] The King James New Testament is remarkably more heavy than the Old Testament in its use of Latin vocabulary, partly from the influence of the Rheims New Testament, partly no doubt due to the comparative lack of Puritan influence on the two New Testament panels. A noted example of this is the familiar 1 Corinthians 13, where the word "charity" is used, instead of "love" which is found in previous English translations. The peculiar thing is that this word "charity" is used for the first time at 1 Corinthians 8:1. "Love" was used throughout the rest of the New Testament, including the first part of 1 Corinthians. But after this point, "charity" is found frequently as an alternative. This might be the influence of the dogmatic Andrew Downes, who had come over from the Apocrypha committee and joined the group doing the Epistles.

Once the individual committees had finished their work, a committee of twelve, two from each group, was appointed to meet in London and go over the whole. Then a committee of two, Miles Smith and Thomas Bilson (who was not among the translators), was to prepare the final copy for the printer. Finishing touches were added at this stage. Miles Smith wrote the preface, which is one of the most remarkable documents in the history of the Bible. The whole subsequent history of the Bible in English might well have been different had the preface continued to be printed with the text of the Bible.[15]

The preface is a defense of the translation against anticipated objections. The translators were aware that their work likely would not be well-received because it was new—people do not take to novelties in their religion. Charges were answered that the translation was unnecessary, that the old version was good enough, and that the translation was done by heretics. Also, several technical matters that called for attention were taken up.

First, there was the matter of marginal notes. The preface defends the practice of putting alternate readings in the margin. Actually the King James Version margin contained three kinds of notes: alternate translations based on a literal rendering of a phrase rendered freely in the text, readings of manuscripts other than that on which the text was based, and cross references. No doctrinal notes are given. People who thoroughly castigated the RSV in 1952 for its textual notes were simply unaware that the King James Version had such notes also, and that it was never intended that the Bible should be published without them. The preface makes it clear that they are there to alert the reader that uncertainty is involved in places, and that "dogmatizing" is not in order. One of these notes, by the way, has taken on an immortality of its own. The text of Isaiah 26:4 reads: "Trust ye in the Lord for ever: for in the LORD JEHOVAH is everlasting strength." By that last phrase, "everlasting strength" there is a marginal note which reads, "Heb: Rock of ages." The RSV renders it in the text: "the Lord God is an everlasting rock."

This suggests another matter dealt with in the preface: the matter of freedom of expression. In the example above, it was a matter of Hebrew metaphor ("rock of ages" is the literal Hebrew) which the translators felt would not be clear in English. Hence they render it as "everlasting strength," with the literal rendering in the margin. Another example may be found in the familiar 23rd Psalm: "I will dwell in the house of the LORD forever." "Forever" has a note appended: "Heb: Length of days." (The Hebrew actually doesn't say "forever," and versions before and since have not rendered it that way). A striking example occurs in Psalm 25, since it illustrates how different committees dealt with the same translational problem. In 25:6, the text reads, "Remember, O LORD, thy tender mercies." A note on "tender mercies" reads, "Heb: thy bowels." The reason for this is clear. In the biblical languages, the heart, not the head, was the seat of intelligence and the bowels were the seat of emotion and feeling. The translators should perhaps have gone one better, translating the Hebrew "heart" by the English "mind"; but at least they recognized the problem for English readers of saying, "Remember, O Lord, thy bowels." So they put the interpretation in the text and the literal meaning in the margin. The committee that translated the epistles handled the problem differently. In 1 John 3:17 the text reads: "Whoso seeth his brother have need, and shutteth up his bowels *of compassion* from him, how dwelleth the love of God in Him?" The words *"of compassion"* are italicized, meaning that there is nothing in the Greek text to correspond to them; they have been inserted by the translators for clarification. Rather than to interpret, with a literal reading placed in the margin, this New Testament committee elected to insert a clarifying phrase into the text after the word "bowels." But the first Westminster committee, doing another part of the Old Testament, recognized no problems with a literal rendering and created a difficult situation in places, such as Genesis 43:30 where we find, "And Joseph made haste, for his bowels did yearn upon his brother."

A close study of the methodologies of the six committees would probably yield many examples of such inconsistency. Yet none of the groups was wedded to a literal rendering of anything, and this is another point that the preface makes clear. They have not tried to render the same word in the original with the same English word. "Thus to mince the matter," the preface explains, "we thought to savor more of curiosity than wisdom. Is the kingdom of God become words or syllables? Why should we be in bondage to them if we may be free?"

Some examples: the Greek word *logos,* "word," is used 331 times in the New Testament. It is rendered in the KJV by some twenty-eight different devices: Not only word, but preaching, saying, rumor, tidings, utterance, game, account, cause, question, treatise, and intent.

Similarly in the Old Testament, the Hebrew *nephesh,* usually translated "soul," although that is not quite its meaning, is rendered by about thirty devices: not only soul, but also words like life, pleasure, person, lust, dead body, beast, creature, self, fish, mind, and ghost.

In each case the translators are simply adapting the meaning to the context. They were well aware that words had meaning only in context, and were quite sensitive to its demands. This is apparent on a larger scale than mere words. In the Hebrew Old Testament, there are a number of passages that are identical with other passages, but the King James panels are quite free in their translation of these. For an example, the Hebrew text of Isaiah 35:10 is exactly the same as that of Isaiah 51:11.[16] But compare the two:

> And the ransomed of the Lord shall return and come to Zion with songs, and everlasting joy upon their heads; they shall obtain joy and gladness, and sorrow and sighing shall flee away. (Isa. 35:10)

> Therefore the redeemed of the Lord shall return, and come with singing unto Zion, and everlasting joy shall be upon their heads; they shall obtain gladness and joy, and sorrow and mourning shall flee away. (Isa. 51:11)

The Hebrew is exactly alike, but the translations are quite different. Examination of context will show some interesting points, however. In 35:9 the word "redeemed" already had been used. The translators did not want to repeat the word in so short a compass of time, so they chose "ransomed." There are subtle differences in the rhythm of the lines; the first is more lyric; the second more stately. But each fits the pattern and mood of the context. The more wooden ASV renders them both exactly alike, and most unmusically. The RSV also renders them exactly alike, but the literary quality is immensely improved.

It was the duty of the final committee to iron out inconsistencies, but many are still apparent. For instance, major characters of the Bible are called by different names. Elijah, the important Old Testament figure, is called Elijah in the Old Testament, but Elias in the New Testament. Even worse, the Joshua of the Old Testament is referred to as Jesus in the New Testament (Acts 7:45; Heb. 4:8), making for some confusion. (The two names are the same: Jesus is an anglicization of a latinization of a grecization of the Hebrew name. Joshua is direct anglicization of the Hebrew.) On this point, the principle laid out in the beginning about the spelling of proper names was not faithfully observed.

For better or worse, the final editors Smith and Bilson (who wrote the chapter headings) submitted their work. But trouble was coming. Bishop Bancroft, who had never particularly liked the idea anyway, was now Archbishop Bancroft, of Canterbury. He managed to get his hands on the text and introduce some changes in places he did not like. Smith was furious when he learned about it, but said, "he is so potent there is no contradicting him!" An example of this pettiness and suspicion appears in Acts 1:20, where, speaking of Judas, the text now reads, "His bishopric let another take." Bancroft, ever suspicious of Puritan anti-episcopal tendencies insisted, Smith said, "on the glorious word bishopric."[17] It was a most unusual place to find insistence upon the word. Geneva had read "charge," with a marginal note, "ministry." This is the only time in the KJV where the word "bishopric" occurs. Elsewhere the Greek word is translated "visitation" or "office of bishop." The latter phrase certainly shows the superior sensitivity of the translators to the English language than Bancroft's technical and pedantic "bishopric." The word actually occurs in a quotation from Psalm 109:8, where the KJV renders "office."

The Bible was printed in folio, with two columns of black-letter type. This was a reversion from Geneva, which had been set up in Roman. The KJV did follow the Geneva in dividing the text into verses (a modern innovation), but unfortunately also followed Geneva's idea of printing each verse as a separate paragraph. Older versions had used sense paragraphing, as have versions since the KJV.

The printer may have allowed himself a little exuberance. On the title page appears the phrase, "appointed to be read in churches," from which derives the name commonly used in Great Britain: the Authorized Version. Actually it never had any official authorization; Barker apparently just took it on himself to say this.[18]

The Bible was intended, at least in James' conception and that of most of the translators, to be framed in a style of language elevated and ringing, so as to match the eloquence of the collects of the Prayer Book. To this end, the final committee read the text aloud to each other to catch infelicities that might appear only when read aloud.[19] To this end, the first edition was heavily punctuated, to assist the reader in placing sense units together. Although sense paragraphing was abandoned in favor of verse paragraphs, the printer's paragraph mark was placed at the proper points for sense paragraphing, at least up to a certain point. The last of these marks appear at Acts 20:36, and no one yet knows why. First editions are divided into two categories, He Bibles and She Bibles, referring to two printings of a page in Ruth 3:15, where some read, "He went into the city," and others, correctly, "She went into the city." Other misprints abounded.

The KJV continued to be plagued by typographical errors. One edition read, "Thou shalt commit adultery." Another substituted "condemnation" at one point for "redemption." Instead of Jesus' saying, "Let the children first be filled," one printing read, "Let the children first be killed." As late as 1702, Cotton Mather in America was complaining about the inordinate number of such errors, and a great many people did not trust this Bible because of the reputation for printer's errors it acquired. One famous misprint summed it up. Where the Psalmist says, "Princes have persecuted me without a cause" (119:161), one edition read, "Printers have persecuted me without a cause."

One misprint caused a political scandal. Acts 6:3 has the apostles speak of the selection of certain men, "whom we may appoint." One edition from the period of the Commonwealth read, "whom ye may appoint," thus having the apostles speak to the congregation. Rumor, no doubt apocryphal, had it that Oliver Cromwell bribed the printer with £1000 to make that change. One typographical error, we are told, has remained: Matthew 23:24, "strain at a gnat," was supposed to be "strain out a gnat." But the error persisted.

The Bible did not enjoy a kind reception. Bishop of London Hugh Broughton wrote that the translators had put all the errors in the text and the correct readings in the margins, and declared: "The late Bible was sent to me to censure; which bred in me a sadness that will grieve me while I breathe it is so ill done. I had rather be rent in pieces with wild horses, than any such translation by my consent should be urged upon poor churches. The new edition crosseth me. I require it to be burnt." Broughton, whose comment is frequently quoted, should probably be ignored. He was consumed with resentment over not having been invited to work on the translation. He was not invited because he was so irascible that others found it hard to get along with him.

Others took up the cause. Izaac Walton tells of his translator friend Kilbye attending a small country church one Sunday soon after the publication, and hearing the preacher deliver a sermon against the new Bible, pointing to one particular place he thought mistranslated, and citing three reasons why it should have been done otherwise. Kilbye met him at the church door, introduced himself, and assured the gentleman that the committee had in fact noted the three points he mentioned in the sermon, but felt that these were outweighed by thirteen other considerations, which he proceeded to cite.[20]

"Zeal to promote the common good receiveth but cold entertainment in the world," began the preface, and so it was. Nobody seems to have been particularly fond of it. The Puritans distrusted it because it was too catholicizing. Some scholars did not like it because it was not accurate enough; as early as 1645 Parliament was being urged to sponsor yet another revision of the Bible, so that people could have the Scripture in an "exact, vigorous, and lively translation," which presumably the KJV was not.[21] Literary critics complained of the KJV's archaic and unnatural language. One wrote that it was composed "in a most gothic and barbarous taste," and the noted John Selden, otherwise appreciative, noted that it was "a translation into English words rather than English phrase."[22] Robert Lowth, who wrote what was really the first prescriptive grammar of the English languge, drew almost seventy of his examples of bad grammatical usage from the KJV.[23]

Some of this was unfair. Lowth laid down his pretended rules about 100 years later; there was no reason why the divines of 1611 should conform to those rules, many of which were imposed on English from the classical tradition anyway. I have not been able to discover the source of the "gothic and barbarous taste" remark, but it sounds like the author may not have liked the tendency of the KJV, in most sections, to stay away from words of classical derivation and use plain English instead.

As for archaism, that is valid enough. It is not true, as one often hears today, that the KJV was written in the language of its day. It was not. This was largely assured by the principle laid down that the Bishops' Bible be revised, rather than that a new translation be made. This meant that the language goes back really to William Tyndale of 100 years earlier; word count studies that have been made estimate that in the New Testament, as much as sixty percent of KJV's phraseology derives from predecessors all the way back to Tyndale.[24] Moreover, the version was intended for the liturgical purposes of the high church wing of the Church of England, which had, in the Prayer Book, afforded old-fashioned language an air of religiosity. The translators intended to forge their style to match that of the Prayer Book. One would have to say, however, that much of what was archaic then has been revised out. What sounds archaic to us today may have been quite normal then.

The fact is that the KJV that we read today is not the version of 1611. This Bible has been revised many times. The version we read today is the Oxford Standard Edition of 1769. In between 1611 and 1769, a large number of changes were made in the text. The greater number consisted of modernizing language and spelling. A goodly number, however, reflected changes in the text of a more substantial nature, correcting translations that were simply poor, such as Mark 10:18, which originally read, "There is no man good, but one, that is God." Later this was revised to read, "There is none good."

After 1611, the King James Version gradually came to replace the Bishops' Bible in the pulpits of the Church of England, because no more folio editions of that version were printed after that date. But it was not taken up with any enthusiasm, and the Geneva Bible continued to be published and cherished by the ordinary Christian and defended by the Puritans. But as anti-Puritan as the King James Version was, it gradually began to win its way even with the Puritans. It was almost two generations before it was evident that the King James Version and not the Geneva Bible would win the day. In 1644 the last edition of the Geneva came off the presses.[25]

But the decisive date is 1662. That year, Convocation of the Church of England voted to replace the Scripture readings of the Prayer Book, still from the Great Bible, with readings from the King James Version (except in the Psalms). That virtually assured the future successful fortunes of the version.

But its success was deserved. It won its way on its merits, which were considerable. It was finally accepted, though well after the death of its translators, because it was so clearly a superior translation to anything else then available. There are a number of firsts about it that make it in a way the first of the modern translations, or at least, ways in which it adumbrates the translations of today.

1. It was the first English Bible, so far as I can determine, that contained the books of the Bible and the Apocrypha in the same order and in the same classification that Protestant usage is familiar with today. Tyndale's New Testament in 1525 rejected four books of the New Testament, and there was always a good bit of confusion about the limits of the Old Testament canon. Even the Geneva Bible incorporated The Prayer of Manasseh into the Old Testament. But the King James Version contained the Apocrypha, as was customary until 1825, when the British and Foreign Bible Society determined to publish Bibles without it. This means that it was really not until the mid and late nineteenth century that one could find Bibles in common use pretty much as we know them today: without the Apocryphal books, but with the books of the two testaments in the familar order.

2. It was the first translation known to draw up principles of translation before the work began, to guide the work. This is standard procedure now.

3. It was the first Bible to be published without doctrinal notes, now common practice in Protestant Bibles.

4. It was the first Bible to be produced largely by a corps of professional scholars rather than solely by ecclesiastics.

5. It was the first Protestant Bible to make extensive use of both Jewish and Catholic scholarship.

6. It is the first to take such liberties with translation itself.

The translators did not live to see the success of the Bible on which they expended so much hard labor. Indeed, they seem not to have used it a great deal. The preface to the King James Version, when quoting the Bible, always quotes from the Geneva Bible. (This may have been the Puritan-leaning Smith's way of getting back at James' determination to strike down the Puritans with this Bible.) In the surviving sermons and other writings of these men, their own version is very seldom quoted.

True, it was not a new translation, and did not claim to be. But it was a most creative revision. The effects of that revision, both for good and ill, on our own culture and language have been incalculable. That is our judgment on their work. But when we look at the preface, at their own judgment of their work, we discover that these were scholars who were concerned above all to deliver an accurate version of God's word in language that people understood. Circumstances have changed greatly since the conflicts within the Church of England of 1611. The language that they wielded so well has changed dramatically, and scholars have a wealth of knowledge about the ancient texts, more so than scholars of 1600 could have dared to dream. But their preface is a friendly hand laid firm on the translator's shoulder: "If we building upon their foundation that went before us, and being holpen by their labors, do endeavor to make that better which they left so good, no man, we are sure, hath cause to mislike us; they, we persuade ourselves, if they were alive, would thank us."

APPENDIX 2

A Comparison of Versions

LLOYD R. BAILEY, SR.

Perhaps it will be useful to the readers of this volume to see a comparison, at selected points, of the versions which have been discussed above.

1. Editions Available

version	available in paperback (publisher)	available with Apocrypha (Deuterocanonicals)	new translation (not a revision)
KJV	X (American Bible Society)	early editions only	O
RSV	X (American Bible Society)	X including 3-4 Macc.; Ps. 151	O
NEB	X (Oxford)	X	X
NAB	X (Nelson)	X Deuterocanonical	X
JB	X (Doubleday)	X Deuterocanonical	X
TEV	X (American Bible Society)	X	X
NASB	X (Cambridge)	O	O
NIV	X (American Bible Society)	O	X
NJV (JPS)	X	does not apply	X
LB	X (Tyndale)	X	new paraphrase
Thompson Reference	O	O	KJV text
Ryrie Study	O	O	KJV and NASB text
Oxford Annotated	O	X	RSV text
Oxford Study Edition	X (Oxford)	X	NEB text
Scofield	O	O	KJV text

Key to chart: cross marks (X) = yes; circles (O) = no.

2. *Clarity of Translation*

The selection of a text for comparison came about in the following way. Using the KJV, I began reading one of Paul's letters and selected a text (1 Cor. 5:9-11) which, because of sentence structure and archaic vocabulary, required two or three readings for the meaning to become clear. I have italicized those points at which, for me, the text was unclear for one or the other of these reasons. Readers may use their own judgment about which of the versions cited has the clearest alternative. Note the amazing similarity between RSV and NASB, and how little they have departed from KJV.

KJV: I wrote unto you in an *epistle* not to company with *fornicators;* Yet *not altogether with* the fornicators of *this world,* or with the *covetous,* or extortioners, or with idolaters, for then must ye needs *go out of the world.* But now I have written unto you not to keep company, *if* any man that is called a brother be a fornicator, or covetous, or an idolater, or a *railer,* or a drunkard, or an extortioner; with such an one *no not to eat.*

RSV: I wrote to you in my letter not to associate with immoral men; not at all meaning the immoral of this world, or the greedy and robbers, or idolators, since then you would need to go out of the world. But rather I wrote to you not to associate with any one who bears the name of brother if he is guilty of immorality or greed, or is an idolator, reviler, drunkard, or robber—not even to eat with such a one.

NASB: I wrote you in my letter not to associate with immoral people; I did not at all mean with the immoral people of this world, or with the covetous and swindlers, or with idolaters; for then you would have to go out of the world. But actually, I wrote to you not to associate with any so-called brother if he should be an immoral person, or covetous, or an idolater, or a reviler, or a drunkard, or a swindler—not even to eat with such a one.

NIV: I have written you in my letter not to associate with sexually immoral people—not at all meaning the people of this world who are immoral, or the greedy and swindlers, or idolaters. In that case you would have to leave this world. But now I am writing you that you must not associate with anyone who calls himself a brother but is sexually immoral or greedy, an idolater or a slanderer, a drunkard or a swindler. With such a man do not even eat.

JB: When I wrote in my letter to you not to associate with people living immoral lives, I was not meaning to include all the people in the world who are sexually immoral, any more than I meant to include all usurers and swindlers or idol-worshippers. To do that, you would have to withdraw from the world altogether. What I wrote was that you should not associate with a brother Christian who is leading an immoral life, or is a usurer, or idolatrous, or a slanderer, or a drunkard, or is dishonest; you should not even eat a meal with people like that.

TEV: In the letter that I wrote you I told you not to associate with immoral people. Now I did not mean pagans who are immoral or greedy or are thieves, or who worship idols. To avoid them you would have to get out of the world completely. What I meant was that you should not associate with a person who calls himself a brother but is immoral or greedy or worships idols or is a slanderer or a drunkard or a thief. Don't even sit down to eat with such a person.

NEB: In my letter I wrote that you must have nothing to do with loose livers. I was not, of course, referring to pagans who lead loose lives or are grabbers and swindlers or idolaters. To avoid them you would have to get out of the world altogether. I now write that you must have nothing to do with any so-called Christian who leads a loose life, or is grasping, or idolatrous, a slanderer, a drunkard, or a swindler. You should not even eat with any such person.

NAB: I wrote to you in my letter not to associate with immoral persons. I was not speaking of association with immoral people in this world, or the covetous or thieves or idolaters. To avoid them, you would have to leave the world! What I really wrote about was your not associating with anyone who bears the title "brother" if he is immoral, covetous, an idolater, an abusive person, a drunkard, or a thief. It is clear that you must not eat with such a man.

LB: When I wrote to you before I said not to mix with evil people. But when I said that I wasn't talking about unbelievers who live in sexual sin, or are greedy cheats and thieves and idol worshipers. For you can't live in this world without being with people like that. What I meant was that you are not to keep company with anyone who claims to be a brother Christian but indulges in sexual sins, or is greedy, or is a swindler, or worships idols, or is a drunkard, or is abusive. Don't even eat lunch with such a person.

3. Accuracy of Translation

One must be cautious about generalizations in this area, since a given version may have rendered the original Hebrew, Aramaic, or Greek with precision at one point and not so well at another. Instances can be selected to the comparative advantage or disadvantage of any modern translation. Thus potential purchasers should rely upon the more extensive discussions above more than the single instance presented here. Nonetheless, I have selected a text for comparison which, from the grammatical point of view, is not ambiguous, and one which the various translation committees (or paraphraser) will have considered with special care. It is Isaiah 7:14.

a. *The historical situation of the text.* King Ahaz of Judah (735-715 B.C.) is considering how he should respond to an impending invasion of his country. His neighbors, Israel and Syria, have threatened to intervene in his country unless he joins them in a coalition against the Assyrians (7:1-2). He is advised by the prophet Isaiah to ignore them, since they will be defeated by the Assyrians before they can mount an attack upon Judah (vss. 3-9). When Ahaz voices skepticism about this response, the prophet announces a sign of what God is about to do. The approaching time of security will be reflected in the name which will be given to a child: Immanuel, that is, "God [is[1]] with us" (vs. 14). Before the child reaches the age of moral discretion, the enemies will have been defeated (vs. 17).

b. *The wording of the text: hā-'almāh hārāh wᵉyōleḏeṯ bēn.*

c. *Crucial elements in translation.*

(1.) *hā-*. This element is the definite article, attached to the initial noun *('almāh).* It is crucial to interpretation and should not be ignored in translation. It indicates a definite person, known to Ahaz and Isaiah, and likely mentioned in a part of the conversation that has not been preserved: *"the* [aforementioned] *'almāh."* It is not some indefinite or future person (as if it were "an *'almāh*").

(2.) *'almāh.* This is a noun, the center of the argument about the meaning of this verse. Does it describe a female's sexual status (virgin), or her age status (young woman)? When viewed objectively, in the context of its occurrences throughout the Hebrew Bible, all the evidence favors the latter understanding.[2] The only reason for seeking to assign it the meaning "virgin" is that Matthew (1:23) quotes this text in connection with the birth of Jesus, and hence it has become traditional to view Isaiah as predicting the virgin birth. But this is not a legitimate means of recovering what Isaiah meant by the word *'almāh,* for the following reasons. (1) Matthew is not quoting from the Hebrew text of Isaiah, but from a later Greek translation called the Septuagint (LXX), which uses the noun *parthenos to translate 'almāh.* In no sense, therefore, is the text of Matthew a direct "translation" of Isaiah. (2) Even the word *parthenos* was originally an age designation ("young woman") and not one of sexual experience or lack thereof.[3] Mary's status as virgin does not rely upon the use of this word in the Gospel, but upon the explicit statements: "before they came together" (vs. 18), and "seeing I know not a man" (Luke 1:34).[4] Thus Mary's biological status is secure, and has no bearing upon the meaning of the word *'almāh* in Isaiah 7:14.

(3.) *hārāh.* The word is an adjective ("pregnant") in a noun-clause, i.e., where the verb "to be" is to be supplied by the modern English translator in the tense appropriate to the context.[5] In the present instance, it would be either the present or the immediate future. Hence: "The young woman (is) pregnant. . . ."

(4.) *wᵉyōleḏeṯ.* A participle of the verb "to bear a child," this verb form is often used for actions on the verge of happening. It is not a future tense. Thus we should translate: ". . . (is) pregnant, and (is about to) give birth to. . . ."

d. *The versions compared and evaluated:*

version	translation	evaluation				correctness
		hā-	*'almāh*	*hārāh*	*wᵉyōle-ḏeṯ*	
KJV	*a virgin shall* conceive, and *(shall)* bear a son	O	O	O	O	0%
NASB	*a virgin will* be with child and *(will)* bear a son	O	O	O	O	0%
LB	a child *shall be* born to *a virgin*	O	O	?	O	0%?
RSV	*a young woman shall* conceive and *(shall)* bear a son	O	X	O	O	25%
NAB	*the virgin shall* be with child, and *(shall)* bear a son	X	O	O	O	25%

version	translation	evaluation				correctness
		hā-	*'almāh*	*hārāh*	*w^e yōledeṯ*	
NIV	*the virgin will* be with child and *will* give birth to a son	X	O	O	O	25%
NEB	*a young woman is* with child, and she *shall* bear a son	O	X	X	O	50%
TEV	*a young woman* who *is* pregnant *will* have a son	O	X	X	O	50%
JB	*the maiden is* with child and will *soon* give birth to a son	X	X	X	X	100%
NJV	*the young woman is* with child and *about to* give birth to a son	X	X	X	X	100%

Key to chart: cross marks (X) = yes; circles (O) = no.

Annotated Bibliography

LLOYD R. BAILEY, SR.

1. General

Austin Seminary Bulletin, May 1981 issue (ed. John Jansen and Prescott Williams) contains a series of articles on recent translations.

Beegle, Dewey M. *God's Word into English.* Grand Rapids: Eerdmans Publishing Company, 1960. Deals primarily with translation problems and with the history of English versions since Wycliffe. Appendix F deals with "More Recent Translations," a section that is now outdated.

Branton, J. R. "Versions, English" in *The Interpreter's Dictionary of the Bible* (hereafter: *IDB*), IV, 760-771. Good though brief treatment to the time of the RSV.

Bratcher, Robert G. "One Bible in Many Translations" in *Interpretation,* XXXII (1978), 115-129. Insightful but unsystematic comments on most recent important translations (does not include the NJV).

Brown, Raymond E. "Recent Roman Catholic Translations of the Bible" in *McCormick Quarterly,* XIX (May 1966), 282-292.

Bruce, F. F. *The English Bible.* New York: Oxford University Press, 2nd ed., 1970. A helpful discussion of versions from the Old English Period through the NEB, concerned primarily with historical background and matters of style. The discussion of KJV is particularly helpful. However, so many versions are covered that little detail can be given to them, and the author's allocation of space is sometimes curious: NAB is given but 2 pages; TEV less than a single page; NJV but 6 lines. On the other extreme, some less important works such as the "Berkeley Version" are given 4 pages! Often there is no discussion of textual base or accuracy of translation, and the author's "evangelical" stance sometimes is evident in his evaluations.

Crim, Keith R. "Versions, English" in *IDB,* Supplementary Volume, 933-938. Good format; brief discussion of major recent versions (NEB, NAB, NJV, TEV, JB, NIV, and LB). Tends to avoid justifiable negative evaluation.

———. "Old Testament Translations and Interpretation" in *Interpretation,* XXXII (1978), 144-157. More a discussion of a few translation problems (and how they are handled by the major recent versions) than of translations as a whole.

Davies, Paul E. "A Descriptive List of Bible Translations Since 1901" in *McCormick Quarterly,* XIX (May 1966), 309-325.

Greenslade, S. L., ed. *The Cambridge History of the Bible, III.* Cambridge: University Press, 1963. See esp. pp. 141-174 ("English Versions of the Bible, 1525-1611") and 361-382 ("English Versions Since 1611"). Deals primarily and excellently with historical background.

Lewis, Jack P. *The English Bible: From KJV to NIV.* Grand Rapids: Baker, 1981. Thorough and helpful discussions. 400 pages.

May, Herbert G. "Authorized Versions" in *IDB,* Suppl. Vol. A good discussion of this term, which is often mistakenly limited in application to KJV.

Review and Expositor, LXXVI (Summer 1979), entitled, "Recent Study Bibles and Translations." Articles of some length on RSV (including the Oxford Annotated Edition), JB, NASB, NIV, LB, TEV, and NEB (including the Oxford Study Edition), plus an introduction entitled "Englishing the Bible" (by Robert Bratcher).

Sakae, Kubo, and Walter Specht. *So Many Versions?* Grand Rapids: Zondervan, 1975. Covers RSV—NIV, giving approximately 10 pages to each version. Generally, a helpful guide.

Williamson, Lamar, Jr. "Translation and Interpretation: New Testament" in *Interpretation,* XXXII (1978), 158-170. (See the previous remarks concerning Crim's article in the same issue.)

2. The Jerusalem Bible (JB)

Danker, Frederick W. "The Jersualem Bible: A Critical Examination" in *Concordia Theological Monthly,* 38, #3 (1967), 168-180. Examines NT section only, considering such areas as English grammar, consistency of lexicography, difficult passages, punctuation, and textual base. Critical at specific points, but general praise.

Fitzmyer, Joseph A. Review of JB in *Theological Studies,* XXVII (1967), 129-131. Commends the version for "over-all excellence."

Grant, Frederick C. Review of JB in *Journal of Biblical Literature,* LXXXVI (1967), 91-93.

di Lella, Alexander. Review of JB in *Catholic Biblical Quarterly,* XXIX (1967), 148-151. Regards the version as "a good annotated Bible" with "adequate introductions." The review focuses upon a number of problems, usually in relation to an over-reliance upon the French edition.

Metzger, Bruce M. "The Jerusalem Bible" in *Princeton Seminary Bulletin,* 60, #2 (1967), 45-48. A general description of the historical background of the version, and a positive appraisal of its scholarship.

Rhodes, Erroll F. "Text of NT in Jerusalem and New English Bibles" in *Catholic Biblical Quarterly,* XXXII (1970), 41-57. Discusses the two versions in relation to their nearest relatives (e.g., for NEB: KJV, RV, and RSV) in terms of agreements and deviations; then compares the two as to their use of the Greek text.

Vawter, Bruce. Review of the French edition *(La Sainte Bible)* in *Catholic Biblical Quarterly,* XVIII (1956), 315-317. As of the date of the article, the author remarks that this is "the most authoritative and respected Bible translation in existence today."

3. The Living Bible (LB)

Bowman, Robert C. "The Living Bible—a Critique," in *Brethren Life and Thought,* XVIII (Summer 1973), 137-142. Lists a number of passages where the evangelical theology of the paraphraser (Kenneth N. Taylor) "has been imposed upon scriptures at the cost of accuracy." Indeed, it is remarked that this version attempts to "correct" the scriptures! (There is a response by Kenneth Taylor at pp. 143-144.)

Crim, Keith R. Review of LB, in *The Bible Translator,* XXIII (July 1972), 340-344. Concludes that, overall, this is a "responsible work."

Ellington, John. "The Living Bible Examined" in *Presbyterian Survey,* Oct. 1978, 9-11. Applies three criteria for an adequate version of the Bible: readability, textual basis, and accuracy of interpretation. The author gives high marks (generally) for the first criterion as applied to LB, but failing marks for the other two.

Epp, Eldon Jay. "Jews and Judaism in the *Living New Testament*" in Gary A. Tuttle, ed., *Biblical and Near Eastern Studies* (Grand Rapids: Eerdmans, 1978), 80-96. Epp quotes ample evidence of "evangelical terms and revivalist cliches" which have been introduced into the text with no "direct textual . . . warrant" (p. 81); of Jewish apocalyptic background which has been "obscured or even removed by the translation or paraphrase" (p. 82); of a "marked . . . tendency to cloud the historical and ideological milieu of the New Testament" (p. 84); of misunderstandings of Judaism so serious as to offend Jewish readers, mislead Christians, and "Have a deleterious effect on contemporary Jewish-Christian relations" (p. 87).

Smart, James D. "The Invented Bible" in *Presbyterian Record,* July-Aug. 1976. The article has been reprinted in its entirety in the present volume.

4. The New American Bible (NAB)

Arbez, Edward P. "The New Catholic Translation of the Old Testament" in *Catholic Biblical Quarterly,* XIV (1952), 237-254.

Barr, James. "After Five Years: A Retrospect on two Major Translations of the Bible" in *The Heythrop Journal,* XV (Oct. 1974), 381-405. One of the best comparisons, by a scholar of the first rank, concentrating primarily upon the NEB from the point of view of excessive use of comparative philology in deriving new semantic possibilities. He finds the NAB to be more cautious in this and in textual matters, and properly so.

Crim, Keith. Review of NAB in *The Bible Translator,* 23 (1972), 444-448. Examines the version under the headings: "Textual Basis of the Translation"; "Meaning of the Text"; "Reproducing the Message in the Target Language"; and "Introduction and Notes."

Dahood, Mitchell. "Northwest Semitic Notes on Genesis" in *Biblica,* 55 (1974), 76-82. Laments that the translation of the book of Genesis in this version has not utilized the evidence provided by the Ugaritic texts.

Danker, Frederick W. Review of NAB in *Catholic Biblical Quarterly,* XXXIII (1971), 405-409. Generally high praise, including the judgment that the version deserves, for the present, the designation "*the* American Bible."

Metzger, Bruce M. "The New American Bible, 1970" in *The Princeton Seminary Bulletin,* LXIV (March 1971), 90-99.

Peifer, Claude J. "The New American Bible" in *Worship,* XLV (Feb. 1971), 102-113. After a number of minor criticisms, the author agrees with "objective critics" that the NAB is "a competent and reliable rendering in good contemporary English."

Reumann, John. Review of NAB in the *Journal of Biblical Literature,* XCII (1973), 275-278.

5. The New English Bible (NEB)

Barr, James. "After Five Years: A Retrospect on Two Major Translations of the Bible" in *The Heythrop Journal,* XV (Oct. 1974), 381-405. (For a summary, see under NAB.)

Bratcher, Robert. Review of NEB in *The Bible Translator,* XII (July 1961), 97-106.

Brockington, K. H. *The Hebrew Text of the OT: The Readings Adopted by the Translators of the NEB.* Oxford: University Press, 1973. Gives the emendations (of the Masoretic Text) which the translators accepted, but without explanation (a great pity).

Burrows, Millar. Review of NEB in *Journal of Biblical Literature,* LXXXIX (1970), 220-222.

Daiches, David. "Translating the Bible" in *Commentary,* May 1970, 59-68.

Hunt, Geoffrey. *About the New English Bible.* Oxford: University Press, 1970. Concentrates upon the work of the committees which produced this version, as well as upon the format of the version.

Macintosh, A. A., Graham Stanton, and David L. Frost. "The 'New English Bible' Reviewed" in *Theology,* LXXIV (April 1971), 154-166. A substantial analysis of the accuracy and literary quality of this version.

Metzger, Bruce M. "The New English Bible, 1970" in *The Princeton Seminary Bulletin,* LXIII (1970), 99-104.

Rhodes, Erroll F. "Text of NT in Jerusalem and New English Bibles" in *Catholic Biblical Quarterly,* XXXII (1970), 41-57. (For a description, see under JB.)

Sanders, James A. Review of NEB in the *Christian Century,* March 18, 1970, 326-328.

Tasker, R. V. G. *The Greek New Testament.* Oxford: University Press, 1964. The Greek text upon which the NEB is based.

Taylor, Charles L. "The New English Bible Translation of Psalms" in *Anglican Theological Review,* LIV (July 1972), 194-205.

Terrien, Samuel. Review of NEB in *Union Seminary Quarterly Review,* XXV (1970), 549-555.

Van Ness Goetchius, Eugene. Review of NEB in *Anglican Theological Review,* LII (July 1970), 167-176. Compares NEB with RSV and JB, giving higher marks to NEB on the basis of several criteria.

See also *The Journal of Jewish Studies,* XXIV (1973) for a review *(nv).*

6. The New International Version (NIV)

Bratcher, Robert. "Review Article. The Holy Bible—New International Version" in *The Bible Translator,* XXX (1979), 345-350.

Deboer, Willis P. Review of NIV in *Calvin Theological Journal,* X (April 1975), 66-78. Covers the New Testament portion of the version only. Finds the differences from RSV not very significant.

Lasor, William Sanford. "What Kind of Version Is the New International?" in *Christianity Today* (Oct. 20, 1978), 78-80. The author finds the NIV "not . . . measurably superior to the RSV" in readability, and that the accuracy of translation is generally reliable.

Lewis, Jack P. "The New International Version" in *Restoration Quarterly,* 24 (1981), 1-11. Generally a very positive appraisal.

Newman, Barclay M. "Readability and the New International Version of the New Testament" in *The Bible Translator,* 31 (1980), 325-336. Examines NIV from the perspective of sentence length, distance between subject and predicate, sentence order, pronominal ambiguity, use of prepositions, biblicisms, inconsistency of language level, etc., and concludes: the translation is dependable, but "It does not communicate clearly; the English style is unnatural and hard to read."

Ryken, Leland. "The Literary Merit of the New International Version" in *Christianity Today* (Oct. 20, 1978), 76-77. Gives generally low marks to the translation and prefers the RSV.

"The New International Version—Nothing New" in *Concordia Theological Quarterly,* 43 (1979), 242-245. Speaking from the perspective of "confessional Lutherans," the reviewer commends the NIV's "basically conservative approach" in matters of doctrine, but laments its "subtle inclusions of Reformed theology." In sum, it "does not appear to be any improvement over what is currently available."

7. The New Jewish Version (NJV)

Borowitz, Eugene B. "Theological Issues in the New Torah Translation" in *Judaism,* 13, #3 (1964), 335-345. Looks at passages where the translators have been charged (1) by Protestant fundamentalists with ignoring theological (largely Christological) implications, and (2) by Orthodox Jews with not adhering to Rabbinic interpretation.

Crim, Keith R. "The New Jewish Version of the Scriptures" in *The Bible Translator,* XXVI (Jan. 1975), 148-152.

Ginsberg, H. L. "The New Jewish Publication Society Translation of the Torah," *Journal of Bible and Religion,* 31 (1963), 187-192. Observations on specific problems by a member of the translation committee.

Greenberg, Moshe. Review Essay in *Judaism,* 12, #2 (1963), 225-237, based on the Torah-volume. Lauds the page format, footnotes, clarity of language, understanding of Hebrew idiom. Characterizes the whole as a "grand work."

Meek, Theophile, J. "A New Bible Translation" in *Journal of Biblical Literature,* 82 (1963), 265-271. "The translation is assuredly the best that has been produced thus far."

Orlinsky, Harry M. *Notes on the New Translation of the Torah.* Philadelphia: Jewish Publication Society, 1969. Discussion of some of the translation problems, by a member of the committee.

———————. "The New Jewish Version of the Torah: Toward a New Philosophy of Bible Translation" in *Journal of Biblical Literature,* 82 (1963), 249-271.

———————. "Some Recent Jewish Translations of the Bible" in *McCormick Quarterly,* XIX (May 1966), 293-300.

Sanders, James A. "Textual Criticism and the NJV Torah" in *Journal of the American Academy of Religion,* XXXIX (1971), 193-197. Basically a review of Orlinsky's *Notes* (above), focused upon the stage of textual development which a particular translation attempts to recover (e.g., Urtext vs. Masoretic Text).

8. The Revised Standard Version (RSV)

Ackroyd, Peter R. "An Authoritative Version of the Bible" in *Expository Times,* LXXXV (Sept. 1974), 374-377. Discusses the goals and durability of the RSV "Common Bible" against the background of the diversity of readings to be found in ancient manuscripts and version.

Burrows, Millar. "The Revised Standard Version of the Old Testament" in *Supplements to Vetus Testamentum,* VII. Oxford: University Press, 1960, 206-221. A general discussion of the differences between the RSV and its parent versions (KJV and ERV/ASV): removal of archaic language, clarification of ambiguities, up-dated lexicography, footnotes to indicate when the ancient versions are being followed, etc.

Cooper, Charles M. "The Revised Standard Version of Psalms" in *Seventy-Fifth Anniversary Volume of the Jewish Quarterly Review.* Philadelphia, 1967, 137-148. Lauds the version's scholarship, but laments limitations in its use of English poetic language.

Larue, Gerald A. "Another Chapter in the History of Bible Translation" in *Journal of Bible and Religion,* 31 (1963), 301-310. A study of the vituperous responses to RSV by some Protestant fundamentalists. Larue's purpose is "to present the central issues that appear over and over again in more than two hundred pamphlets."

May, Herbert G. "The Revised Standard Version After Twenty Years" in *McCormick Quarterly,* XIX (May 1966), 301-308.

———. "The Revised Standard Version Bible" in *Vetus Testamentum,* XXIV (1974), 238-240. Reviews the ongoing work of the RSV Bible Committee.

Metzger, Bruce M. "The RSV—Ecumenical Edition" in *Theology Today,* XXIV (Oct. 1977), 315-317.

———. "The Story Behind the Making of the Revised Standard Version of the Bible" in *The Princeton Seminary Bulletin,* N.S., I (1978), 189-200.

9. Today's English Version (TEV)

Bratcher, Robert. "The Nature and Purpose of the New Testament in Today's English Version" in *The Bible Translator,* 22 (1971), 97-107. A response to specific criticism as the 3rd edition is being prepared. Discusses the nature of a dynamic equivalence translation, text base, contextual consistency, etc. Also cites specific instances of revision since the 1st edition.

Bullard, Roger A. "Sex-Oriented Language in TEV Proverbs" in *The Bible Translator,* XXVIII (April 1977), 243-245.

Dahood, Mitchell. Review of *The Psalms for Modern Man* in *Catholic Biblical Quarterly,* 34 (1972), 240-242. He says that the translation is "philologically thirty years out of date."

Legrand, L. "The Good News Bible. A Reaction from India" in *The Bible Translator,* XXIX (1978), 331-336. A brief look at three passages. The result is praise for the translation.

May, Herbert G. Review of TEV in *Interpretation,* XXXII (1978), 187-190.

10. The New American Standard Bible (NASB)

Bratcher, Robert G. "The New American Standard Gospel of John" in *The Bible Translator,* 13 (1962), 234-236. Lists the kinds of revisions that have been done (mostly modernizations of language), then gives several grammatical "atrocities" and typographical errors. Concludes that RSV has already done, and excellently, what NASB sets out to do.

Hodges, Z. C. Review of the NT in *Bibliotheca Sacra,* 121 (1964), 267-268. Praises the clarity of its English vocabulary, but criticizes the dullness of its syntax. Doubts that it "is sufficiently excellent to become the standard for general use."

11. Study Bibles

Beegle, Dewey. *Prophecy and Prediction* (Ann Arbor: Pryor Pettengill, 1978), Chapters 12-13. A discussion of Dispensationalism and how it is reflected in the Scofield Bible's notes. Beegle is quite unsympathetic with the approach.

English, E. Schuyler. *A Companion to the New Scofield Reference Bible.* New York: Oxford, 1972. Basically a summary of the ideas about God, Satan, the Millennium, etc., as found in the Bible as viewed by Scofield (Dispensational Pre-Millennialism).

Polhill, John B. "The Revised Standard Version and the Oxford Annotated Bible" in *Review and Expositor,* LXXVI (1979), 315-324.

Reumann, John. "Review of The Oxford Annotated Bible" in *Journal of Biblical Literature,* 82 (1963), 238-239.

Tate, Marvin E. "The Oxford Study Edition of the New English Bible with Apocrypha" in *Review and Expositor,* LXXI (1979), 325-339.

Notes

2. The Revised Standard Version

1. The King James Version contains more bad grammar than is commonly realized. Much of it is failure to observe agreement in singular and plural number, the rule for which was very loosely observed in the sixteenth and seventeenth century. In Luke 9:17 we read that "there was taken up . . . twelve baskets." Peter was astonished at the miraculous draught of fish "and so was also James and John" (Luke 5:10). Jesus is reported as saying, "This is an evil generation; they seek a sign, and there shall no sign be given it" (Luke 11:29). Likewise "Whom do men say that I am?" (Matt. 16:13) should be "who."

2. The use of "was" with the second person singular pronoun occurs occasionally in authors of earlier centuries.

3. An example of a much less important difference between the two committees is the following. The King James reading in Gen. 22:23, "These eight Milkah did bear to Nahor," was changed by the English Revisers to "these eight did Milkah bear to Nahor," despite the Americans' objection that, when read aloud, this sounded like "did milk a bear"!

4. This was Moffatt's second translation of the New Testament. In 1901 he had issued a modern speech version with the books arranged in the sequence in which many scholars think they had been written.

5. Ropes resigned from the Committee in 1932.

6. At the time of publication of the RSV Old Testament a limited number of changes were introduced into the RSV New Testament. For example, because of euphony the translation of Acts 17:28 "In him we live and move and are" was changed back to the King James phraseology "we live and move and have our being." Of more consequence was the restoration of the words "sanctify" and "sanctification" to certain passages, in order to preclude mistaken inferences that had been drawn from their replacement by "consecrate" and "consecration" and to agree with the Committee's retention of the term "sanctify" in the Old Testament.

In 1959 the Committee authorized a number of changes, chiefly in connection with matters of punctuation, capitalization, and footnotes. Some examples of such changes are "without" changed to "from," Job 19:26; "loaf" to "bread," Matt. 7:9 and 1 Cor. 10:17; "be he" to "is he," Matt. 21:9 and parallels; "the son" to "the Son," Matt. 27:54 and Mark 15:39; "married only once" to "the husband of one wife," 1 Tim. 3:2, 12; 5:9 and Titus 1:6.

7. See the *Congressional Record,* vol. 106, part 6 (April 19, 1960), pp. 8247-8284.

8. The third edition, prepared in 1969 by K. Aland, M. Black, C. M. Martini, S. J., B. M. Metzger, and A. Wikgren, was finally published in 1975, but the changes from previous editions were known in 1971 through the publication of Metzger's *A Textual Commentary on the Greek New Testament* (London, 1971).

9. Herbert G. May and Bruce M. Metzger, editors, *The New Oxford Annotated Bible, with the Apocrypha,* Expanded Edition, Revised Standard Version (New York: Oxford University Press, 1977).

10. See Ginn and Company, "Treatment of Minority Groups and Women"; Holt, Rinehart and Winston, "Guidelines for the Development of Elementary and Secondary Instructional Materials: The Treatment of Sex Roles"; Houghton Mifflin Co., "Avoiding Stereotypes"; McGraw-Hill Book Co., "Guidelines for Equal Treatment of the Sexes in McGraw-Hill Book Company Publications"; Macmillan Publishing Co., "Guidelines for Creating Positive Sexual and Racial Images in Educational Materials"; Random House, "Guidelines for Multi-Ethnic/Nonsexist Survey"; and Scott, Foresman and Co., "Guidelines for Improving the Image of Women in Textbooks."

One can also call attention to *Sexism and Language,* by Alleen P. Nilsen, Haig Bosmajian, H. Lee Gershuny, and Julia P. Stanley, and published by the National Council of Teachers of English, Urbana, Illinois, 1977.

3. The New English Bible

1. Such as Leo Rosten, *Treasury of Jewish Quotations* (New York: Bantam Books edition, 1977), p. 75, where one Donald Ebor is cited as Chair of the Joint Committee. Of course, there is no reason in the world for Rosten to have been aware of the problem.

2. Information on the background and policy of the NEB is drawn from Coggan's preface; from a small leaflet, *The Story of the New English Bible* (Oxford and Cambridge, 1970), published in conjunction with the issuance of the Bible; and from F. F. Bruce, *History of the Bible in English* (New York: Oxford, 1978).

3. The term "reading" is used in the technical sense of a variant in the manuscript tradition, either of the original or of an ancient translation. It is to be distinguished from "translation," "version," or "rendering," which refer to differences in translation of a given text.

4. The NEB follows the tradition of the KJV and RSV in representing the Hebrew name of God, Yahweh, by the word "LORD," capitalized. On the few occasions where the name is really crucial to the passage, e.g., Exodus 6:3, the Anglicized form JEHOVAH is used, again capitalized.

5. Interestingly, a noted Arabist was among the translators of the KJV.

6. On this matter one should consult the important article by James Barr, "After Five Years: A Retrospect on two Major Translations of the Bible," *The Heythrop Journal* XV (1974), 381-405. The other major translation is the New American Bible.

7. On matters of English style, the most informed review I have seen, though not especially appreciative, is that of David Daiches, "Translating the Bible," *Commentary,* May 1970, pp. 59-68.

8. On this question, see the review article by J. A. Sanders, "The New English Bible: A Comparison," *Christian Century,* March 18, 1970, pp. 326-328.

5. The New American Standard Bible

1. But at Matthew 1:23, in the quotation of Isaiah 7:14, the word "Son" does receive a capital. The same thing is true of Hosea 11:1, where "My son" appears in Hosea, but in the quotation at Matthew 2:15 "My Son" is the rendering.

2. Observe the lack of cohesion in the following paragraph, where three diverse topics are discussed in four sentences.

Textual Revision: Words are the vehicle of thought, and most languages, especially the English, have a flexibility which economic and cultural progress utilizes. Passing time with myriads of inventions and innovations automatically renders obsolete and inexpressive words that once were in acceptable usage. The ever present danger of stripping divine Truth of its dignity and original intent was prominently before the minds of the producers at all times. An editorial board composed of linguists, Greek and Hebrew scholars and pastors undertook the responsibilities of translation.

Observe also the ambiguity of the pronoun "they" in the second sentence of the paragraph below. Initially one assumes that its referent is "the words of Scripture" of the previous sentence, which is not the case. The problem could easily have been resolved by restructuring the second sentence to read: "Since the Holy Scriptures are the eternal Word of God, they speak. . . ."

The New American Standard Bible has been produced with the conviction that the words of Scripture as originally penned in the Hebrew and Greek were inspired by God. Since they are the eternal Word of God, the Holy Scriptures speak with fresh power to each generation, to give wisdom that leads to salvation, that people may serve God to the glory of Christ.

3. "Readability and the New International Version of the New Testament," *The Bible Translator,* vol. 31, no. 3, pp. 325-336.

4. The note attached to "shall be born to you" (1 Kings 8:19) is, fortunately, somewhat more delicate: "Lit., *is to come forth from your loins.*" Three other related notes provide spiritual and scholarly help for the reader: at Joshua 10:19 "attack them in the rear" has note "Lit., *smite their tail*"; at 1 Kings 14:10 "every male person" is "Lit., *him who urinates against the wall*"; at 1 Chronicles 29:24 "pledged allegiance to King Solomon" is "Lit., *put a hand under Solomon.*"

At first glance the note at Lamentations 1:9 appears also to relate to the posterior portion of the anatomy: "Lit., *did not remember her latter end*" (for text: "did not consider her future"). Worse than these notes is the translation of Proverbs 5:3-4:

For the lips of an adultress drip honey,
And smoother than oil is her speech;

But in the end she is bitter as wormwood,
Sharp as a two-edged sword.

5. In the Hebrew Old Testament the word *Qesitah* is found also at Genesis 33:19 and Joshua 24:32, where NASB provides the same note, except in these two passages the word is spelled with lower case "q."

6. According to the overall format of NASB Reference Edition, the punctuation, should have been "Gk.," instead of "Gr." However, the margin is loaded with numerous typographical inconsistencies and errors. Notice that in the following two examples in this paragraph the abbreviation "v." is used in Exodus 16:31, while "vs." occurs at Exodus 16:15. Generally, the form for textual notes is to punctuate with a semi-colon between alternatives as at 2 Samuel 4:1 ("So some ancient mss.; MT, *he*"), but this form is not always maintained: see, for example, 2 Samuel 3:7 ("So some ancient mss and versions MT, he") and 2 Samuel 3:18 ("So many ancient mss and versions MT, he"); compare also the form at 1 Samuel 16:7 ("So with Gk.; Heb., *He sees not what man sees*") with that at 1 Samuel 22:14 ("So with Gk., Heb., *turns aside to*"). At 2 Chronicles 7:20, the errors are compounded ("Ancient versions, Heb. read, *them*"). The note at 1 Kings 6: is unique: ("So with Gk & versions: M.T., *middle*"). Observe also "reads;" (Isaiah 30:7); "reads:" (Isaiah 30:19); "read," (Isaiah 33:2); and "reads:" (Isaiah 33:11).

7. At Job 40:15, in the context of "Behold now, Behemoth, which I made as well as you. . ." the same note is repeated in conjunction with the phrase "as well as."

8. Observe that the translation of Ezekiel 6:11 suffers also from the transfer into English of the singular "hand" and "foot"; in English one claps his "hands" (plural).

9. In NASB note "a Hebrew idiom" is italicized, but it should not be.

10. This marginal note at 26:4 is interesting, especially in light of 27:3 and the two notes there:

For as long as [1]life is in me,
And the [2]breath of God is in my nostrils,

1 Lit., *breath*
2 Or, *spirit*

Whereas at 26:4 the Hebrew word under discussion is literally "breath," another Hebrew word is literally "breath" at 27:3, and the Hebrew word under discussion is translated "breath" at 27:3 with the alternative "Or, *spirit*" offered in the margin.

11. ASV, the feigned progenitor of NASB, is honest with the text and note here: "They say" with note "Heb., *saying*."

12. In all fairness to NASB, "God" may be italicized in the text, but the use of the oversized capital letters for the word gives the impression that it is not in italics.

13. In the same verse "were taking place" also translates an aorist indicative; this is in fact the *same* verb form translated "was occurring to."

14. Actually, the definite article is lacking in all the Hebrew constructions mentioned in this and the above paragraph, even though in the literal renderings of NASB, the article is included.

15. At Job 3:11 the translation reads "at birth" with the marker for the note before "at"; at Psalms 22:10 the translation is "from birth," with the note marker before "birth." This accounts for the absence of "from" in the note at Psalms 22:10.

16. In the "Explanation of General Format," there is a paragraph relating to the use of italics; the first sentence reads:

> ITALICS are used in the text to indicate words which are not found in the original Hebrew or Greek but implied by it.

This principle is utilized only at random and always in a rather haphazard manner, especially with regard to forms of the verb "to be," which are sometimes not required in Hebrew or Greek, but which must be rendered in English. Moreover, the literal form of the original is frequently by-passed without marginal notation.

The absurdity of attempting to use italics in this way, as well as the impossibility of consistent marginal notation of literal renderings, may easily be indicated from the NASB rendering of Jeremiah 1:5-6.

> Before I formed you in the womb I knew you,
> And before you were born I consecrated you;
> I have appointed you a prophet to the nations.
> Then I said, 'Alas, Lord God!
> Behold I do not know how to speak,
> Because I am a youth.'

At least the following items should be noted, if these principles are to be fully activated: (1) "the womb" is literally "a womb"; (2) "you were born" is literally "came from the womb"; (3) "appointed" is literally "gave"; (4) "then" is literally "and"; (5) "how to speak" is literally "a word"; (6) "am" is not in the Hebrew text and should be italicized; and (7) "I am a youth" is literally "a youth I."

17. According to Bruce M. Metzger, *A Textual Commentary on the Greek New Testament,* p. 757, the spelling *Armageddon* is "based on one form of the late Byzantine text."

6. The Jerusalem Bible

1. The *Codex Iuris Canonici,* a codification in 2414 separate *canones* of centuries of ecclesiastical legislation, took effect in the Latin church May 19, 1918, a year following its promulgation. Theoretically it is still in effect, subject to subsequent specific revisions (such as those which have virtually abolished the *Index Liborum Prohibitorum* and seriously modified the *censura praevia* of books and other writings), pending an overhaul that may or may not come to fruition in our times.

2. A commentary on the Code, much used in Catholic seminaries at the time, further made it quite clear that the provision applied to anybody: "omnes, tam sacerdotes *quam tirones* [my emphasis] et alumnos, qui habitualiter studia biblica et theologica, sive in scholis *sive privatim* [again my emphasis], seria mente excolere et augere nituntur." See Uldaricus Beste, *Introductio in Codicem* (Collegeville: St. John's Abbey Press, 1946) on can. 1400.

3. An interesting example typical of many others was recently called to mind by the 500th anniversary of the Bible in Catalan, printed at Valencia in 1478 (and translated a long generation before). Though proclaimed in its colophon to be "the most true and Catholic Bible" and published with the highest available ecclesiastical approbation, it fell prey to the Spanish Inquisition which was extended to Valencia in 1484 and which consigned to the flames vernacular Bibles along with Jewish Talmuds and Arabic works of alchemy. Cf. Guiu Camps, "Cinccents anys de la primera edició catalana de la Bíblia," *Revista Catalana de Teologia,* 3 (1978), 3-16.

4. Article I of the Constitution of the American Bible Society, established in 1816, states that the sole object of the Society shall be "circulation of the Holy Scriptures without note or comment." See Creighton Lacy, *The Word Carrying Giant* (South Pasadena: Willim Carey Library, 1977), pp. 10, 16-17, 84-95, 252-253, 256, 259-260, 262, 288.—Ed.

5. In its Fourth Session, April 8, 1546. Cf. Denzinger-Schönmetzer, *Enchiridion Symbolorum* (34th ed., Freiburg: Herder, 1967), §§ 1504, 1506.

6. *Divino afflante Spiritu* in Denzinger-Schönmetzer, § 3825.

7. More particulars than the reader may be interested in knowing about this history can be found in Hugh Pope, O.P., *English Versions of the Bible* (2d ed.; St. Louis: Herder, 1952), 355-378, 386-441, 464-496.

8. *Die Bibel. Die Heilige Schrift des Alten und Neuen Bundes. Deutsche Ausgabe mit den Erläuterungen der Jerusalemer Bibel* (Freiburg: Herder, 1968).

9. In *Bibel und Kirche* 32 (1978), 135, Anton Steiner, responding to the familiar question "welche Bibel kaufen," also chides the "Jerusalemer Bibel" for having acquiesced in introductory material and annotation that was already outdated in 1968.

10. Cf. Herbet Haag, *Biblische Schöpfungslehre und Kirchliche Erbsündenlehre* (Stuttgarter Bibelstudien 10; Stuttgart: Katholisches Bibelwerk, 1966), 49-54, referring also to pp. 13-37. There is an English translation, *Is Original Sin in Scripture?* (New York: Sheed & Ward, 1969), but in the substitution of English for German sources the force of the contrast has largely disappeared.

7. Today's English Version (The Good News Bible)

1. See the four relevant items in the bibliography under "Zion, Daughter of," *Interpreter's Dictionary of the Bible,* Supplementary Volume, p. 985; also W. F. Stinespring, "The Trials of Translation: Modern English Versions of the Bible," *St. Andrews Review,* Vol. 1, No. 4 (1972), pp. 65-69.

2. Anchor Bible, *Proverbs and Ecclesiastes,* by R. B. Y. Scott, Doubleday & Co., New York, 1965.

3. *The Old Testament, A New Translation,* Vol. I, 1924, Vol. II, 1925, *The New Testament, A New Translation,* New Edition Revised, 1925, by James Moffatt, George H. Doran Co., New York; all later issued in one volume as *The Bible, A New Translation.*

4. Scott, *Proverbs and Ecclesiastes,* pp. 192-193.

5. Doubleday & Co., New York, 1977.

6. See Note 1, above.

7. Anchor Bible, *Job,* by Marvin H. Pope, 3rd edition, Doubleday & Co., New York, 1973.

8. Doubleday & Co., New York, 1971.

9. *The New Testament, An American Translation* by Edgar J. Goodspeed, University of Chicago Press, 1923. Included in *The Complete Bible, An American Translation,* Chicago, 1939.

10. Harper and Brothers, Publishers, New York and London, 1933, pp. 90, 302.

Appendix 1. "Zeal to Promote the Common Good"

1. The Puritans were repelled by the formalities, the archaism, and especially the theological bent of the versions used in church. The High Church wing found the anti-episcopal leanings of the Geneva Bible abhorrent. These diverging approaches to patterns of worship and church government drove the two parties far apart during Queen Elizabeth's long reign.

2. David Daiches, *The King James Version of the English Bible* (Chicago: University of Chicago Press, 1941), p. 65; James Baikie, *The English Bible and Its Story* (Philadelphia: J. B. Lippincott, 1928?), pp. 263-264.

3. The notes were published by William Barlow, Dean of Chester, as *The Summe and Substance of the Conference . . . at Hampton Court.* See Edmund Venables, "Barlow, William," *Dictionary of National Biography* (Oxford, 1917), I, 1152.

4. Bancroft's letters may be found in Alfred W. Pollard, *Records of the English Bible* (Oxford, 1911), pp. 331-334. On some of the money problems, see Pollard, pp. 56-58; and Harriett Chaplin Conant's undeservedly forgotten *The English Bible* (New York: Sheldon, Blakeman and Co., 1856), pp. 427-432.

5. Stuart B. Babbage, *Puritanism and Richard Bancroft* (London: SPCK, 1962), p. 68.

6. The rules are conveniently available in Geddes MacGregor, *A Literary History of the Bible* (Nashville: Abingdon Press, 1968), pp. 184-185. Cf. the list of eight rules later presented to the Synod of Dort in 1618, given in Pollard, *Records,* pp. 336-339.

7. For example, Isaac was Izhak; Jacob was Iaakob.

8. Material in the following paragraphs is largely drawn from biographical data available in Gustavus S. Paine, *The Learned Men* (New York: Crowell, 1959), now published as *The Men Behind the KJV* (Grand Rapids: Baker, 1977). Much of the material is also to be found in MacGregor, *Literary History*. Many of the translators have entries in the *Dictionary of National Biography*, where bibliographical details are available.

9. T. S. Eliot, "Lancelot Andrewes," *Essays Ancient and Modern* (London: Faber and Faber 1936), pp. 11-30.

10. Paine, *Learned Men*, p. 113.

11. These notes were edited, translated (from Latin), and published with photographic reproductions, by Ward Allen, *Translating for King James* (Nashville: Vanderbilt University Press, 1969).

12. S. L. Greenslade, "English Versions of the Bible, 1525-1611," *Cambridge History of the Bible* (Cambridge: University Press, 1963), III, 167; Daiches, *King James Version*, pp. 171-172.

13. Daiches, *King James Version*, p. 173.

14. Greenslade, *Cambridge History*.

15. The preface is most easily available today in MacGregor, *Literary History*, pp. 220-242.

16. These examples are studied by Charles C. Butterworth, *The Literary Lineage of the King James Bible 1340-1611* (Philadelphia: University of Pennsylvania Press, 1941), pp. 220-221.

17. Paine, *Learned Men*, p. 128; Conant, *English Bible*, pp. 439-440.

18. On the question of authorization, if any, see Pollard, *Records*, pp. 59-60; Baikie, *English Bible*, pp. 282-283; F. F. Bruce, *History of the Bible in English* (New York: Oxford University Press, 1978), pp. 99-100.

19. We owe this information to John Selden in his *Table Talk* under "Bible." See Robert Waters, ed., *John Selden and His Table Talk* (New York: Eaton and Mains, 1899), p. 73.

20. MacGregor, *Literary History*, p. 199.

21. *Ibid.*, p. 208.

22. Selden, *Table Talk*, p. 74.

23. *A Short Introduction to English Grammar* (London: J. Hughes, 1762).

24. Butterworth, *Literary Lineage*, p. 230.

25. Except for reprints of some portions originally prepared for Cromwell's troops in 1643, which were distributed to soldiers in the American Civil War.

26. The substance of this essay was originally prepared and delivered as the annual Faculty Lecture at Atlantic Christian College, November, 1977.

Appendix 2. A Comparison of Versions

1. The verb "to be" is not literally present in this sentence, as it often is not in Hebrew. It is to be supplied by the English translator, in the tense appropriate to the context. Here, it could be "was" or "will be," as well as "is."

2. Readers can easily consult the evidence in the article "Virgin" in *The Interpreter's Dictionary of the Bible,* Supplementary Volume.

3. This can be verified by anyone who cares to check Liddell and Scott's Greek-English lexicon.

4. There is no objection, either grammatical or theological, to translating Luke 1:27 as, ". . . to a maiden *[parthenos]* betrothed to . . . Joseph . . . and the maiden's name was Mary." (See TEV.)

5. See above, footnote no. 1.

Index

I. Hebrew Bible (OT)

II. Deuterocanonicals, Apocrypha

III. New Testament